WRITING ACROSS CULTURES

WRITING ACROSS CULTURES

ROBERT EDDY
AND AMANDA ESPINOSA-AGUILAR

UTAH STATE UNIVERSITY PRESS
Logan

© 2019 by University Press of Colorado

Published by Utah State University Press
An imprint of University Press of Colorado
245 Century Circle, Suite 202
Louisville, Colorado 80027

 The University Press of Colorado is a proud member of
the Association of University Presses.

The University Press of Colorado is a cooperative publishing enterprise supported,
in part, by Adams State University, Colorado State University, Fort Lewis College,
Metropolitan State University of Denver, University of Colorado, University of Northern
Colorado, Utah State University, and Western State Colorado University.

∞ This paper meets the requirements of the ANSI/NISO Z39.48–1992 (Permanence of
Paper).

ISBN: 978-1-60732-873-5 (paperback)
ISBN: 978-1-60732-874-2 (ebook)
DOI: https://doi.org/10.7330/9781607328742

Library of Congress Cataloging-in-Publication Data

Names: Eddy, Robert, author. | Espinosa-Aguilar, Amanda, author.
Title: Writing across cultures / Robert Eddy and Amanda Espinosa-Aguilar.
Description: Logan : Utah State University Press, [2018] | Includes bibliographical refer-
    ences and index.
Identifiers: LCCN 2019005793 | ISBN 9781607328735 (pbk.) | ISBN 9781607328742
    (ebook)
Subjects: LCSH: English language—Rhetoric—Study and teaching—Evaluation. | Critical
    discourse analysis—Social aspects. | Multiculturalism in literature. | Racism in language.
Classification: LCC PE1404 .E284 2018 | DDC 808/.042071—dc23
LC record available at https://lccn.loc.gov/2019005793

This book is dedicated to future teachers and students of FYW and successor FY courses. May you cocreate relationships and texts of radical equality, dynamic democracy, and collaborative rhetorics. May you share evidence, resources, and counterreadings with respect, full engagement, and rhetorical listening.

To Dada, Lisa, Mama, and Nuggle

CONTENTS

ACKNOWLEDGMENTS

Robert Eddy: Thanks to all the students who allowed us to use their writings in this book. All student names in this text are pseudonyms, so I cannot thank individual students by name. I made every effort to contact the student with the pseudonym of Adhita Sharma. I request that the rights holder contact the authors through the publisher. I thank Tom Broadbent for an unshakeable support of this project in its initial development. I thank Michael Spooner for being an enabling and crucial reader. I thank Rachael Levay for a sureness of vision and for the strength and confidence to follow a distinguished predecessor as acquisitions editor and for doing so with generosity and understanding. I thank coauthor Amanda for always telling your truth and always practicing and teaching equality with and to everyone. I thank the anonymous external reviewers for generous and sustained attentiveness and for uncompromising and insistent insight and counterreadings. I thank Eileen Eddy for help decoding the digital, chasing resources, dealing with the smooth surface of arguments, and reteaching me the complexities of being multiracial in the midst of the uninterrupted white privilege of an American systemic racism and your father's interrupted but always present white privilege. Last and most important, I thank An Lan Jang for never giving up on this project, for never giving up on me, for providing the most searching and insightful reading of the multiple contexts of this work, and for always redirecting tests and blessings back to their source and to the need for answering this question: Fabi'ayyi 'Ālā'i Rabbikumā Tuka<u>dhdh</u>ibān? (Quran 55:13).

Amanda Espinosa-Aguilar: I join Robert Eddy in thanking our many collaborators over the years, including our editors and the staff at Utah State University Press, the external readers, los estudiantes que enfrentaron el desafío de convertirse en un pensador crítico, and our friends. Without their feedback throughout our careers, this work would never have been completed. A big hug and shout-out go to two Bobs. One is the brother who coauthored this book with such determination and tenacity, and the other first led me down the rhet/comp rabbit hole. Finally, my enduring gratitude and respect goes to Dave, whose love defies definition. Whether I'm a success or a flop, he has provided me with unlimited support throughout many decades. It's finally time to pour the Cointreau, Hon!

Preface

HOW *WRITING ACROSS CULTURES* POSITIONS ITSELF IN CURRENT RHETORIC, WRITING, RACISM, AND DIVERSITY SCHOLARSHIP

Robert Eddy and Victor Villanueva, in their edited collection on racism and representation in writing spaces, remind us that

> universities now tend to have something like an Office of Equity and Diversity. That's an interesting title—Fairness and Difference. We would wish for the "and" in Equity and Diversity to be replaced with "despite" or "within." But right now, the Office betrays the precise problem, diversity detached from equity, two different subjects: fairness (what we all want) and difference (with those differences maybe or maybe not treated fairly). Separate out the two and all there is is the acknowledgement of power differences, of a sorting mechanism that decides who is most likely to get parceled out, separated, othered. . . . Acknowledging difference is not the same as acting on those differences—substantively. Diversity is something other than Equity.
>
> Whatever the euphemism, whatever individual sensibilities about difference as of no real contemporary consequence, the language betrays the ways that othering is in the word and gestures of diversity. . . . But all that has really changed—and it is a significant change, all in all—is the social sanction of racism. The social sanction of gender discrimination has altered, not as significantly as it has of racism (if the prevalence of the word *bitch* has any significance). Yet the inability of society to allow for something other than heterosexuality remains as strong as ever, as public debate takes place about whether or not gay couples should be treated fairly. And social safety nets for the poor have become threadbare. The effects of bigotry and exclusion remain. (2014, 5)

Since it remains true that the overwhelming majority of teachers of college writing and multimedia authoring are white but students are increasingly of color, and that these same white writing teachers are often early-career graduate students or other early-career writing professionals who might "graduate" out of teaching first-year writing after a few years, this current book intends to support teachers, especially early career, in

DOI: 10.7330/9781607328742.c000a

embracing the challenges and exciting opportunities of instructing in increasingly multiracial writing spaces.

But with reference to the two paragraphs quoted above from Eddy and Villanueva, how do we best understand this crucial disconnect of "fairness and difference"? In a television interview in March 1964, Malcolm X noted that "you can't drive a knife into a man's back nine inches, pull it out six inches, and call it progress. If you pull it all the way out that's not progress. Progress is healing the wound that the blow made. And they haven't even pulled the knife out much less healed the wound. They won't even admit the knife is there" ("Malcolm X on Progress"). How must we acknowledge and understand racial oppressions, and how might we provide alternatives to unearned privileges and disrespectful Otherings? This book examines the unearned racial and cultural privileges that come from demonstrated competence with Standardized American English. White writing teachers and administrative support professionals need and often desire a better understanding of and engagement with the exciting demographic changes that make the United States and our learning spaces look increasingly like the planet as a whole. When we say the current volume frames racial and cultural unearned privileges as complicating and disrupting the rhetorical and literacy work of college writing courses, we are not saying all the interconnected privileging or Othering dynamics related to gender, class, sexuality, generation, religion, and all the other Others are less important to us. Rather, we are saying this book foregrounds racial and cultural complexities/disruptions to educational, rhetorical, and social justice occurring in our college learning spaces. In any event, all the Otherings are always present in any foregrounded examination of power, privilege, and difference.

This book argues that as all of us live and work in the present white-majority United States but thoughtfully prepare for a color-majority/white-minority United States that is quickly approaching, we are all in the midst of an emerging shared fate on a vulnerable planet divided by racism and by war (Eddy 1996). One vivid indication of this significant demographic transformation is that white children are already in the minority of births in the United States (Yen 2012). We argue that as we move rhetorically and politically/economically from structures of a largely uncontested as well as unearned white privilege to a complex and doubtless messy shared fate in which white privilege must be completely dismantled, we must also acknowledge our idea(l)s as teachers/scholars/activists/public intellectuals who affirm and challenge student writing and students as whole people. The new framework this text elucidates foregrounds a way for creating writing spaces in which critical mentoring and collaborative revisions of identity are nurtured in the midst of challenging, resisting, and dismantling unearned white privilege.

This is not to say that the coming color-majority/white-minority status will end white power dynamics; the change in demographics will certainly not itself mean the end of our racist system. In the introduction, which follows this preface, we give our definition of racism: a "political-economic reality of discrimination, segregation, and exploitation based on membership in a racialized group that leads to vastly different life chances." Many folks of color define systemic racism as systemic white privilege. Many white folks define and understand racism as individual acts of insult or attack, thus denying or ignoring the systemic and institutional realities of racism. The completely routine linguistic, rhetorical, educational, media, healthcare, housing, policing, legal, and literal violence of systemic racism against the minds and bodies of people of color will not end with a white-minority United States. Systemic racism in this country will only end when we end it collectively. The number of US races and cultures included in the "we" of the previous sentence who will increase and better coordinate current antiracism work so as to end racism in this country will determine the heart of the US political economy in the present and the coming decades. At the heart of this "we" who commit to ridding this country of racism will be people of color and white allies working as equals. What percentage of white Americans and white writing teachers are committing and will commit to racial justice for all/ending unearned white privilege? This is an open question that will define the collective destiny of this country in the present and in coming decades. The coauthors of this book *reject the oppression of people of color right now* and work for that reality in classrooms, in coalition work, and in prison writing. We are not waiting for any demographic changes to fight racism in learning spaces and the public sphere generally. We remind our readers of the coming white-minority status because it matters in learning-space politics and national politics generally; whites who do not commit to racial justice and the common humanity of all will engage in more than routine enactments of white privilege and resistance to loss of white power. The median net worth figures for blacks and whites in Boston represent disastrous inequality: African Americans—just $8.00 (not a typographical error); Whites—$247,500 ("Spotlight" 2017). What percentage of wealth and power will whites lose if unearned white power is replaced with justice for all? What percentage of whites are willing to work for racial equality if the price in classrooms and in net worth is the total loss of unearned white privilege?

The danger to us all, especially people of color and white allies (who are seen by white supremacists as race traitors to be hated most), is white supremacy in the form of overt violence. More common, however, are covert or indirect forms of white privilege in classrooms and the national culture generally, and these indirect challenges to openness are of central importance to dynamic learning and functioning equality. In writing classrooms mainly or significantly composed of white students, a powerful manifestation of white privilege and white discomfort and resistance is simple and sustained silence in response to any multiracial work that critiques typical unearned white privilege. Such silent resistance and the racial dominance of white-student collective responses are challenges for writing teachers whether they are early-career or more experienced instructors. These white-student silent resistances to emerging demographic equality are increasing as a color-majority United States emerges. The solutions or antidotes to such white rejection of multiracial realities in the present and stronger demographic richness in the near future are versions of demonstrating to white students how they can begin to become experts-in-training in cross-racial rhetorics and code meshing as the direct and democratic cross-racial communication of radical equals. Yet to take on this newer role, white students must engage as equals in dynamic and sustained communication with students of color in the classroom or other learning spaces they share. The learning goal to foreground here is best put in query form in end-of-course student-evaluation questions: How has our intense but temporary learning community been an approximation of the American Dream of education, engagement, equality, and openness? How have we fallen short of that ideal? What adjustments will you make in your future work experience to accentuate the positive elements of our experience and avoid the negative? Jason Esters describes a race- and gender-centered writing center:

> Writing centers work when their practitioners have built community. And there is no community if race or gender is an elephant in the room. They should be safe spaces, liberating spaces, not silent ones that never address the issues of race that imbue the center, its tutors, its clients, and its administrators. Community needs to be built, and it needs to be just as much a part of the strategic plan as computers and salaries and legal pads. (2011, 299)

As we use the term *unearned white privilege*, coauthors Espinosa-Aguilar and Eddy, a woman of color and a white man, are referring to structural realities. As former graduate students ourselves, both from working-class backgrounds, and as teacher/scholars who have gone on to work with our own graduate students, we are more than aware that white grad students rarely feel as if they are living a life of privilege and excess resources. So, given that white graduate students, new teachers especially, very often bristle at the term *white privilege*, what happens when the term *unearned* is added? White privilege and the ideology of liberalism are such that readers by and large take this term personally and start thinking about how hard they've had it or are having it as graduate students, balk at the suggestion that they enjoy privilege, and miss the structural point—that it's *unearned* because social structures persist that afford whites the access and power denied people of color who face systemic racism, classism, and other isms all the time. Privilege is a given—is literally *given*—on the basis of melanin and heritage. We all must remember that what is unearned—by gender privilege and by race privilege—must be put back in circulation openly and fairly if we wish to be a democracy of equals.

The politics of language diversity is an unavoidable challenge in multiethnic and multiracial writing spaces in our contemporary country, our continent, our hemisphere, and our planet generally and will become increasing so as we move toward, for example, a color-majority/white-minority United States. Given the significantly and increasingly diverse population in the United States, especially among the Latinx population, what are rhetoric and writing studies doing to engage, support, and challenge what Cristina Kirklighter calls the "dynamic heterogeneity" of North American Latinx? The answer is still far too little. Thankfully, dynamic work has emerged in the field. A groundbreaking book is Cristina Kirklighter, Diana Cárdenas, and Susan Wolf Murphy's *Teaching Writing with Latino/a Students: Lessons Learned at Hispanic-Serving Institutions* (2007). Focusing on schools with at least 25 percent Latinx student populations, the editors and contributors studied appropriate graduate preparation—or its absence—for teaching students, the relationships of English, Spanish, Spanglish, and language-status issues to the great varieties of cultural and linguistic groups within and among Latinx in the United States, and the effects of racism in complicating, interrupting, and challenging student engagement, persistence, and success.

Similarly, Michelle Hall Kells, Valerie Balester, and Victor Villanueva's *Latino/a Discourses: On Language, Identity, and Literacy Education* engages the international and intercultural, the classroom and the community, scholarship and family life, Spanglish and public discourse, and the politics of language diversity, as well as practical strategies for learner success. In his afterword to the volume, Villanueva concludes with this invitation and insistence:

> And we create and come to understand our own [Latino] discourses—much
> more than language—and entreat you to join us in that understanding,
> so that we might come together as one, despite our differences, which we
> also claim with pride, so that we can receive the respect and dignity that
> is our due. (2004, 143)

How do teachers in multiracial, multilingual settings honor language diversity and acknowledge the power of Edited American English (EAE)? How do linguistic power status, nationalism, and racism influence and problematize our intentions and our practices in writing spaces? Geneva Smitherman and Victor Villanueva's *Language Diversity in the Classroom: From Intention to Practice* uses the work of Eduardo Bonilla-Silva and Tyrone Forman to remind us "that *appearing* racist is the taboo, not racism itself" (Smitherman and Villanueva 2003, 3).

In *Literacy and Racial Justice: The Politics of Learning after Brown v. Board of Education*, Catherine Prendergast presents literacy as a white property controlled and marketed by white political and economic powers. In examining what can only be seen as the myth of assimilation through literacy as constructed in immigration cases she studies and in the full variety of Supreme Court rulings in the Civil Rights time frame, she clearly and vividly foregrounds the routine racial injustice she uncovers. What to do? Prendergast insists on inclusive literacies that engage systemic racism rather than blink away routine racial oppressions. What is an inclusive literacy?

> At its best, literacy is a process of lifelong learning, a source of potential
> social engagement and critique, fuel for self-affirmation, and a means to
> restore justice to the law. At its worst, and too often in the present national
> dialogue on the subject, it is an excuse to delay long overdue reparations.
> (2003, 176)

Prendergast's argument uses Eric Yamamoto's *Interracial Justice: Conflict and Reconciliation in Post-Civil Rights America* (1999) and ends her book with the word *reparations* to provide a reality check for us as professional educators and whole human beings. Malcolm X's key line in many speeches, "no justice, no peace," is where we are standing in the present. So what might justice literacy and its assessment look like, especially in writing studies?

In *Vernacular Insurrections: Race, Black Protest, and the New Century in Composition-Literacies Studies*, Carmen Kynard argues that how "the story of the relationship between composition studies and the Black Freedom Movement is told bears important consequences as it provides an insightful reading into the epistemological breakthroughs and remaining cognitive closures surrounding a continued color line in language and literacy education" (2013, 6). Kynard's affirming of the crucial effects of the continued color line in literacy instruction gives us a sense of where we all stand in the second decade of the twenty-first century as we prepare for new ways of being together, or not together, especially in literacy instruction in the context of equity within diversity.

In *Race and Writing Assessment* (2012), Asao Inoue and Mya Poe provide the background, current scholarship, and future challenges for assessment practices that do more than pretend scientific fairness in the midst of political-economic injustices in access to college, retention in college, and evaluations of college work, especially in writing spaces. In her chapter in Inoue and Poe's collection, Zandra Jordan reminds us that appreciation and engagement with language-diversity issues and opportunities is not just for historically white colleges and universities (HWCUs) but for all college settings and concludes:

> We can help students by understanding their attitudes toward AAE and our own; engaging them in dialogue about language diversity through readings and writing; helping them identify unfamiliar EAE conventions and then modeling those conventions, while also honoring the language of their heritage; and bringing these new approaches into the way we assess student writing in the classroom. To college composition instructors wondering how to respond to African American English speakers, [my student Shanika] offers these words: Don't just knock 'em down. Give 'em something that they can change. They can develop greatly over a semester but the opportunity of just changing completely over a semester is just slim. So, just understand, maybe, where that person is coming from. (2012,108)

Shanika gives crucial advice by insisting that we work harder in writing spaces to understand and appreciate "where that person is coming from," in both the case of a whole human being playing the role of student and a whole human being playing the role of teacher. In this book, teachers and students are invited and supported—but also challenged—to do much more work analyzing their own racialization and cultural constructions. Cathy Davidson and David Theo Goldberg (2010) call this racialization analysis work "mobilizing networks" of as much real complexity and hoped-for consonance in as wide an array of coalitions with multiple rhetorical audiences as is possible. They affirm the goal of equity within diversity in which all the key players, as well as all the currently Othered voices and groups, intermesh.

It is clear that in dynamically interacting with current demographics in a contemporary multiracial United States, and in equitably preparing for a color-majority United States, we must reinvent our country, reinvent our universities, and reinvent our discipline to end all unearned group privileges of race, gender, sexuality, and culture. In Christopher Schroeder's *ReInventing the University* (2001), we see one colleague's struggle to decenter the existing political economy of our classrooms. We must decenter our learning spaces because routinely they represent only one possible voice—a white hegemonic monologue—but, working with students, Schroeder wants new voices, new practices, new standards, and new legitimacies.

As we reinvent our country, universities, and discipline, Jacqueline Jones Royster and Gesa Kirsch's *Feminist Rhetorical Practices: New Horizons for Rhetoric, Composition, and Literacy Studies* can help point the way. In exploring the "tectonic shifts in rhetorical practices" (2012, 29), the coeditors use the analytical tools of critical imagination, strategic contemplation, social circulation, and transnationalism to open up rhetorical inquiry and ethical responsibility to each other and to our multiple evolving identities and plural environments as a robust interdisciplinary project of survival. *Writing Across Cultures* offers several survival scenarios and assignments that include alternative rhetorical ways to imagine and plan coalitions of adaptability to changing identities and increasing group-responsibilities. See for example Context-Building Writing Activity 20: The Migrant as Our "Rescuer" in Our Course and in Our Country and Context-Building Writing Activity 21: Renaming the United States of America.

As we go about this crucial and exciting work of evolving multiracial alternative rhetorics and pedagogies, teaching narratives become an important resource for cross-group teacher dialogue. Lisa Guerrero's edited collection *Teaching Race in the 21st Century: College Teachers Talk about Their Fears, Risks, and Rewards (2008)* provides stories of dominant racial discourses and how these discourses are studied, resisted, countered, complicated, and challenged by individual instructors.

For a teaching-narrative book that is single-author, Frankie Condon's *I Hope I Join the Band* does the crucial work of affirming the voices of students of color and exploring ways to avoid unintentionally erasing voices and languages of color. Condon shares potent honesty throughout the book, including her admission that she is "sometimes baffled by the depth and degree of anger many white folks express when they are invited or provoked to consider the matter of complicity with racism" (2012, 89). Condon is the lone author until the last chapter, when she suddenly and dynamically engages dialogically with Vershawn Young, particularly on the subject of racialized identity, for a powerful closing to the book. The dialogue narratives demonstrate that "we humans tend to tell a story in order to understand a story" (141). The work of

Writing Across Cultures is to multiply these cross-group stories and to give students and teachers options for organizing dynamic stories and rhetorical analyses for new coalitions and new forms of collective actions for racial justice within learning spaces and beyond them.

Schroeder's *Diverse by Design: Literacy Education within Multicultural Institutions* includes a fascinating narrative by Neida Hernandez-Santamaria, which includes this response to how her Hispanic-serving institution (HSI) welcomes the cultural diversity of its students:

> Taking into consideration the fact that we are promoting Latino students' success, we are morally required to be aware of environmental and social factors that impact the diverse members of the Latino community. By being aware we can more effectively help our students succeed in college and eventually as professionals by tailoring for example the Seminar classes to meet specific needs (Schroeder 2011, 119).

The teaching narratives in Schroeder's book, and the book overall, exemplify the relationship of the reality of systemic racism to colorblind racism in teachers and students. Teaching narratives that share and complicate the rich experiences of teaching and learning at HSIs and HBCUs compared with teaching and learning at HWCUs can provide a way to see the alienation of poor students of color and how critical mentoring has survival value for all involved. The following are excerpts from Carmen Kynard's take on institutions that proclaim diversity yet are threatened by any evidence of it in action. She writes,

> Before the first day of my very first semester, I had already grown accustomed to the endless public proclamations of this place being THE MOST diverse university in the country. And while this is certainly true of the students, it certainly does not accurately describe the faculty, pedagogies, ideologies, or mission of this university.

After meeting with a student who suggests it is unusual that Dr. Kynard has maintained her identity while working in the academy, she reflects,

> I almost fall out of my chair. I really don't even know how to answer at first. The only thing I can come up with to tell her is that I am wondering and concerned about what has happened at this university that she must even ask this, how could I appear as such an anomaly to her? I tell her quite frankly that I REALLY am NOT sure how "comfortable" I am these days but I DO know that I won't be giving up any part of myself in order to exist in a place that gives so little to people like me—somehow that kind of equation just don't balance out so I don't do no math like that, not for nobody, especially the white racists who roam at large at this university under the guise of diversity. . . . This rhetoric of diversity that infects the campus but seems to really be nothing more than a celebration of the production of a multilingual bourgeois ethno-class who can now attract

a more colorful populace in a consumer capitalist market. I also want to talk about what it means to prepare student teachers, student teachers of color, who will teach in working class urban communities of color, but who have never experienced a liberatory education at our campus, not even by our department. . . . For me, when it comes to transformation and impact, it's all about the classroom. Teaching in this place will mean that I have to draw from another space, be here but be from somewhere else pedagogically, politically, and historically and so I keep coming home late on Friday nights, talking to more students, understanding more and more about where I am, and what it will mean to intervene in all of that through my teaching (Kynard and Eddy 2009, W33).

If we collectively labor to reinvent our discipline as a multiracial inter-disciplinary project of survival and productivity for all, we must connect Kynard's charge that "this rhetoric of diversity that infects the campus but seems to really be nothing more than a celebration of the production of a multilingual bourgeois ethno-class who can now attract a more col-orful populace in a consumer capitalist market" with Villanueva's claim, "Racism, its tie to colonialism, its tie to language and language-in-action, its corrosive effect, it's leaving holes in memory, like empty pockets in the brain" (2008, 84). The political-economic attempt to construct mul-tilingual folks of color as a "bourgeois ethno-class who can now attract a more colorful populace in a consumer capitalist market" in the pres-ence of a "corrosive," colonial systemic racism that controls language and memory is a reality that cannot be blinked away. We need to resist and replace corrosive colonial racism with dynamic networks of equity within diversity. All races and cultures among both teachers and students deserve material equity, not mere symbolic diversity.

If we are to pursue a multiracial interdisciplinary project of survival and productivity for all of us, we must redirect and speed up our claimed support for real equity within diversity: true pluralism, including of lan-guage. In our discipline we all do versions of rhetorical language and literacy work. Therefore, it is a good idea to revisit and redefine contras-tive rhetoric. Clayann Gilliam Panetta's *Contrastive Rhetoric Revisited and Redefined (2001)* reviews the history of the use of contrastive rhetoric with international students studying in the United States. But the book intends a more inclusive audience than ESL colleagues alone. Panetta and other contributors to the volume connect contrastive rhetoric to the various "native" Englishes of American writing classrooms and graduate programs in interesting and innovative ways. Contrastive rhetoric can and should be a powerful analytic tool for foreground-ing, exploring, and respecting—in pluralist settings—the key issue of difference. Juanita Comfort's chapter develops several case studies of

African American women in their midforties in doctoral programs and concludes that

> while schooling students in the conventional discursive rules that even the students themselves believe they will need to acquire to be successful academics, graduate faculty should be prepared to help them to consider more carefully the consequences of internalizing the rules of the "Master's" discourse. . . . Faculty readers might further do more to help writers transcend the traditional dichotomy of academic versus nonacademic discourse. Many African-American women in the academy increasingly desire to compose their texts in ways that encourage interpersonal and intercultural *interaction* with their audiences. In order to feel confident about using all the resources at their command, these writers need the assurance that their readers are cognizant and appreciative of the nuances of other ways of knowing and being that writers bring to acts of composing. Engendering trust at this level also means developing strategies for helping writers exploit effectively their culturally distinct resources in composing texts designed for academically oriented purposes and audiences (2001, 102–3).

Writing teachers, especially white writing teachers, must understand that being "cognizant and appreciative of the nuances of other ways of knowing and being that writers bring to acts of composing" requires a sense of shared fate, of pluralism, and of real equality, as well as code meshing of standardized English with any and all the Other(ed) Englishes. Vershawn Young, Rusty Barrett, Y'Shanda Young-Rivera, and Kim Brian Lovejoy's *Other People's English* supports writers of color and helps all of us theorize and make pedagogical the overcoming of "linguistic double consciousness" (2014, 55). Code meshing is not merely code switching because the meshing acknowledges and demonstrates more accurately the complexity that creates who we are and how we judge rhetorical possibilities. What are we, then? We are—all of us—multiple amphibians living in many worlds and communities at once who badly need to be recognized as vast and complex. All of us. Code meshing acknowledges and performs our complexity, while code switching can oversimplify our identity across race, culture, and power differentials.

We need to move more committedly toward an increasingly multiracial reinventing of our country, universities, and discipline. John Trimbur's *Solidarity or Service: Composition and the Problem of Expertise* is crucial for helping our discipline reimagine how a multiracial reinvention of our work in a code-meshing context might look and what bottlenecks of privilege must be overcome. How might multiracial equalities influence and transform current relationships of experts and everyday people through a social process of shared critical literacies and shared expertise in various, perhaps circulating, features of our multiple amphibian lives of solidarity and shared survival? What might such a goal and task of constructing a multiracial social process of equity within diversity look like within and beyond learning spaces? According to Trimbur, we need to understand how institutions set boundaries between professionals and ordinary people, how ideologies organize expert and lay knowledge into cognitive and cultural hierarchies, and what the implications of these actual and symbolic economies of expertise might be for teachers, theorists, and program administrators who believe writing instruction should promote rhetorical agency and popular participation in public life (2011, 1). On this matter of equitable and open relationships of expert and lay knowledge, *Writing Across Cultures* agrees with Han Yu in his "How to Define a Teacher" that we must open up definitions and expectations of a "teacher" and a "student" and realize that "everyone [is] a teacher of what each person kn[ows] best" (2014, 167).

When David Harvey, in his *A Brief History of Neoliberalism*, reminds us about prospects for freedom, he insists that social justice must become a "definite goal rather than a distant ideal" (2005, 183) and that public discourse in the United States, and internationally, is "impoverished" by refusals to debate "concepts of freedom . . . appropriate to our times" (184) as opposed to freedom equaling only free-enterprise affirmation of wealth quests. Affirming rights, especially "alternative rights," must be carefully defined—think here of our profession's 1974 affirmation of Students' Right to Their Own Language (National Council of Teachers of English 1974) and the degree to which our profession has upheld commitments to thoughtful language diversity. Harvey argues that alternative rights require "an alternative social process within which" such rights "can inhere" (2005, 204).

The challenge, as Goldberg makes comprehensively clear and appropriately complex in *The Threat of Race: Reflections on Racial Neoliberalism*, is understanding that the "principle charge facing the modern state, then, has been how to conceive of and manage its population" (2009, 328). If neoliberalism "is the undertaking, then, to maximize corporate profits and efficiencies by reducing costs—most notably as a consequence of taxes, tariffs, and regulations," (332), this means that "'trickle-down' charitability" (332) is the only structurally affirmed gesture toward social justice. And who are the least protected citizens? Those who don't "belong." And those who don't belong get labeled as Other. And who is the latest Other who has surely been made to feel not to "belong"?

Deepa Kumar, in *Islamophobia and the Politics of Empire* (2012), shares with readers her frequent commodification and demonizing after 9/11.

Though she is neither Arab nor Muslim, her sense of shared fate with despised Others and with all people of color made her determined under all situations not to disclose to attackers that she is not Muslim. This is the kind of solidarity that needs to inspire all of us as we move toward color-majority United States and possibilities for commitments to equity within diversity. Such solidarity is not pretending we are someone we are not; it instead involves a refusal to abandon sisters, brothers, and trans others from disrespected groups not one's own at moments of crisis and assault. Individual survival by separating our identity from an under-attack member of another oppressed group would be a deeply conflicted form of self-preservation that could result in credible survivor guilt.

What are we to do about we the people of the United States at our worst when we engage in rhetorics that characterize others as the less than human? David Livingstone Smith's *Less Than Human: Why We Demean, Enslave, and Exterminate Others* begins by quoting the ending of Ali Alizadeh's poem "Your Terrorist":

> I understand
> what you want your filthy slave to be. I am
> your barbarian, your terrorist;
> your monster. (quoted in Smith 2011, ix)

When we dehumanize others, we share this thinking pattern: we use Othering labels to describe those unlike ourselves as barbaric, terrorists, monsters. Smith argues that the rhetoric of the less than human—which all of us are susceptible to falling into—involves these stages:

1. We see Othered humans as dehumanized animals.
2. We engage in a sympathetic imagination that others with our phenotype have similar inner lives, values, and commitments.
3. We see dehumanized groups as a "means" to our group's desires with our having no moral obligations toward them.

Seeing others as less than human takes place on college campuses all too often. It is manifest in our texts, assignments, assessments, fraternities, sororities, student clubs, and the hiring and judging of faculty colleagues. Smith ends his book with an understated but desperate plea:

> The study of dehumanization needs to be made a priority. Universities, governments, and nongovernmental organizations need to put money, time, and talent into figuring out exactly how dehumanization works and what can be done to prevent it. Maybe then we can use this knowledge to build a future that is less hideous than our past: a future with no Rwandas, no Hiroshimas, and no Final Solutions.

Can this be done? Nobody knows, because nobody's ever tried. (2011, 273)

And it is here in *Writing Across Cultures* that we intend to make our contribution, however modest in scope or possible results, toward addressing all persons involved in rhetorical work across race and culture as radically full human beings. We also hope for and will work toward Davidson and Goldberg's "mobilizing networks" of shared work and shared fate (for an example of the importance of alliance and coalition work, see Malea Powell [2004]).

What is a concrete image of the goal of multiracial, subordinated groups as full equals? Writing home during his Pilgrimage in 1964, Malcolm X described what race relations are like when there is equality.

> There were tens of thousands of pilgrims, from all over the world. They were of all colors, from blue-eyed blondes to black-skinned Africans. But we were all participating in the same ritual, displaying a spirit of unity and brotherhood that my experiences in America had led me to believe never could exist between the white and non-white. America needs to understand Islam, because this is the one religion that erases from its society the race problem. Throughout my travels in the Muslim world, I have met, talked to, and even eaten with people who in America would have been considered white—but the white attitude was removed from their minds by the religion of Islam. I have never before seen sincere and true brotherhood practiced by all colors together, irrespective of their color. (1965, 340)

The answer to Islamophobia and all the other rhetorics of the less than human, in our learning spaces and outside them, is multiracial, subordinated groups working toward coalitions of equality. We must coconstruct a new sociological imagination of what it means to be American, democratic, and pluralistic, as the mobilizing networks of the twenty-first century invite and, finally, demand. *Writing Across Cultures* supports teachers of writing as we individually and collectively invite students to rewrite all the Americas, North and South, within and among cultures of equity within diversity. The goal, not as a distant ideal but as a current necessity, is classrooms and nations in which we are all welcomed and valued as dynamic beings from the same extended family, which is currently barely functional but which wants something much better: justice with common humanity open and acknowledged.

WRITING ACROSS CULTURES

Introduction

PLURALIST RHETORICS FOR WRITING TEACHERS AND THEIR STUDENTS

Congratulations. You've been assigned a first-year writing (FYW) course, possibly even your first. You know you need to instruct students on the fundamentals of composing, from paragraphing to organizing, to revision, to editing and proofreading. However, as first-year writing instructors, dare we say composition specialists, we sincerely hope our book takes you far beyond this. For many of your students, completion of your course assignments is the roadmap for their journey to and through a new place and in a new culture. The place is college and the new culture is academic life and language, rhetorical work, and the art of persuasion in multiracial settings of unequal power relations.

This book is an exception to the majority of rhetorics on the market. First, it is intended to help all composition instructors, regardless of previous experience, become better teachers in the highly racial setting that has become the first-year writing course. Specialists know that, historically, composition has been taught by novices and those lacking training in the field (TAs, adjunct faculty trained in literary studies, retirees, former high-school teachers, faculty spouses). Beginning teachers rarely have developed a philosophy of teaching; they teach the way they were taught. Until we develop a teaching philosophy, we teach by trial and error. Most faculty still come from white, middle-class backgrounds, are second- or third-generation college graduates, and earned advanced degrees with the mistaken notion that they would land a tenure-track appointment at a research university. Rarely have such folks interacted with students whose demographics do not reflect their own. Yet, they are members of the demographic that is statistically becoming the minority at US colleges. In this way US higher education is beginning to reflect South African apartheid: an empowered minority holding all the cards over the soon-to-be racial majority. Consider this reminder from Asao Inoue and Mya Poe:

> Across the U.S., the educational system is undergoing a major demographic shift. For example, this year in Texas, 52% of entering first-year

DOI: 10.7330/9781607328742.c000b

students are students of color. . . . According to the U.S. Census Bureau, 47% of children under the age of 5 in the U.S. are children of color with 25% of those children being Hispanic (U.S. Census, 2009, para.1). Overall, 44% of children under the age of 18 in the U.S. are "minorities." Among college-age students, the National Center for Educational Statistics (2009) estimates that by 2018, the enrollment of traditionally underrepresented minorities in higher education will include a 26% increase in black students, a 38% increase in Hispanic students, a 29% increase in Asian Pacific Islander students, a 32% increase in American Indian students, while only a 4% increase in white students. (2012, 1)

These racial trends are speeding up, leading to the United States as a color-majority country in approximately twenty-five years. Our book, and future editions of it, can become a leader in helping teachers, students, and administrators navigate the real challenges and wonderful opportunities of multiracial learning spaces, multiracial workplaces, and multiracial hiring committees in the present and more so in the near future.

THE DEFINITIONS WE WILL USE

Rhetoric: the art of persuasion in multiracial settings of unequal power relations.

Ideology: a set of strongly held beliefs and values, a world-view, especially dealing with governance of society. Ideology includes beliefs that influence us through language and image to see things in a way that is only truly rational to those in power. It is the majority group's hustle, which they claim is natural and inevitable.

Racism: a political-economic reality of discrimination, segregation, and exploitation based on membership in a racialized group that leads to vastly different life chances. Many folks of color define systemic racism as systemic white privilege. Many white folks define and understand racism as individual acts of insult or attack, thus denying or ignoring the systemic and institutional realities of racism. A powerful and constructive anonymous reviewer of this book during the prepublication review stages defines racism as "a complex, intersecting, institutionalized, and *strategic* system of advantage and violence based on race."

White privilege: unearned, more or less unconscious and automatic racialized preference, power, and comfort of being the norm possessed by all white-phenotype people regardless of their relative wealth, status, and reputation. Yes, wealthy and connected whites have more white privilege than other whites, but all whites have serious and sustained white privilege. White privilege is the last power, and it is a crucial asset of otherwise powerless, poor whites, an asset that can open doors to training, jobs, housing, and public assistance ahead of people of color in a racist system whose safety net for the poor of any color is threadbare. Many experts, educators, and activists describe white privilege as the other side, the opposite side, and the enabling side of racial discrimination. On one hand, white privilege is a huge political-economic benefit for white people. On the other hand, it is personally and spiritually damaging to everyone and is especially destructive to the humanity of white people. It has deformed the white psyche, and the white elite have used it to separate working-class whites and people of color in a classic divide-and-conquer strategy. It must be eliminated for there to be human liberation in this country and the chance for coconstructing multiracial equality.

Culture: ways of living, especially behaviors and beliefs over generations, of people in any human group: a nation, race, religion, profession, club, sport, or any other human group. Cultures are complex, historically contingent, and not essentialized except by detractors or outright enemies or by fundamentalists within the culture who essentialize their own group. When a culture essentializes itself and thereby becomes fundamentalist, thinking it has 100 percent of the truth, as in religious or political extremist cultures, it thereby declares at least rhetorical war on all other groups, if not literal war. It is the slowly changing stories of identity and purpose, which appear more or less unchanging, that lead cultures to pluralism or fundamentalism, to coalitions and cooperation, or to contestation and war.

Democracy (in academia): an exciting reality in many FYW courses in which the multiple student and teacher voices explore, dialogue, encourage, critique, and develop individual and group arguments about evidence and persuasion in common readings and multiple class members' texts. On the political-economic and structural levels, democracy in academia is more often a goal and an ideal than a current reality. The ideal of democracy is that all voices are structurally equal. In such democratic equality, the relative value of particular texts and of all academic work is collaboratively determined based exclusively on verifiable evidence and convincing argumentation that includes careful listening to naysayers and dissonant voices of disrespected outsiders in the shifting centers of power and openness. Among contemporary college faculty overall, democracy is sadly lacking in an era of mostly contingent, underpaid, underinsured, non-tenure-track faculty positions in the corporate university run by an increasing number of corporate administrators using the venture-capitalist model. Among college students, the exponential growth of student-loan debt is indentured servitude and is the opposite of democracy. Democracy in academia is a currently receding but worthy ideal that must not be romanticized nor seen as part of a distant future but must be fought for in the present, made real and viable, and opened to constant review by all interested individuals and groups.

WHO BENEFITS FROM THIS BOOK

A significant percentage of graduate-student teaching assistants and early-career teachers are assigned first-year writing classes and are often in need of support when working dynamically and spontaneously in multiracial classrooms. This text was written by two teachers who wish to teach other teachers, regardless of their years of experience, how to more fully use both home and academic cultures to teach writing. Writing program directors and instructors with more experience will find the book appealing for a number of reasons. First, these teachers often don't want to be confined by the material in a textbook. Traditionally, composition rhetorics are designed to include rhetorical modes, paragraph development, theses, and so forth. Experienced teachers often tell us they prefer to go without a book than be forced to use those that continue to suggest effective writing is merely the sum of its parts.

Second, experienced teachers rarely use an entire textbook because textbooks try to cover too much. Our book remains focused consistently on a writing model developed by Robert Eddy called the Eddy Model of Intercultural Experience in academic writing, and we provide examples of student-produced sequenced writing using the model. This text is designed to allow experienced instructors to take multiple approaches to teaching writing about culture and race and is designed to mentor newer teachers in enabling successful student negotiation of the academic terrain that is college.

KEY TERMS AND THE EDDY MODEL

As college campuses become ever more multiracial, our book's key concept, namely the Eddy Model of Intercultural Experience, is increasingly needed. The realities of a mainly white teaching staff and an increasingly multiracial student body mean that authentic cross-racial communication is crucial. Our text is unique in that its primary focus is helping students become engaged members of a new culture, namely the discourse community of college/academia.

There are three key terms we use throughout this text. They are *metaculture*, *polyculture*, and *interculture*. Many compositionists are familiar with metacognition, or the act of thinking about how we think. Borrowing from that definition, we use *metaculture* to suggest the act of thinking about how our thoughts construct the ways in which we adopt certain cultural behaviors or values. Similarly, we understand that the prefix *poly* suggests many, as in *polyglot*. We explore, using the Eddy Model of

Intercultural Experience, the concept that culture is rarely uniform; we acquire not just a culture of origin during our lives but many others that intertwine to make up our personal world-view. We leave behind the duality of biculturalism and purposefully reject the politically loaded term *multiculturalism.* Intercultural experiences ultimately result in a metacultural being able to actively consider the origins of their values, beliefs, and key behavioral operating concepts and express them in ways that respect difference and foster polycultural understanding.

AIMS AND UNIQUE FEATURES

There are three unique aims to this book. The first is that we intend this text to be seen more as a conversation among colleagues about how best to enculturate first-year students to college and academic discourse than as a lecture. Second, it remains true that the vast majority of incoming students are inexperienced about academic culture. We intend that this unique conversation challenge our profession about how it has, or has not, gone about teaching collegians how to negotiate multiple boundaries and audiences in self-conscious ways. As instructors with several decades of teaching experience, we have spent years engaging our students and colleagues in this often uncomfortable but creative conversation. We ask them to compare a first-year student's exposure to academic culture to visiting another country or to living in that new place for nine months to four or five years. Living in is very different from visiting or imagining a place. As travelers who choose to become residents of the subtle, complex culture called *college,* which uses the foreign language called *academic discourse,* students will be changed by the experience. This new culture especially requires a student to conceptualize how their home culture creates their sense of who they are and how the world works.

These concepts did not occur to us overnight. Here is a little about our own experiences with teaching writing and immersion in other cultures. Amanda and Robert have each taught college writing for a number of decades and are Americans; Robert began his college teaching career at an eastern US college, then lived outside the United States for more than a decade, where he taught for about an equal number of years in England, China, and Egypt. Since returning to the United States, he has taught at a historically black university in the Southeast and is currently teaching at a large research university that is predominantly white on the West Coast. Amanda's career has included appointments at one private and several public US universities and two-year colleges located in nearly every geographic region of the United States: the Pacific Northwest, the West, the Midwest, the Northeast, and the Southeast. These schools use both open and exclusive admissions policies, ensuring that Amanda has worked with students from a wide range of racial, ethnic, religious, socioeconomic, immigrant, linguistic, gender, and age backgrounds. The methods this book employs apply equally well to the different cultures within the United States or the cultures of other countries. To come to college is to enter a new culture and to be required to learn a new language, no matter where you come from.

Another key feature of our text is that it uses student samples, not professionally authored ones, to demonstrate in action the framework of the Eddy Model of Intercultural Experience. Our book springs from the conviction that most first-year students have a limited idea or misinformed ideas about the customs, language, expectations, and nuances of university life. Some will live in residence halls and have to negotiate that culture as well as the academic one. Some will be in a new city, state, or country and will have to negotiate that culture as compared to the one left at home. Our book's strength lies in highlighting this awkward, often painful, yet rewarding journey. As students learn to negotiate their real-world adaptation to their new culture(s), they must also learn skills for coping with academic culture. We follow several students from prewriting and brainstorming through drafting, revising, and editing a final draft. The entire sequence is presented not as perfect examples but as real examples, warts and all, of how several students struggled to adapt to the culture of academic writing by using the Eddy Model of Intercultural Experience. The focus on real-world cross-cultural experience and the foregrounding of student texts make our novel approach worthwhile and productive.

The other unique quality of this text, and the competitive advantage to this framework, is its simplicity. Instead of being an unwieldy and bloated textbook, this one utilizes a streamlined, classroom, and interculturally tested method of introducing students to academic writing via sequenced assignments that aren't confined by traditional and static approaches such as modes, templates, and genres often found in competing texts. Since our book presents information without the more lock-step features of an FYW textbook, it focuses just on the stages necessary for a student to experience becoming a fully functional member of academia and user of its discourses. Although some of this text discusses best practices for teaching the fundamentals of writing processes, we believe we write as people trying to reach other people and that students benefit most from seeing composing as an act of engaged communication, not just detached processes.

AN OVERVIEW OF THIS BOOK

Most of the chapters demonstrate the Eddy Model in action. Before we get into the specifics of the model, we provide some context. In chapter 1 ("Home Culture(s), Academic Discourse, Critical Reading, and the Eddy Model of Intercultural Experience"), we discuss how one's identity is shaped and changed after engaging new cultures. We introduce the major theme of this text, namely that entering college is akin to visiting a foreign land for the first time. Then the chapter examines the concepts of how home language and academic language differ and why including practice in critical reading is essential for teaching students audience awareness, which enables them to be able to re-view their own and others' writing. Learning to read critically trains students to see they must make thoughtful choices in their language and adapt it for different audiences, such as home and school. The chapter ends by fleshing out Eddy Model of Intercultural Experience, which is an innovative way of meshing the study of writing with the study of other cultures. The objective is explaining the chart outlining the method, which is the driving force behind the pedagogy that follows.

In chapter 2 ("Entrance to the Preliminary Stage: Brainstorming about Culture"), we discuss a parallel model, borrowed from anthropology, called the Kluckhohn Model. The Eddy Model was directly influenced by this highly regarded chart and is an adaptation of it. This chapter demonstrates how to use the Kluckhohn Model to teach invention methods, such as brainstorming about one's key cultural assumptions, and shows student samples of some Kluckhohn Model-inspired freewrites. These samples demonstrate students examining how their values shape their culture and vice versa. While the Kluckhohn Model can be an effective tool in helping us understand other cultures and our own, we ultimately suggest that the Eddy Model goes further in its ability to create intercultural, metacultural, and polycultural awareness. The chapter concludes by demonstrating how to use the Eddy Model to teach a wide range of invention techniques. It demonstrates both individual and group prewriting techniques based on the Eddy Model, notably focusing on one Eddy used while teaching FYW in China and in Egypt.

Chapter 3 ("The Preliminary Stage, Part 2: Prewriting Using the Eddy Method") demonstrates how to incorporate the invention techniques from the previous chapter along with the Eddy method to create brainstorming drafts that ask students to reflect on their observations. After examining some student samples of freewriting, we present the analogy that compares essay writing to travel.

By the time chapter 4 ("The Spectator Stage: First Draft") begins, students and their instructors already understand the parts of the Eddy method and have used their freewrite essays and other prewriting techniques to get a grasp of the origins of their home cultures. This chapter challenges students to move from mere observation to active engagement or interaction with their new collegiate culture. This engagement happens when students interact with others by planning and eventually sharing their thoughts via a working draft that may be full of false starts. Two student samples are presented that demonstrate the journey from planning to drafting, or the preliminary and spectator stages.

The focus shifts next to talking with students about critical reading, evaluation, feedback and revision. Chapter 5 ("The Increasing-Participation Stage: Working Drafts and Revision") focuses exclusively on the concept of revision being tied to the concept that as changes occur in the writer, those changes are reflected back in the writing. While many writing textbooks look at revision as merely a linguistic exercise—moving ideas, cutting paragraphs, adding more detail—this chapter suggests change happens organically. As authors interact with more people in the new culture, this interaction alone enables writers to more fully comprehend what compels their readers. We suggest that genuine revision can only occur when writers are so fully engaged with their new culture that they can actively solicit feedback from readers. Writers must become dual ambassadors, knowing when to talk and share and when to listen and keep silent. Ultimately, revision is viewed as openness to change and not just moving or cutting sentences. This approach creates polycultural authors who can navigate between their home culture and others with ever-growing fluency.

Experienced instructors know most novice college writers are reluctant to change anything they have written. Chapter 6 ("The Shock Stage: Writer's Block and Fear of Change") takes this on. Many people fear any change, and many students resist making changes to initial drafts. Often these fears result in writer's block. This chapter helps students work through these fears by demonstrating various techniques for guiding students to specific and global places in their draft on which to focus their revision. Student samples of exercises to alleviate writer's block are also discussed.

Chapter 7 ("Convincing the Audience by Using Edited American English") covers supposed best practices in teaching fundamental EAE composing skills, source citation, mechanics, and even grammar and usage. This chapter focuses on why the fundamentals continue to hold a false binary opposition. This binary is perpetuated by those whose language prejudice leads them to believe that imprecision with EAE affects readers, usually negatively; thus, for students who choose to code switch, or who feel forced to code switch by teachers or institutional or other audience requirements, attention to usage and the like must be learned and valued just as they are by professionals, regardless of background. Amanda asserts that such code switching promotes a language of power instead of the power of language prejudice. Amanda does not want her first-generation students, especially of color, to be victims of routine white-power language prejudice, so she endorses code switching. Robert believes in and practices code meshing. Robert agrees with Kim Brian Lovejoy's reading of Suresh A. Canagarajah: "Code-meshers 'don't expect commonalities in form or convention' (p. 18) and what allows them 'to communicate across difference is that they instantaneously construct the norms and conventions. . . . For them meanings and grammars are always emergent' (Canagarajah 2009, 18)" (Young et al. 2014, 134). Likewise, Robert affirms that successful code meshing must be "intelligible, purposeful, and effective" (Young et al. 2014, 144). This chapter revises our initial metaphor of culture as a backpack that needs repacking to one of a culture's similarity to a computer operating system.

Chapter 6 looks at ways of using feedback to rework an essay to overcome writer's block. Chapter 8 ("The Adaptation Stage: Final Drafts and Congruence") returns to the Eddy Model to look at how to create final drafts by defining congruence and identifying and removing the three major congruence blocks that occur in many final drafts: undefined abstractions, logical fallacies, and unexamined alternative explanations. We look at student attempts at incorporating these revisions and end the chapter by presenting the final draft of one of the student essays that has been examined throughout the book.

Serving mostly as a theoretical conclusion, Chapter 9 ("The Reentry Stage: Future Compositions and Dissonant Voices") examines return shock and dissonant voices. The dissonant voice sees knowledge as a continual process, not as an individual commodity loaned by experts who retain ownership. Knowledge is always contested ground. Students who are developing their own dissonant voices add new points to the existing conversations that produce knowledge, making knowledge construction more open and fair. Return shock, the lack of harmony with one's original culture, happens when the dissonant voice tries to impose its values on the home culture. The greater the degree of adaptation to one's new college or geographical culture, the greater the degree of return shock one will experience. Since dissonant voices utilize polycultural and pluralist rhetorics, a dissonant voice will have significant to extensive inharmony with its new culture of college, especially college's white-supremacist attitudes toward language and power. Dissonant voices, which are polycultural and pluralist, do not perfectly fit anywhere and need to seek coalitions for freedom, openness, and degrees of community as alternatives to white supremacy, which is why dissonant voices tend to choose code meshing.

In chapter 10 ("Cultural Meshing or Switching in Poly- or Intercultural Writing Classes"), we revisit the major points of each coauthor. Amanda argues that the Eddy Model makes possible for all students, but especially students of color, linguistic agency and independence. Robert claims that a writer's decision to code mesh or code switch is rhetorical, ideological, and involved with the politics of representation—how we are, whether we like it or not, a representative of our race, religion, sexuality, nationality, or immigration status.

The Eddy Model ensures that first-year writing teachers are able to develop tools to do academic and cultural work. One way we do this is by providing a section titled "Context-Building Writing Activity" at the end of each chapter in the book. These activities are written for students and are meant as a built-in teaching manual for practicing the Eddy Model. They utilize the same terminology and order as the model, providing everything from revision-workshop guidelines to classroom writing prompts to brainstorming exercises to extended essay assignments. We don't expect anyone will use all these activities in preparing or even teaching their individual courses. However, those in bold font are intended to map out for instructors an entire semester's use of the Eddy Model.

You might be asking, What does all this culture stuff have to do with writing courses and with academic writing processes? We believe it has everything to do with them. One could say that the only means we humans have of sharing our values, beliefs, and even identities is through language. Just as they must learn to navigate the cultural assumptions unique to their home and school lives, our students must develop the ability to choose language appropriate to reach or affect the audiences in each culture they inhabit or to code mesh those language choices so they can speak with the fullness of their being and knowledge-making ways. This book is designed to help you teach your students how to develop the language skills necessary to move effectively from one environment to the next or to mesh them all and to be consciously intentional in choosing code meshing or code switching. This book suggests that one's personal power and one's ability to use language are effectively interchangeable. Those students who increasingly become intercultural, metacultural, and polycultural thinkers will understand that their control over language impacts their life choices politically, economically, racially, and academically. But—our students need to be consciously intentional about choosing code switching or code meshing.

Since academic discourse is steeped in the ideology of white power as systemic racism, which in our definition of ideology we describe as the "majority group's hustle," student internalizing of new college values is highly conflicted in an oppressive and racist American system. Can students, as they internalize academic discourse, be changed in only positive ways by learning systematic analysis and taking naysayers seriously without also internalizing racist language and power values? Patricia Bizzell foregrounds the difficult and perplexing challenge FYW teachers face: "In short, our dilemma is that we want to empower students to succeed in the dominant culture so that they can transform it from within; but we fear that if they do succeed, their thinking will be changed in such a way that they will no longer want to transform it" (1992, 228). Given the adaptability of systemic racism in this country, Bizzell's dilemma is or should be recognized as the dilemma of all FYW teachers and students except those who want to try to assimilate and accept the status quo. Any students, but especially first-gen students of color who do not seek to assimilate but who intend to construct a position somewhere along the continuum of resistance, separation, and pluralism, must deal with the ideology of white power, privilege, and values. Here is how Jason B. Esters, a black academic specializing in writing center work, accurately dramatizes the enormity of the rhetorical and analytical work that must be done to interrupt the power of systemic racism over our students and over all of us in our racial expectations. Here a student—Cecil—reflects on the visit of Esters to the student's class to do a writing center workshop. How do racial expectations function in academic writing settings?

> I guess it may seem odd for a student to want to write a reaction on a regular presentation. I wanted to bring to light a part of Systemic Racism that is instilled on us as students, (particularly black students) from when we are young. Beverly Daniel Tatum poses a great question in her book, *Why are All the Black Kids sitting Together in the Cafeteria?* "How did academic achievement become defined as exclusively white behavior?" (Tatum, 65). From when we are young we develop these racial notions that to be successful is white and to be a failure is black. Rarely is being black associated with academic success, "Racist arguments about contemporary intelligence levels are grounded in nearly four hundred years of viewing blacks as having intelligence inferior to that of whites" (Feagin, 95).
>
> Now you may still ask yourself, so what? Why this paper. Even now as I become a more learned individual than I had been merely four weeks

ago, I find a century of Systemic Racism acting on my subconscious. When Professor Taylor initially spoke to the class about a Jason Esters coming to the class to talk to us from a writing center, I had no assumptions of who he was and what he looked like. Yet, as Professor Taylor kept mentioning this man's name and how smart this man was, I then began to build up an image of this "writing genius." White, tall thin man; well dressed (suit, business casual); nice dress shoes; golden blonde hair; blue eyes; and well-spoken. Ah-ha! The joke is on me. Yes Jason is well spoken, oh and yes he did seem to be the "writing genius" Professor Taylor made him out to be, but I was happily mistaken. As he walked toward our classroom, I watched him, and thought, "Look at this guy, what week are we in at school, and he still doesn't know where his class is?" He didn't know because he was our guest. A short black man with dreadlocks and Timberland boots. Was it because the color of his skin and the freeness of his hair why I asked myself that question? Honestly, I don't know.

This incident served as a basic reminder to me, that I am still at the beginning of my journey in knowing not only who I am, but who my people are. In erasing all of the negative stereotypes imbedded in my head of this evil black man that is me. If I were to walk down the street with another black man and we are looked upon by a white stranger, we are just two black men. What ever stereotype they make of that black man, they will be making of me. So if can look at a fellow brother who shares a similar history as me, and share the same thoughts of an ignorant white man, then I am still bound in slavery of the mind, with the white man's ideas/beliefs. (2011, 293–94)

POLYCULTURALISM, LANGUAGE, AND POWER

This book is based on the conviction that writing faculty are joining multiracial political-economic forces that are changing Edited American English. We are collectively changing the nature of available rhetorics, opening up conservative white privileged conditions, and creating possibilities for the constructing of knowledge by extending, complicating, and making multiracial what historically white universities in particular, and what a white United States in general, understand EAE to be. Polycultural rhetorics include interpersonal difference, but the complex contexts for personal identity issues are the collective ideologies and practices constituted in and by systems of power. On the matter of intersectionality, this book insists on the following: the intersecting of social identities of race, class, gender, sexuality, and the others constructs the specifics of systemic oppression experienced by individuals. The power culture of college does not exist, as it claims, in a nonideological space. Colleges and universities serve to perpetuate the political economies of white power. Immersion in college culture is immersion in white dominance, patriarchy, capitalism, and all directly related power forces. This book intends to make cross-cultural rhetorical exercises and activities equally empowering for students of color and white students, as difficult as that necessary goal is in a national setting of uninterrupted and unacknowledged white privilege, which is often racial privilege flowing through the teacher.

An anonymous external reviewer of an earlier draft of this book challenged us with two strong questions. "How can immersing oneself in 'white dominance, patriarchy, and capitalism' be empowering? What exactly does it mean to cross cultures with oppression?" Here is where Bizzell's dilemma and the black student's—Cecil's—response to Esters and to his own internalized racism illuminate the challenge for FYW teachers at every phase of our careers—early, middle, late.

White teachers unpracticed in multiracial teaching and living tend to deploy an unconscious white-privileged maneuvering to control language and curriculum and control the responses of students of color to language and to the white teacher's authority. A deep responsibility for all of us involved in the challenge of equitable and effective college writing classes for both students of color and white students is the central matter of not only a student's right to their own language but also their right to ideologically position themselves as they wish on a continuum of assimilation, resistance, separation, or pluralism. Eddy has argued elsewhere, along with Carmen Kynard, that "our idea(l)s have been shaped within very specific rewritings of race, access, and educational equality that HBCUs have attained while Historically White Colleges and Universities (HWCUs) still struggle to participate in such a practice of social justice and shared fate" (2009, W25). When Eddy and Kynard insist that "HWCUs tend to be competitive, independent and isolating, and HBCUs are typically noncompetitive, interpersonal and interactive," they are thinking, for example, of the following:

> Our first address [was] from Sista Prez Johnetta B. Cole. . . . As is characteristic of speeches to incoming first-year students, she instructed us to look to our right and to our left. We dutifully gazed upon each other's brown faces. She spoke: "other schools will tell you one of these students will not be here in four years when you are graduating. At Spelman we say we will all see to it: your sister *better* be at your side when you *all* graduate in four years!" Loud cheers erupted—we were our sisters' keepers. (Jamila 2002, 387)

To repeat, because of its central importance: not only do students have a right to their own language, they have the right to ideologically position themselves as they wish on a continuum of assimilation, resistance, separation, or pluralism. Young, Barrett, Young-Rivera, and Lovejoy construct a compelling case for code meshing as liberatory and integrative, as acknowledging our wholeness, complexities, and person-hood, and, by contrast, view code switching as "separating languages according to context" and as "acting White." Writing teachers at HBCUs, HSIs, tribal colleges, and HWCUs must acknowledge that it is students who decide where and how to position themselves ideologically, lin-guistically, and rhetorically. When Robert Eddy, who is in deep support of code meshing, taught for ten years at an HBCU in North Carolina, he had to accept that most conservative black students chose to code switch. These students did not consider code switching as "linguistic segregation" or as involving their "racial self-concept," (Young et al. 2014, 3) and neither does coauthor Amanda. Throughout her career, Espinosa-Aguilar has encouraged code switching to help all students, especially those from underrepresented backgrounds, successfully navi-gate higher education and its norms. Unlike white coauthor Eddy, she too experiences the systemic racism students of color face and believes teaching students to use the master's tools, especially his language, will always provide a path toward the power that traditionally and recur-rently has been denied people of color. Like Robert's HBCU students, Amanda regards code switching as a common-sense and rhetorically sophisticated way of acknowledging how white power and privilege oper-ate not only in white communities but also for most members of the cur-rent professional class of color and for the next generation in training. Robert did not agree with his students' choice, but he had to completely acknowledge their right to decide for themselves.

The anonymous reviewer's two challenging questions—"How can immersing oneself in 'white dominance, patriarchy, and capitalism' be empowering? What exactly does it mean to cross cultures with oppression?"—must be answered by the coauthors of this book in terms of student language and ideology rights. We claim that the continuum of ideological positions from which students can choose an ideological commitment within the cross-currents, complexities, and challenges of the politics of representation are assimilation, resistance, separation, and pluralism. For students who try to assimilate, especially first-gen students of color and first-gen white students who to varying degrees accept and/or ignore "white dominance, patriarchy, and capitalism" and instead focus on trying to become successful and rich in the pre-vailing racist system, immersion in college culture is the credentialing they believe they require for upward mobility. Such students often have vague, distant-future commitments as self-justification for address-ing "social problems" after they become super rich and members of the 1 percent. For students who choose ideological placing along the continuum of separation, whether through isolating themselves as much as possible with their own community within the borders of this country or by ancestral relocating to Africa, or other continents, immersion in college—white dominance, patriarchy, and capitalism—is empowering because it helps them decide that, yes, the situation is hopeless and they need to isolate themselves or leave what they regard as this national, nonnegotiable nightmare. For students who choose resistance by joining Black Lives Matter, aligning with other protest and countercultural groups and certain hip-hop figures and older icons like Malcolm X, immersion in college white dominance, patriarchy, and capitalism is deeply empowering, not only because it makes political-economic realities much clearer and more comprehensively understood but because such immersion begins or further develops informed commitments to alternative ways of organizing justice work for individual and collective lives and makes beginning that work possible even before graduation. For students who choose pluralism, like those who choose resistance work (the two are closely connected), they use college immersion in crossing "cultures with oppression" to clarify world-views as ontological and epistemological commitments. Students who choose pluralism commit to engagement across key lines of difference in the midst of real social action work around current injustices. One good site that includes resources to help FYW teachers contextualize/problematize student ideological possibilities is the Pluralism Project (Eck 2006).

The black students Eddy worked with in North Carolina, who chose resistance or pluralism as their ideological commitment, code meshed, and often dynamically so. His students who chose separation rather than resistance, pluralism, or attempts at assimilation, often by joining the Nation of Islam (NOI), were nearly all working class, on public assistance, or in the drug trade. These students who chose separation were divided into two roughly equal groups in terms of their language choices. One group chose to communicate orally and in writing exclusively in African American English. They quickly ran up against the middle-class or above black administrators who allowed only code switching, especially in formal writing in course work, but the students also were disciplined severely by many, probably most, black faculty. These committed-to-AAE-only students tended to get grades that eliminated them from the university through teachers committed to code switching only who would not accept meshing and graded it as error, or these students withdrew from the school, tired of struggling with switching-only instructors, or rethought their ideology and language choices. The other group of students who chose separation were committed strongly to code switching. Often formally imitating Malcolm X in his NOI days, they tried to outdo users of EAE in rhetorical use of the standard dialect and often got honor grades.

To be sure, there is tension here between Robert's assertion that students should be given choice between meshing and switching and the anecdotes offered. These brief narratives about one HBCU during Robert's ten years there certainly seem to show that code switching was, ultimately, the more practical choice or that is was at least firmly endorsed by perhaps all black administrators and most black faculty. Students who chose to use their own languages or to code mesh in formal work were effectively filtered out of the university. So how was choosing between meshing or switching a real choice? It was a real choice in Robert's classes and in a small number of other classes. Among Robert's own students, about 75 percent chose to switch because, in the words of one student, "That is what the white world and the leaders of the black world require of us, and what we have practiced in school." Among the 25 percent or so who meshed, more than one or two individuals on their own (with no suggestions from Robert) handed in two versions of the main research writing of the semester: one meshed and one switched and asked Robert either to "choose the stronger one" or to suggest whether "freedom or safety is better." It is the case that none of his students who meshed would agree to let Robert use their texts in this book, a reluctance having to do with naming, including a student who handed in both a switched and a meshed text. This person would not agree to have her name changed if used in this book, nor did she want her real name used, which could have resulted in her "be[ing] exposed to the network of black leaders who would feel ignored and hurt by my meshing; a generation thing, Prof Eddy. Meshing is clearly the future." To see one example of a meshed text by one of Robert's black students at the HWCU where he works now, see Tyrone Aire Justin's "Raps: Sweet Brown and Black" (2014, 34–40). This writer describes his experience of writing multiple drafts of his text, which presents his desire to replace brown on black and black on brown violence both within incarcerated spaces and outside them with friendship or even brotherhood, as an "empowering conscious choice and success on my terms and in my language."

In addition to individual students ideologically and rhetorically positioning themselves in meshing or switching, Eddy, as a white professor and WPA at an HBCU, had black department, college, and university supervisors who all demanded code switching and regarded meshing as error construction. But more than race and social class was at work in the complexity of the context involving white-phenotype Eddy and black administrators in their respective politics of language and power differences. Essential elements of contestation that interpolate race and class at HBCUs are Christianity and Islam. The black administrators were Christian in theory and practice and Eddy is Muslim in theory and practice. Moreover, the one-quarter to one-third of students who were Muslim—either orthodox Islam or Nation of Islam (all local African Americans, not international students) were usually close to Eddy and normally addressed him as Dr. Salah Al-Din, his Muslim name. Students also recognized Eddy as working class when nearly all the black administrators were middle class or above. Also, in a post-9/11 United States, Eddy experiences Islamophobia often and intensely when the race and name privileges he has get seriously complicated by his being Muslim.

One of the student-government leaders, who is Muslim—a traditionally aged undergraduate and local black student who became Muslim in prison—had a meeting with the college dean, a black middle-class woman who was leader of the largest local black church. The meeting—as later related to Eddy by both the dean and the student—was a polite but seriously dissonant talk about code switching and code meshing. The dean continued to insist that code meshing is a fancy name for error construction or "misplaced black pride" and that white professors and white WPAs should not get involved in this crucial aspect of black educational policy. The student responded strongly by saying, "Dr. Salah Al-Din has drunk the milk of mother Africa; you have not; he is working class like nearly all of our students; you come from class privilege, and he is a Muslim leader and an expert on Malcolm X. All your references to Islam are oblique and never complimentary. All Dr. Salah's references to Christianity are appreciative and supportive. We are close to him and trust his teaching and his intentions toward us." When Robert met with the dean in her office about her meeting with the student leader, she did not mention religion but asked Robert about social-class matters and how he got the highest student-evaluation numbers and strongest student written responses among all faculty at the university as a white person at a HBCU. Robert's answer was "mainly three reasons: 1. The power of white privilege; 2. My having lived in Africa, being Muslim, an expert on Malcolm X, and a former undefeated amateur boxer is a big deal to many of our students; 3. As a working-class intellectual worker I love teaching academic writing, and our 99% poor or working-class students recognize our instant class solidarity." The dean asked Eddy his opinion about which of the three was strongest in influencing the positive student-evaluation numbers and comments. Eddy replied, "The first, white privilege, which should outrage all of us; we must eliminate unearned white privilege." But the dean's main purpose in the meeting was to insist on code switching as the policy of the university administration and that it must be strongly enforced by the WPA.

What was Robert's response to this clear black supervisory directive to teach and to (WPA) program code switching? He did what this book advises all writing teachers to do: teach both the rhetoric of code switching and the rhetoric of code meshing and acknowledge student rights to their own language and to ideologically position themselves as they wish on a continuum of assimilation, resistance, separation, and pluralism and thus to consciously choose switching or meshing. Writing instructors are teachers of and for freedom, not enforcers of indoctrination of the Left or Right. College students choose to mesh or switch.

CONTEXT-BUILDING WRITING ACTIVITY 1

Welcome to English 101. As a way of becoming familiar with each other, all of us, including your instructor, will share a brief story from our educational journey. Just give us the summary or basics. Please do not put your name on your story. Instead, put your ID number to receive credit.

After we spend ten minutes writing, your instructor will collect the stories. The teacher will read them out loud asking everyone to write down one question to ask the author about what the student wrote. Everyone will be invited to share their questions with the group. Then, the author will be invited to choose some of them to answer briefly, if they wish to give up being anonymous.

CONTEXT-BUILDING WRITING ACTIVITY 2

This survey is designed to help your writing teacher measure your confidence as a reader and as a writer of research. The following activity is available as a pdf file in our class LMS/Connect course site that should be downloaded and printed to make it easier to turn in. It is reproduced here because we will discuss the survey in class as well.

Confidence Survey

Please rate your ability to do the kinds of assignments listed below. Circle your answer.

Assignments	*Confidence in your ability to do them*			
1. Summarize essential information from a text	None	Low	Medium	High
2. Find the central argument in an essay	None	Low	Medium	High
3. State & support your own argument	None	Low	Medium	High

4. Select a research project or approach	None	Low	Medium	High
5. Do independent research at a college library	None	Low	Medium	High
6. Cite a source (quotation) in your essay	None	Low	Medium	High
7. Cite a source (paraphrase) in your essay	None	Low	Medium	High
8. Cite a source (summary) in your essay	None	Low	Medium	High
9. Revise & edit your own essays	None	Low	Medium	High
10. Suggest effective revision feedback to peers	None	Low	Medium	High
11. Give an oral presentation of your research	None	Low	Medium	High
12. Compile an annotated bibliography	None	Low	Medium	High
13. Compile a "Works Cited" page	None	Low	Medium	High

Adapted from Jennifer Rene Young (2002)

CODE-MESHING ACTIVITY 1

Building Community Using Home Language(s)

If you might code mesh any of the writing in this course, whether formal papers, informal writing tasks responding to readings, responses to multimedia texts, or creative or speculative writing, then as at-home writing you will bring to the next class session, share an anecdote you want other students who may code mesh and the teacher to associate with you as a key to your character or aspirations. This brief story could be code meshed using your home language(s) meshed with Standard English. This anecdote can be brief, a paragraph, but it must have an opening, middle, and ending. Your teacher will also bring a brief story about his own home languages meshed as he uses them in daily life. We will share either with the whole class if everyone produces one or in groups of three people considering meshing while students not considering meshing meet a second time about Context-Building Writing Activity 1.

1

HOME CULTURE(S), ACADEMIC DISCOURSE, CRITICAL READING, AND THE EDDY MODEL OF INTERCULTURAL EXPERIENCE

COLLEGE CULTURE AS FOREIGN TERRITORY

For several centuries in the United States, faculty have expected that students try to assimilate to the best features of college culture, language, and customs. Often these selective assimilation attempts are a struggle, especially for those students who are first generation, nontraditionally aged, or students of color. One reason for this reality is because those students have been historically underrepresented and have had few or no mentors down the generations to introduce them to the complexity of college passage. Although the demographics of US college students are changing to be more inclusive, the life-altering experience of adapting to college culture has not changed. It is white centered, white focused, and white dominated. Functionally relating to white college culture remains a challenging process, resulting in identity-altering dissonance. Whether one is a first-generation American Indian, an immigrant from Algeria, or an Anglo-Irish American from South Boston, success often depends on one's ability to gain fluency and competency in college culture, especially writing. These are the challenges for students who want to attempt assimilation to college culture, who want to learn to code switch, which Espinosa-Aguilar describes as learning audience awareness—when, where and with whom one uses which language. As the introduction of this book insists, students can try to assimilate to college culture and its white ways with language and power, as this paragraph relates, or they can react to white college discourse in terms of separation, or resistance, or pluralism, trying to get from college what they want without accepting the status quo of white dominance.

We know our students will carry their "original" selves to this new place, collegiate culture. Their response to the new culture slowly creates a "new" self that interacts with their "old" self. Most contemporary

DOI: 10.7330/9781607328742.c001

philosophers believe in the linguistic constitution of reality, the concept
that our language creates our reality by defining and naming it. We deli-
cately drape our words and ideas (which are the circulating words and
ideas of the dominant white culture) onto our world, and they become
a map, but also a cage. We think our culture, our "cage," is natural,
objectively real, independent, and inevitable. We assume our views of
our self and of the world are objectively real, just as we perceive them to
be. When we see people from another city, state, or country, we see them
through the cage of our culture, so we stereotype them. We don't see
them as equally complex and as human as ourselves and those who share
our home culture. We Other them. But if we begin to get to know their
language and view of the world, we begin developing additional ways
of looking at their world. In doing so we become metacultural, able to
contemplate how our culture is changed by us and we are changed by it.

The road to metaculturalism starts after moving into the college
world and learning its language, especially written language. For our
first-generation white students, typically working class, they begin seeing
their home culture clearly, perhaps for the first time, because there is
something to compare it to in college culture. First-generation students
of color have no trouble seeing the differences between their home culture and college culture as white and middle class or above. Some of the
ideas our students believed in deeply will be regarded as narrow-minded
by their new college selves. This change will not happen overnight, but
it will happen for many of our students from all racial and class backgrounds. New ideas will challenge the concepts our students think they
are certain about, causing them to see the old ideas for the first time.
We all begin as monoculturally provincial. New college students didn't
even think of foundational ideas as ideas because they just looked at the
world through them. The new does not necessarily turn them against
the old; it just leads to an examination of their culture of origin for
what may be the first time for first-generation white students and more
systemically for first-generation students of color who experience gulfs
between white power and their home culture. When human beings,
like plants, are taken from their original locale and transplanted to a
new place, they must put down roots to survive, and by doing so they
are nourished in an alien soil that will come to be their new "home," at
least for a time.

However, it is not just a matter of "adding" an old culture to a new
one; they do not simply coexist equally. They compete, and the prize
is our students' ethos. The cultures compete for our students' beliefs,
emotions, goals, and dreams, and often for their politics and religion.

We don't wish to be overly dramatic. The experience is dramatic enough, over time. But we say this because we wish it had been clearly stated to us when we were first-year students. Entry into a foreign land and its language inevitably changes how people view fellow humans, read a text, use digital media, and make decisions, as well as how our brains process data. There are big questions: Who am I? What will I become? What values do I believe in most strongly now? How will those values be influenced by my new college culture? Students need to face these questions as central if we are to achieve our most vigorous and effective goal: the development of meta-, poly-, and intercultural beings. Our student colleagues need to consider our argument that the end of college is not just that students earn an educational credential but that they develop a critical ethos for operating in the world as a wholly human, intellectually curious, and fully engaged person.

With this text you will help your students understand that their old and new selves will compete. At home, the old self was sometimes comfortable, in part because things were accepted as habitual. At college, through peer pressure and other cultural power differentials, the new self will become increasingly operative because it seems like the appropriate one to use in that setting. Students, if they want to live a life of code switching, must learn to become consciously intentional when using one culture or language rather than the other, based on which will be the more persuasive given their audience and rhetorical purpose. Even though these two cultural selves will compete, neither can win completely. When they gravitate toward their college selves, students will not be able to pretend they didn't live for years in their home culture(s). Likewise, when rejecting college and trying to regain the monocultural security of their home culture, students won't be able to successfully pretend their college experience hasn't affected them or never happened.

CULTURAL BACKPACKS AND ACADEMIC DISCOURSE

When students come to college, they bring the intellectual and emotional artifacts of their home culture with them. The container for this culture, which we envision as a backpack, is heavier than their literal suitcases stuffed with clothes and other possessions, and even on the most practical level, it is more important. For example, residential students' cultural backpacks probably determine which material belongings they carry to college. For commuting students, their home cultures determine what vehicle they get to classes in or, for online students, how they get to their particular keyboard and whose keyboard it is, personal or public.

To be the strongest and most aware writers, our students need to unpack their cultural backpacks. They need to see how their native cultures structure time, action, and discourse. All cultures have discourses vying for influence and power. Notice we aren't suggesting students lose their cultural backpacks; that is impossible. Instead, students must supplement their luggage set. They need to ask themselves what the dominant discourse of their home culture is and how it will interact with academic discourse and the writing they produce in that discourse. However, before students can answer these questions about discourse for themselves, we must first talk with them about what it is.

We tell students discourse is the formal conversations of groups involving what constitutes legitimate knowledge and who decides which groups benefit from such legitimacy. Academic discourse is the conversation carried on in books, journals, conferences, classrooms, and digital spaces. The characteristics of academic discourse vary depending on discipline. Certainly there are important differences in the sciences compared to the social sciences or to the humanities. But it is important to realize that in spite of differences, there are general characteristics of American academic discourse that are valued across disciplines and majors. Academic discourse is skeptical, analytical, and critical. It is concerned endlessly with the relationships between fact and theory. It will not accept an idea without vigorously looking at the evidence from as many sides as possible. This is the idea US academic discourse has of itself: a dispassionate, multiperspective, scientific search for truth. Unfortunately, the context of academic discourse is white supremacy, and its language rules. Laura Greenfield reminds us that "if 'Standard English' is imagined to be a finite language system when it is not (as no living language is finite), then people in power can always use it as a socially acceptable measure for making decisions about affording access to people of color, obscuring the racist motivations behind their practices" (2011, 42). She wants to make certain we know exactly what she is arguing.

> Black people are not discriminated against because some speak a variety of Ebonics—rather, I argue, Ebonics is stigmatized because it is spoken primarily by black people. It is its association with a particular people and history that has compelled people to stigmatize it. Our attitudes towards language, it appears, are often steeped in our assumptions about the bodies of the speakers. We assume an essential connection—language as inherently tied to the body. In other words, language varieties—like people—are subject to racialization (50).

The negative in academic discourse, invisible to most white students and clearly apparent to most students of color, is that it is steeped in systemic racism and must always be resisted and challenged on that account. The positive side of studying academic discourse for students is that they learn the undeniable value and legitimacy of multiple perspectives, especially linguistic ones, but only within Standard English. They also learn how to be critical readers of texts and the ideas being thrust at them from their college environment. By reading, we don't just mean that physical action in which our eyes take in thousands of bits of data per second as they fall across texts and images. Yes, when we read critically, we interpret what others have written, but more important, we are able to apply this skill to our response to our own writing and also to the responses others give to our work. The more perspectives from which one can read an object, idea, or theory, the better one's chances are of judging them fairly. Most cultures take their values and beliefs for granted and do not want them systematically analyzed. Most people and perhaps all cultures dislike being judged, especially the dominant culture, which wants college culture and our country generally to be "colorblind."

HOW ACADEMIC DISCOURSE AND CRITICAL READING AFFECT COLLEGE WRITING

In a perfect world, from the perspective of many employed in higher education, academic discourse would be based on the scientific method at institutions funded publicly, not through self-interested private funding. But rather than listening to and fairly judging all voices democratically, academic discourse rejects more than only what it regards as untenable. It also rejects what it considers undesirable. Unusual voices that try to enter the conversation of academic discourse, especially to change it, do not have an easy time. Academic discourse wants to weigh evidence carefully before it accepts opinions as facts. If it is truly scientific, healthy, and open to new points of view, academic discourse requires perpetual rereading and review. Academic discourse, thus, is characterized both by the need for criticism and the fear of it. It needs criticism and constant review because if we are to make sense of the world we strive to know, we cannot put faith in those in power and in the status quo; we must constantly question and evaluate them. The white leaders of academic discourse fear criticism because of the loss of power and influence they will experience if currently Othered voices become equal.

Most of the writing produced prior to college in typical large classes is completed as homework assignments. Writing in secondary schools relies on material drawn from experts or authorities of some kind. Students learn to gather information and organize it and often try to make some judgments as well. But often they don't have strong or clear or carefully thought-out views. There is little of their own thinking in their papers. The differences between secondary and college writing are partly a function of biological maturity and of the nature of academic prose, which must demonstrate a voice in which the author is in control of the material and intending an original point of view. College writers are learning how to become equals of the experts by learning their language and sharing their methodologies, such as critical reading and evaluation. They are learning to code switch between EAE and their home languages.

For over thirty years, composition scholars have argued that writers learn how to write by writing and by learning how to read their own, and by extension others', writing. We can't stress enough that effective rewriting of anything is only possible if students know how to critically read and reread their own thoughts. This is also why peer review often doesn't produce meaningful evaluation for many FYW students. If students haven't been trained to read with this level of sophistication before they come to college, it is unrealistic to expect them to be able to do it without training from us. Peers give effective feedback only after being taught how to read a text with the express intention of helping the author review the effects their rhetorical choices have on fulfilling the evaluation criteria, achieving the major assignment requirements, and affecting the audience. Students who can critically read their own texts in this way find no difficulty in doing the same with anything else they read thereafter.

THE EDDY MODEL OF INTERCULTURAL EXPERIENCE AND WRITING PROCESSES

As they become increasingly metacultural, your students will slowly develop a sense of an intercultural space between their home and college selves. This intercultural space creates intellectual choices for them perhaps for the first time because, with the practice of this book, they will be increasingly able to step out of their home culture into newer ones. Real choice of perspectives will show them that as they change their cultural perspective, they change their world. This brings us to the other unique quality about this book. Its primary function is teaching academic writing faculty how to use this intercultural thinking method to guide students toward critical, open-minded, and disciplined writing with multiple perspectives to the questions, problems, obscurities, debates, and dissonances of college study.

Table 1.1. The Eddy Model of Intercultural Experience

Stages of Behavior	Stages of Intercultural Experience	Stages of Writing Processes
	Preliminary Stage→	Prewriting: hope & fear Vague ideas of approach Anticipation but no focus Invention strategies
Must interact with others in class	←Spectator Stage→	False starts Misunderstandings Oversimplifications Writing to learn: first draft
Must understand interactions in class	←Increasing-Participation Stage→	Working drafts Conceptualization Better feedback = more confidence
Must create a role acceptable to class	←Shock Stage→	Writer's block Fear of reality Fear of self-exposure Fear of real questions Conceptual dissonance Fear of clear need for reconceptualization: Where will it lead? What and who will I become?
Self as center of communal responsibility	←Adaptation Stage→	Final draft Identification with the reconceptualization Congruence
The dissonant voice(s)	←Reentry Stage→	Sequence of thematically coherent assignments puts students in a new Preliminary Stage as paper 2 looms ahead

In order to see these skills can be built, let's examine an overview of the Eddy Model of Intercultural Experience.

This chart is a map to this book and to academic composing processes. Since the chart is the map to intercultural exploration in this book, let us suggest how best to study the chart. The left row, Stages of Behavior, lists generalized descriptions of how your students will interact with the people in your class. The middle row identifies the various stages of intercultural experience. The right row suggests what some of the interactions your students will experience may look like in each of the writing stages they encounter. Robert produced the left column of the chart, Stages of Behavior, and the right column, Stages of Writing Processes, but the central column, Stages of Intercultural Experience, was adapted from Tom Lewis and Robert Jungman (1986).

In the Preliminary Stage, your students will explore the roots of their values by practicing various prewriting techniques, and they will be introduced to the context-building writing activities. In one of the first activities, students are asked to construct a cultural-assumptions map. Notice that in the first stage, little work is shared with others. In the Spectator Stage, students begin to interact with others in class as their brainstorming moves from considering the roots of their culture to actually freewriting about them. This interaction involves peer review, a mutually supportive activity for writers and readers.

In stage three, the Increasing-Participation Stage, students complete working drafts of a paper. Their attempts at conceptualizing ideas result in trying to understand interactions in class. These class interactions are increasingly metacultural as students attempt to understand what they were trying to achieve in their own writing while simultaneously learning to compose critical responses to classmates' work. Students also need to understand how their peers responded to their review, and how they responded to their peers' response in return. These interactions should not be regarded as of minor importance. They involve not only your students' learning the craft of academic writing and reading (two sides of one coin) but also their deeper engagement in the collaborative character of writing. In the world outside college, in business, government, and activism for example, writing is a team sport. This is so in the literal sense that groups do much of the writing. But writing in the world outside college is also collaborative through various forms of peer review.

Take this book as an example. It is clearer and stronger because of the peer responses we received from friends, colleagues, students, family members, and anonymous peer reviewers. They did not cowrite or rewrite sections of the book, but they told us how they responded, what questions they had, and what places in the text were unclear, unconvincing, or inconsistent for them and perhaps for other readers. In most cases, our response to the reviews was to rewrite sections or restructure the book. The book is much stronger because of the peer reviews we received. But there is another way this book is collaborative. It relies on the publications of scholars past and present who developed theories of composition central to how we teach writing. It isn't realistic to note all these authors here, but it would be disingenuous for us to pretend they haven't influenced this book. And there are our student samples. This book could not exist without the student work discussed throughout. It should be a pleasure—as well as a clear duty—to acknowledge all the help one receives from other writers.

In the Shock Stage, your students' roles will change as they grapple with the most challenging concept of this framework: the dissonance resulting from reconceptualizing their home culture and/or their world and sense of self. When students enter this stage, they worry that they might wind up rejecting key features of their home culture. They are often literally in shock because of the dissonance from the clash of their "old" and "new" selves. Students must create a role acceptable to class. They must learn how to not only cope with the dissonance but to develop ways of talking about it with others without resorting to merely criticizing unfamiliar views and experiences. They fear giving up generalizations in favor of developing the means of interacting with others in ways that value and respect difference.

After all the angst created by the previous stage, the next one, Adaptation, results in students being aware of themselves as centers of communal responsibility. This is achieved, in part, by gaining a sophisticated understanding of audience and by fully realizing that close analysis is crucial for earning their readers' respect. This stage is marked by how far their peer-review skills have moved beyond safe commentary toward critical interrogation of an author's arguments, be they the author's own or those of another. By now students will also be producing final drafts of essays that examine race and culture, and they will have learned to critically read their own and others' arguments about them. In this stage, students identify with their reconceptualization of their home culture and find congruence by meshing it and their other cultures. They have taken their first steps toward an intercultural, metacultural, and polycultural ethos. The next step toward developing that ethos is the final stage, the Reentry. We know that writing is a recursive process, so it comes as no surprise that students will find themselves back at the Preliminary Stage as they begin brainstorming and inventing ideas about their next assignment, next topic, next culture to be explored.

Unlike the authors of many textbooks in which these individual stages are recursive or blend with one another, we believe each stage serves its own developmental and necessary purpose. We find it hard to believe that the Reentry Stage of Intercultural Experience can take place if a student never goes through the Shock Stage, for instance. As your students study the chart, they should ask each other questions such as the following. Each question is followed by the appropriate stage it interrogates.

What are some of your fears about writing? (Preliminary)

How do I write about a topic when I already know what I think about it? (Spectator)

Why can't I use racial slurs or anti-LGBTQ talk when others do?
(Participation)

How can I overcome my defensiveness toward my home culture?
(Participation; Shock)

What is the emotional toll of challenging or rejecting my core beliefs?
(Adaptation)

When is it possible for disparate cultures to mesh? (Reentry)

Consider your discussion of this chart as the beginning of an ongoing conversation that will shape your students' critical-thinking processes not just throughout college but thereafter. There will be much more in subsequent chapters on using the chart to design assignments and class activities. Our hope is that the exercises and methods in this book make your intercultural journey more dynamic.

Becoming part of a new culture is not easily done nor complete in semester. Nor do we believe all people move through these stages at the same speeds, with the same ease, or even at all. Culture is a spider's web of almost infinite subtlety and complexity. It is a multimodal space of deep complexity, richness, and challenge. Culture is powerful because much of it is unconscious and habitual. But with the practice of the intercultural writing method outlined in the chart above, your students will get better and better at writing academic prose with clarity and insight and learn to cope with the cognitive dissonance they experience along the way. Their writing will improve because they will increasingly understand that the context of critical thinking is provided by the more or less unconscious cultural assumptions that condition their perceptions and conceptions of themselves and the world. They will learn to name these cultural assumptions that compose their world and self and thus will begin to recompose themselves as they wish to be. This consciously intentional adaptation is the goal of our book. There are some people for whom this method will not work since they will not allow their new ways of college seeing to mesh with or critique their home culture. For them there is no overcoming their cultural dissonance. In those cases, the Eddy Model becomes literally an academic exercise, one with little effect since those students choose not to question the values they brought to college, which is their right. People are free to keep changing or to commit to their current way of knowing and being by saying "no thank you" to a polycultural ethos.

The authors of this book went through dissonance themselves. Both are the first members of their families to graduate from college; both were raised in working-class families; both experienced backlash after they first brought vocabulary, theories, and new knowledge back from college and attempted to introduce them into their home environments. Indeed, in order to become fully literate in the language of the academy, the authors decided, mostly unconsciously, to learn ways of negotiating audience, rhetoric, vocabulary, purpose, mechanics, grammar, and usage. In learning this language, they became bilingual in the same way someone moving to a foreign country must do to fit in, survive. To this day, they must consciously work at using what remains an intermittently foreign language to them; they will always project "tells" that they are not native speakers of Standardized American English. They became meta-, poly-, and intercultural beings only after mastering academic language and learning when to use it or when to retain the home, native language no one had to explicitly teach them. While they learned most of this acculturation to college and its discourse in classrooms and professional conferences, opportunities to integrate it with their other cultures, like the one at home, were rare. For instance, since she was a first-generation college student, from the days when that concept did not even exist, Amanda knew success in college carried far greater meaning for herself and her family than it did for most of her classmates. Like many undergraduate students of color in the 1980s, she embraced code switching since it promised academic and socioeconomic success. Thirty years on, Amanda recognizes that the reified norm of linguistic imperialism in higher education throughout the United States may have contributed to her repeatedly revisiting, if not actually taking up residence in, the Shock Stage. Robert, however, who is fully committed to code meshing and whose marriage partner is a Muslim from China, whom he met and worked with there, includes elements, with clear rhetorical intentions, of his working-class white English, especially key idioms, as well as selective use of Chinese and Arabic phrases, in sha Allah, wherever he communicates. Robert meshes because he insists that there must be narrative unity in our life, language, and names. Robert, who is also Mu Jingru 穆鏡如 and Salah Al-Din—all his functioning names and all essential, central elements of his identity and commitments—regards the code meshing he does in his college teaching and activist teaching in prisons as crucial to his intellectual labor with student colleagues and coworkers for racial justice and educational success. Many of Robert's college students, and all his incarcerated students, use all his names in class and in emails (no email access allowed by prison authorities for his incarcerated students), as well as the titles of Professor Eddy and Dr. Eddy when they want a more traditional or formal response from him.

We know that this process of fitting into college culture and discourse, reflecting on how we are challenged by the ambient white supremacy of college, and deciding whether we resist it or try to assimilate is complex and difficult because that is the nature of effective academic writing within the context of our complex cultural assumptions. Cultural assumptions are cultural eyeglasses through which we see the world without even realizing we have the special focusing eyeglasses on. But in addition to reminding you that this is a demanding activity, we invite you to test our claim that such writing processes are also exciting and liberating. Your students will be excited because composing is an activity of profound freedom and therefore power over one's self and world. Writing is liberating in that it is one human activity that enables us to construct and control not just ourselves but to some degree how and what others believe, feel, and do. It conveys freedom by giving us choice, which in turn gives us more freedom. No activity quite marks our humanity, our personality, as how we use language, whether written or spoken.

How do students who choose to mesh rather than switch their language resources experience the work of this chapter differently? In his foreword to *Other People's English*, Victor Villanueva writes,

> Exile. Alienation. What does one do when one becomes fully conscious of the alienation that arises from the exile of being racialized, of knowing something ain't right and there ain't no puttin' it right but can't be no ignoring the wrong? (Villanueva 2008, 84)
> But as this book will make clear, I was meshing more than switching. There is a difference, and it's an important one. I write as I write not to imitate a dialect of my childhood nor because I haven't a repertoire within the standard, but to take rhetorical advantage of the rhythm, to try to be compelling in blending the oral and the literate. I blend, not always consciously, not switch. I don't play with dialect in writing because I know that what one linguist calls Puerto Rican Black English (Ana Celia Zentella) is a living language, that no less than African American English, no less than Standard English changes with time. (Villanueva 2014, ix)

Code meshing does not magically negate racialization, alienation, and exile. Meshing does not end white power dynamics, but it does resist white supremacy as an equal rather than seeking assimilation and so affirms pluralism with equality. In terms of the Eddy chart, the cross-cultural dynamics for meshing are similar to switching, but with some important differences. The very act of meshing affirms the equality of one's home culture with white college culture. Differences remain but with equality affirmed by the meshing student. The key Shock Stage of the Eddy chart remains with its clear need for reconceptualization because of the dissonances of home and college cultures manifested in the student's writing. Moreover, the ontological questions of the Shock

Stage remain as well: Where will reconceptualization lead? What will I become? Who will I become? On the left side of the Eddy chart—Stages of Behavior—the answer to these ontological questions is in the context of the college class alone: must create a role acceptable to class, which is the only cultural acceptance necessary for the code switching student. The student who is consciously intentional in choosing code meshing still wants to create a role acceptable to class but only if the meshing student believes such acceptance by the course environment affirms all their cultural complexity, cultures, and languages. Vershawn Young ends *Other People's English* by insisting that code meshing "can help anyone reduce language prejudice and promote the power of language as opposed to the codes of power" (Young et al. 2014, 156).

Earlier in this chapter, we said our students need to unpack their cultural backpacks. We asked two questions: What is the dominant discourse of one's home culture? and How will it interact with academic discourse? In chapter 2, we discuss how to use invention techniques to begin constructing serious and systematic answers to these crucial questions, and in chapter 3 we examine the rhetorical effects of using the Eddy Model for prewriting. Many of our students have told us they did not begin to consider themselves as truly "educated," as capable of critical thinking in its academic version, until they began this systematic process of looking at their values and thinking processes. Students need to understand how their home culture structures the way they view time, action, and discourse (social relations). This process of charting cultural values is difficult, exciting, and humbling. It is difficult because it is highly complex. It is exciting because students can learn so much about their culture and self. It is humbling because over time, they realize how profoundly they have oversimplified the world by universalizing values, that is, projecting their cultural values onto people and cultures that are different from theirs. To successfully enter the conversation of academic discourse and to excel at college writing, students must practice the closely logical habit of mind of academic discourse. But to practice it, they must understand the "natural" habit of mind they inherited from and practiced with their native culture. Everyday experiences often unconsciously shape or teach us to value one of our cultures over another. The context-building writing activity below invites students to begin illustrating and exploring the influence of their home culture on their thinking and to engage the power of competing cultures.

CONTEXT-BUILDING WRITING ACTIVITY 3

Racial Autobiography Paper in 600 Words Maximum

How has your racial identity influenced your sense of self?

Describe the impact of racial identity in your life—not race generally, but your race, as you define and name it, and any significant experiences, teachings, and values pertaining to that identity. I won't require it, but I strongly recommend the optional source of interviewing two family members about their experiences of and beliefs about being "x" race. If you belong to more than one race, by all means acknowledge that and analyze how having more than one racial identity influences you. 600 words max.

Note: Do NOT hide by saying you see people, including yourself, as individuals and thus ignore race. No one is "colorblind." Do NOT hide by analyzing your culture instead of your race. Yes, they are connected, but they are not the same thing. Most of all, do NOT hide by saying you have a "personal" or "individual" culture. There is no such thing. Culture is the ways of a people, and so is a group activity. If you identify as white, what is your opinion about why many white folks prefer to talk about culture instead of about race? This important brief paper is about how your identity is influenced and largely defined by your race (or races if you are biracial or multiracial). Yes, this is a racial miniautobiography. 600 words max.

For white teachers assigning this racial autobiography to students of color, expect folks of color to be intelligently cautious about how much they share, especially early in the semester before trust has been established. If you are a white teacher inviting cross-racial openness under conditions of unequal power, you must be an accountable reader. Reread or read Nancy Barron's section in her essay with Nancy Grimm, "Addressing Racial Diversity in a Writing Center," for a reflection on this responsibility. Consider "Nancy Barron [a Latina]: In a Latino community, my university [white] colleagues looked like the oppressors, the ones who never listened but always knew what was right for everyone." At the same time, these colleagues persistently assumed everyone saw them as individuals, and not connected to a larger group (Barron and Grimm 2002, 70).

CONTEXT-BUILDING WRITING ACTIVITY 4

NOTE: This form may be used in two ways during the space of a course. We use it to help students learn to critically read peer and professional writings. We encourage instructors to use it as an initial foray into peer review. Second, and more important, we first use this activity to teach students how to respond to assigned professional readings. They will come back to it later in the term when they need to respond to any sources they eventually use in research-based essays.

Responding to Reading Form

Name_____ Date_____

Text responded to (give full citation) _____
_____
_____

What I found most interesting and/or important in this reading _____
_____
_____

The most important question or questions I have after reading this text is or are
_____
_____

The most important question or questions, above, are possibly or definitely connected to cultural rhetorics or racialized communication in the following ways _____
_____
_____

CODE-MESHING ACTIVITY 2

How is your racial identity connected to your home language(s)?

Write 600 words or less as spoken word about your identity connected to your home language.

This should use your home language by itself or meshed with Standard English. You will have the chance to volunteer to read this to the whole class or to your three-student meshing group within the class. Nuff said. Jump in.

2

ENTRANCE TO THE PRELIMINARY STAGE
Brainstorming about Culture

USING THE KLUCKHOHN MODEL TO DISCOVER THE ORIGINS OF OUR VALUES AND BELIEFS

It might seem like a contradiction to say that in studying the college classroom as a foreign culture, the essential first step is to study one's home culture. But how could it be otherwise? First-year students can't help but "construct" their impressions of college as "foreign" by comparison to their home culture. In one sense we are simply stating the obvious: it is during the college years, especially the first year, that people experiment with new behaviors and identities. One of these new identities will embody the behaviors of a collegian instead of, say, a high-school student. Besides negotiating routine tasks like finding their classes on campus, our students quickly discover that success in college requires much more than academic experience; probably more important to this transition are the social as well as cultural experiences with which they will grapple. This is true for all our students regardless of their home culture but even more so for nontraditional, L2, and international students for whom learning the rules and values of standardized English will be akin to learning the values of unearned racial and cultural privilege. We agree with scholar Fan Shen who, when reflecting on learning English composition in the United States himself wrote, "I realize that the process of learning to write in English is in fact a process of creating and defining a new identity and balancing it with the old identity" (1989, 466). Before fully engaging the values of the foreign culture that is college, students need to own the values embedded in the identity they brought with them to this new environment.

In the introduction to this book, we said we would demonstrate what home cultures teach students about social relations and discourse with the help of a model from the field of anthropology. Table 2.1 is an adaptation of the Kluckhohn Model (K Model), which was originally

DOI: 10.7330/9781607328742.c002

produced by the anthropologists Florence Kluckhohn and Frederick Strodtbeck for their book *Variations in Value Orientations*. A couple of decades later, L. Robert Kohls created a simplified version of the model as a tool for helping Americans adjust to living overseas. In his book, *Survival Kit for Overseas Living*, Kohls suggests that what people need most for adapting is "to become aware of your cultural baggage and . . . to avoid tripping over it too often. To do so we need to ask what it is in the American environment that has made you what you are and how an awareness of your Americanness can provide the basis for understanding and coping effectively with your experiences in a foreign country" (1984, 2). In essence, he suggests that a crucial step to intercultural understanding is identifying the assumptions we make about ourselves and our relationship to the world and how those assumptions guide our actions. The Kohls version of the K Model can be used as an elementary tool in helping students understand the origins of their existing values structure.

Let's take a moment to critically study this table, which is read from left to right. The far-left column, labeled Concerns/Orientations, lists categories of human interaction we assign, often unconsciously, to the aspects of a culture. As you can see, these deal with everything from personality types to relationship preferences. For instance, the first orientation, Human Nature, can be classified into a range (identified here as Possible Responses) as evil, mixed, or good. In other words, one's home culture automatically and unconsciously constructs what we instinctually see as the innate predisposition or "basic nature" of other humans and thus determines into which response we place them (seeing humans as basically bad, and unchangeably so, for instance). Our dimensions on the left align most often with only one of the Possible Responses located in the second, third, and fourth columns. To fully understand how we view others, we need to figure out which orientation our culture(s) has trained us to assign to each response.

It is often helpful for our students when we model the mapping of our own cultural constructs by using the K Model. Robert's overseas experiences inform where he would place the cultures he knows best. Table 2.2 maps Robert's application of the K Model to his experiences living and teaching in African, Asian, and European cultures. You will notice that Robert describes Islam as a culture. Islam is a religion first and last to believing Muslims, like Robert, but a culture first to Christian residents of Muslim-majority countries (a population of, for example, 10 percent Coptic Christians in Egypt), nonobserving Muslims, former Muslims or current agnostics or atheists, and international residents

Table 2.1. The Kluckhohn Model

Concerns/ Orientations	Possible Responses		
Human Nature: What is the basic nature of people?	**Evil**. Most people can't be trusted. People are basically bad and must be controlled.	**Mixed**. There are both evil people and good people in the world, and you have to check people out to find out which they are. People can be changed with the right guidance.	**Good**. Most people are basically pretty good at heart; they are born good.
Human-Nature Relationship: What is the appropriate relationship to nature?	**Subordinate to Nature**. People really can't change nature. Life is largely determined by external forces, such as fate and genetics. What happens was meant to happen.	**Harmony with Nature**. Humans should, in every way, live in harmony with nature.	**Dominant over Nature**. It is the great human challenge to conquer and control nature. Everything from air conditioning to the "green revolution" has resulted from having met this challenge.
Time Sense: How should we best think about time?	**Past**. People should learn from history, draw the values they live by from history, and strive to continue past traditions into the future.	**Present**. The present moment is everything. Let's make the most of it. Don't worry about tomorrow: enjoy today.	**Future**. Planning and goal setting make it possible for people to accomplish miracles, to change and grow. A little sacrifice today will bring a better tomorrow.
Activity: What is the best mode of activity?	**Being**. It's enough to just "be." It's not necessary to accomplish great things in life to feel your life has been worthwhile.	**Becoming**. The main purpose for being placed on this earth is for one's own inner development.	**Doing**. If people work hard and apply themselves fully, their efforts will be rewarded. What a person accomplishes is a measure of their worth.
Social Relations: What is the best form of social organization?	**Hierarchical**. There is a natural order to relations; some people are born to lead, others are followers. Decisions should be made by those in charge.	**Collateral**. The best way to be organized is as a group, where everyone shares in the decision process. It is important not to make important decisions alone.	**Individual**. All people should have equal rights, and each should have complete control over their own destiny. When we have to make a decision as a group, it should be "one person one vote."

Adapted by Kohls (1984, see chapter 7 and appendix A).

generally. Especially in North Africa and the Middle East, where different dialects of the dominant Arabic language make communication routine from Morocco to Oman, four thousand miles as the bird flies, there is a significant shared culture. Robert is happy to agree with Edward

Said in the preface to the twenty-fifth anniversary edition of *Orientalism*:
that "I have no 'real' Orient to argue for. I do, however, have a very high
regard for the powers and gifts of the peoples of that region to struggle
on for their vision of what they are and want to be" (1994, xviii–xix).

For Robert, traditional Chinese culture is best reflected in the orienta-
tions found in the fourth column of the table. Yet, his read of modern
Chinese history is that the Communist government is attempting to move
Chinese values to the far-right side of the chart in the orientations of Time
Sense, Human-Nature Relationships, and Human Nature. Mainstream
Islamic culture is also rooted in the fourth column of the chart. The main
cultural struggle in Islamic countries is between traditional values—past
oriented—and self-defined, not Western-imitated, modernization, as
represented by the future-oriented right side of the chart. Anglo-America
is firmly located in the fourth column of the chart because it believes in
individualism, activity, future orientation, mastery over nature, and the
basic goodness of people, if they are treated in the right way, and all are
controlled by faith in change as Progress with a capital P.

Amanda's map of the K Model, table 2.3, is quite different from
Robert's, especially given that she has only lived in Western cultures. In
fact, although she considers him a great friend, Amanda's response to
US culture resembles Robert's only in the orientation of activity, which
they both see as one of doing. Also unlike Robert, whose responses
to the orientations are very similar across the cultures in which he
has lived, Amanda's responses to the K Model orientations are literally all over the map, or table as it were, and she refuses to be limited
to one. Since her cultural constructs are informed by her role as an
historical US "minority," Amanda's cultural mapping reflects that. So,
although she sees human nature as falling mostly in the middle range
of responses, as neither good nor bad but a true mix, she also knows
from lived and cultural experience that in the United States, at least,
people like her—namely, a working-class woman of color raised on food
stamps—have historically been dehumanized and discriminated against
by the dominant majority. Thus, she wavers between seeing the basic
nature of humanity as mixed most days and as extremely evil on far too
many others. She has little patience for those whose time sense is stuck
in the present and also has issues with the futility of mere future thinking. While her time sense isn't solely rooted in looking to the past, she
does think most humans should strive more to learn from it. Similarly,
while she doesn't believe people can live in complete harmony with
nature, nor that they should succumb to the delusion of que sera, sera,
they certainly do invent ways of manipulating nature, and usually not

Table 2.2. Robert's Map of Chinese, Islamic, and American cultural constructs

Orientations	Possible Response Traditional Chinese	Possible Response Islamic	Possible Response American
Human Nature	Good	Good	Good
Human-Nature Relationship	Dominant over Nature	Dominant over Nature	Dominant over Nature
Time Sense	Future Oriented	Past/Future Oriented	Future Oriented
Activity	Being	Becoming	Doing
Social Relations	Collateral	Collateral	Individual

Table 2.3. Amanda's Map of Ethnic American Cultural Constructs

Orientations	Possible Response American
Human Nature	Mixed
Human-Nature Relationship	Dominant>Harmony
Time Sense	Past Oriented>Future
Activity	Doing
Social Relations	All (Multimodal)

always for the best. Finally, Amanda believes human relationships are multimodal, reflecting each of the possible responses, since some situations call for individualism while others might benefit most from a collateral or even hierarchical orientation. For instance, while she is directing her writing center, Amanda makes no bones about that social setting being hierarchically organized, as was her birth family. Her own family is organized collaterally; she sees the neighborhoods where she lives and works as individual and will fight social mores that foster discrimination or forms of inequality within them.

After allowing time for our students to ask questions and discuss the table and our maps, we invite them to create their own map of their home culture(s) using the K Model. Initially, their classmates are their audience since they are likely still getting to know one another. To create their map, students just need to choose cultures they are members of and use the chart to map the value orientations of those cultures. Although Robert and Amanda emphasize racial and national culture in theirs, students could map a subset of a larger culture, as is demonstrated in the one in table 2.4 created by one of Amanda's students.

This student completed both the composition courses required for graduation with Amanda. It was during the second course that Corey

Table 2.4. Corey's Map of American Gay Cultural Constructs

Orientations	Possible Response Gay American
Human Nature	Mixed
Human-Nature Relationship	Harmony
Time Sense	Present
Activity	Being
Social Relations	Individual/Collateral

completed this map. Corey was a first-generation student of color whose lived experience and budding acceptance of his sexuality led him to these observations. By outlining and sharing their own cultural constructions with others, students like Corey begin to understand that their perceptions of new cultures are entirely conditioned by their existing cultural conceptions of themselves and the world.

CONTEXT-BUILDING WRITING ACTIVITY 5

Prewriting: Key Cultural Assumptions Map

This activity asks you to use the K Model to map your assumptions about the culture you are most familiar with, your home culture. What are your key cultural assumptions? What has shaped them? Where do they come from? How do you think you learned them? First, look at the K Model to see where your cultural assumptions fall, just as the authors of this book have. Do you agree with Robert Eddy's belief that Anglo-Americans believe in individualism, doing, future orientation, dominance over nature, and the basic goodness of people? If not, how does your view differ? What is a key cultural assumption that has been determining your values and behavior? Religious doctrine? Gender roles? Book versus street smarts? Is there a key cultural assumption you would consciously like to modify or eliminate from your home culture? Is there one you would like to explore during your time in the class? Is there one you wish to avoid at all costs? Which do you approve of, admire or love most? By mapping your cultural assumptions, you begin gaining more conscious control of your thinking, writing, and behavior.

While students create their maps, we remind them of our responsibility to be careful, however, not to use the K Model and this mapping exercise as a machine to produce stereotypes. Every culture is profoundly complex and has at least some individual members who demonstrate the full range of values included in the K Model. But, likewise, we must acknowledge that every culture has a mainstream value structure that changes with time. What those values should be is the essential conversation of the discourses in that culture. So as long as we do not think of a culture's values as unchangeable, and so long as we remind ourselves that there will always be important minority variations on mainstream views and that these minority voices are competing with each other and with the mainstream to be heard, the Kluckhohn Model will be, at least initially, an excellent tool for systematically exploring one's home and previously unexplored cultures. We remind the students that culture is a spider's web: touch any part and the whole vibrates.

In the next chapter we revisit the cultural-map exercise and use it to start drafting a freewrite. For now, though, we want to move away from the use of the K Model to using the Eddy Model, which teaches writing about culture in a more complex way. When discussing academic writing processes, instructors usually refer to the first steps as *invention* since it is during this phase that authors often ask questions of themselves and others in order to create new ways of seeing and discussing the world around them. Much of the rest of this chapter discusses a number of individual and group prewriting activities that will help your students gather data about the new culture(s) they are experiencing, most notably collegiate culture. We have included examples of most of these methods that were written by our students; we return to some more of their work later in the book. As a reminder, the excerpts from student work in this text are not perfect examples; they are provided to demonstrate the concepts and how some of our students completed these assignments. We do not expect any instructor to use all these methods. The wide variety is intended to provide instructors with many options for engaging students in the Preliminary Stage of the Eddy Model, which focuses exclusively on invention.

USING THE EDDY MODEL—THE PRELIMINARY STAGE: INDIVIDUAL INVENTION STRATEGIES

Brainstorming through Listing

One common prewriting activity is listing, which is often done alone. Often these initial forays into invention reflect the most common stereotypes about people or topics. For instance, after ten minutes of brainstorming about the topic "Islam," your American-born students will likely produce a list consisting of stereotypes or ideas that might look like this, just as ours did:

1. religious fanatics
2. terrorists
3. hostage takers
4. pray all the time
5. rock-throwing Palestinians
6. Saddam Hussein or Osama bin Laden
7. "moderate" Arabs
8. oppressed women covered by veil
9. wife walking behind husband
10. towelheads
11. murderers
12. war lovers
13. anti-American
14. anti-Christian

As we noted above, while we don't want students to merely rely on stereotypes to interrogate a subject, we also should not encourage students to hide their stereotypes because that is how stereotypes retain at least some of their power. We should make stereotypes public, at least to ourselves, and if possible, in a way sensitive to others. Later we must try to "unpack" these stereotypes so we can get beyond them, beyond their false simplicity and lack of sophistication. But initially, we simply need students to acknowledge that they have them.

Even such a simple list, so briefly arrived at, reveals several embedded or possible focuses that can be developed further in a freewrite. Encourage your students to look for connections or common threads in their brainstorming to find a focus, or dare we say it, a thesis, to explore later when they begin freewriting. For instance, a student might want to look at women and Islam, items eight and nine. If she pursues such a thesis in an actual working draft or essay, she will eventually learn that the subject is much more complex than she might believe if she continues to only accept the simple media stereotypes of women and Islam. For instance, a passage (53: 21–25) in the Quran reproaches pre-Islamic Arab men for practicing female infanticide, while a number of passages (4: 1, 6: 98, 7: 189, 16: 72, 30: 21, 31: 28, 35: 11, 39: 6, 42: 11, 78: 8) (Nasr et al. 2015) suggest that men and women are equals because they originate from the same cell and the same soul. From these passages, one can see ready evidence exists to contradict a simplistic assumption that women are somehow considered inferior in Islamic culture.

Examining items two, three, five, eleven, and twelve from this same brainstorming list also shows a possible connection between Islam and violence. Related to a possible focus on violence, item seven repeats a term we find often in the media in relation to Arabs: "moderate." That term alone could be the focus for a freewrite or even a fully developed essay. What exactly does "moderate" Arab mean? What does it imply is the norm for Arabs? Doesn't it imply that the norm is violent or terrorist? "Moderate" terrorist? "Moderate" fanatic? This student could already have a (very tentative) plan to write about "Images of Violence in Our Perception of the Arab," or "Who Created the 'Moderate Arab'?"

Journalist's Questions as Invention

Another prewriting technique that is sometimes appropriate, especially when looking at distinct or brief events, is using the so-called journalist's questions,—who, what, when, where, why, and how—as an invention strategy. As with other brainstorming methods, students can use this strategy working alone or in groups. Let's say one of your students wants to explore the murder of Malcolm X. The journalist's questions would give them a structure to focus their brainstorming inquiry. Here are some samples:

Who might have been involved in the planning and carrying out of the murder?

What were the possible motives of the people or groups suspected of the crime?

When and under what conditions did Malcolm X begin to believe his life was in danger?

Where in the Audubon Ballroom in New York did the shots come from, according to the many witnesses?

Why do some who study the assassination (like George Breitman and Spike Lee) wonder about a wider conspiracy?

How did the murder of Malcolm X influence the spread of Islam in the United States and the civil rights movement?

The highlight of this method is in the immediate amount of data it provides students from which to work. The questions allow students to narrow their research, sharpen their thesis or purpose, and begin organizing how the information is interconnected.

Particle, Wave, and Field Invention

Another interesting invention structure that helps us decide what is constant and what changes in the study of a subject, idea, or experience is the particle, wave, field method. It was introduced in an innovative textbook called *Rhetoric: Discovery and Change* by Richard E. Young, Alton L. Becker, and Kenneth L. Pike. A significant percentage of Eddy's students have found this prewriting method useful and creative, according to course evaluations. Teachers will see that in some ways this method mirrors the journalist's-questions technique.

Whatever the potential focus they are exploring in their invention strategies, a student's subject can be considered as a particle—the unchanging aspects of a subject, as a wave—the changing aspects of a subject, and as a field—the context of the subject's web of relationships. The **particle** dimension of a subject, for example—culture—would yield questions like these:

> What does the term *culture* mean?
> How was the term *culture* formulated?
> What are the characteristics of a culture?

The **wave** dimension of the subject—culture—would yield questions like these:

> Today, how is the definition of the term *culture* being contested?
> What forces or groups are contesting the definition?
> What are likely to be the future issues in the definition?

The **field** dimension of the subject—culture—would yield questions like these:

> How do changes in the thinking of what constitutes a culture relate to issues in American politics and education?
> Should changes in cultural identity be seen as evidence that the United States is becoming more open to multiracialism or is resisting diversity?
> What are the social, economic, political, and religious influences on attitudes toward multiracialism?

Using this strategy, then, requires students to take any subject and apply the particle, wave, field method to invent questions that help them narrow their views. In turn, this helps them determine what it is they want to explore about the subject and want to discuss about the topic when they start freewriting their working drafts.

At this point, we'd like to introduce the work of one of our student authors, Brian Jones, who used the Eddy Model during his FYW course.

His writing is explicated throughout this book. Later we see him take this topic through the other stages of intercultural experience when he develops a working draft and creates a revised, final essay. For now, let's first examine how this student used the particle, wave, field invention strategy to brainstorm the topic of drug culture.

Particle (unchanging aspects)

Why is the selling of illegal drugs so constant as to seem eternal?

Why did I sell drugs?

Why wasn't I afraid of jail, killing someone, or of being killed?

Wave (changing aspects)

What are the changing characteristics of the drug trade?

Are drug dealers crazier and more daring than they used to be?

What matters more to drug dealers now? Money or their reputation?

Field (context)

How have high tech developments influenced drug dealers?

How is drug dealing related to race and economics?

How is drug dealing related to trends in suicide and random violence?

Brian took the material he constructed from the particle, wave field invention strategy and developed it into the following plan:

Why I sold drugs:

1. I was afraid of being considered a nobody.

2. I was afraid of poverty.

3. My environment schooled me in it.

4. To prove I was a real man in the hood, prepared to die for my friends and rep.

5. To prove I was not afraid of death.

6. To survive and reach the age of 25.

As we see in chapter 4, Brian eventually uses this scratch outline to compose his first working draft in which he depicts what he now considers a nightmare of destructiveness, most of it self-directed. He feels lucky to have survived. Now let's look at another student's work that uses a formal outline to brainstorm about a topic.

OUTLINING AS INVENTION

Traditionally, outlining is taught to students based on the classical model wherein rhetoricians or writers classify and divide their main points from supporting ideas and details by organizing their points into subordinating levels. These levels are often stated in complete sentences, use topic sentences to separate body paragraphs from introductory and concluding ones, and utilize letters and numbers to indicate levels of generality and importance. Here is an excerpted example of a formal outline written by one of Amanda's students:

Thesis: Students who bring weapons on campus should not be allowed to continue their schooling because they threaten the safety and learning experience of others.

I.   Gun deaths at public schools have increased dramatically in the last twenty years and is not isolated to one area of the United States.

A. Colleges
   1. Virginia Tech
      a. number of people killed
      b. cause
   2. Seattle Pacific University
      a. number of people killed
      b. cause
   3. University of Alabama
      a. number of people killed
      b. cause
B. High or Middle Schools
   1. Columbine High School
      a. number of people killed
      b. cause
   2. Berrendo Middle School
      a. number of people killed
      b. cause
   3. Red Lake Senior High School
      a. number of people killed
      b. cause
B. Elementary Schools
   1. Sandy Hook Elementary School
      a. number of people killed
      b. cause
   2. Cleveland Elementary School
      a. number of people killed
      b. cause
   3. Essex Elementary School
      a. number of people killed
      b. cause

II. Bullying and its connection to school shootings

   1. Motivates most shooters
   2. Victims of bullying are twice as likely to bring a weapon to school
   3. Sometimes distracts from other causes like mental illness . . .

Robert's students have also created outlines, but they often combine elements of formal outlining with brainstorming techniques like listing and the journalist's questions. This next example of outlining was composed by Adhita Sharma, an American born in India, who speaks the languages of both countries and powerfully identifies herself with each. As part of a college-wide interdisciplinary project that focused on modernization in Western and Eastern nations, and which gave students the chance to write about their own primary culture or another culture presented in the project, Adhita, a practicing Hindu, chose to write about another culture, specifically Islam and modernization, because she planned to work in the future at helping resolve the centuries-old conflict between Hindus and Muslims in India. She believed this work would be more successful if she understood Islam better.

During campus Interdisciplinary Week, which included campus lectures, readings, movies, group work, and research, Adhita took notes and marked passages in her texts. One quotation in particular she found striking and clarifying was the following from Pierre Nora's *Les lieux de la memoire*:

> Memory is life. It is carried by groups of living people, and therefore it is in permanent evolution. It is subject to the dialectics of remembering and forgetting, unaware of its successive deformations, open to all kinds of use and manipulations. Sometimes it remains latent for long periods, then suddenly revives. History is the always incomplete and problematic reconstruction of what is no longer there. Memory always belongs to our time and forms a lived bond with the eternal present.

Adhita was fascinated by the idea that history as group memory could be considered selective and always in evolution. Without really having said it to herself clearly, she had assumed that history was basically objective unless it was turned into propaganda or lies. She also copied a line in her notebook from a movie she saw while working on an interdisciplinary project: "Men want to forget things they don't like." When Adhita put these two quotations together, and since she had decided to write her paper about Islam and modernization, she wrote down the following journalist's questions in her journal:

What does Islam teach about memory?
What does Islam try to remember (or forget)?
How do these questions relate to modernization?

These three questions constituted what she most wanted to learn about Islam and provided Adhita with the basis for constructing a formal outline and an organizational diagram. The structure of this brainstorming evolved through her attempts to understand, answer, and condense her questions into what seemed most relevant. Here is Adhita's brainstorming over these concepts:

> Imagine if we could remember everything. It would be hyperintense; we would be drowning in a sea of sensations; insanity surely. Certainly there could be no meaning in, no relationships between—everything! Therefore memory must be
>
> 1. **Selective**
>
> and it must involve the making of
>
> 2. **Meaning**
>
> order, relationships, interconnectedness, touching the world and other people.
>
>> Memory is to touch life.
>> If memory is selective and involves the making of meaning, then what meaning does Islamic memory select?

In its final form, Adhita's outline included a diagram of three key Arabic words. Here are her outline and diagram:

Intro
1. Memory is selective and involves the making of meaning.
2. Remembering everything would be drowning in a sea of apparently unrelated events. Intense but insane.
3. Hypnosis, certain forms of psychotherapy, might indicate that much or all previous experiences, memories, are present in the subconscious, if we could reach them.
4. It appears that we **remember** certain events so as to **hide**, to cause to remain invisible, multitudes of other events that would overwhelm us with their number. [But maybe it is not just a question of number; remember the line from the movie: "men want to forget things they don't like." Also, think about the number of people, especially young people, who deny for political or anti-semitic reasons that the Holocaust ever took place.]

Body
1. In the contemporary West we have two major views of self and memory.

    a. The scientific, materialist, atheist, no core self view. In this view there is no soul, just socialization and genetic predisposition. A form of "Fate"? In the materialist's view, memory doesn't involve a soul, an original nature, it just involves discrete events in the process of one's socialization or the inevitable results of genetic factors.

    b. The religious position. There is a soul, as well as the processes of socialization. Memory for this group will involve the events from birth onward, but will also involve the fact of a soul, an essential and eternal core of being which is the "real self." But in the Judeo-Christian tradition this real self or human nature is fallen—Original Sin. The Fall. Memory canNOT be a guide because **our core is corrupt**.

2. The situation according to Islam is not materialist, as you would expect from a religion, but also there is no concept of Original Sin in Islam. The core of human nature is Pure, indeed Heavenly. We carry paradise at the center of our Being. But we have **forgotten** our original nature. A chart of memory and meaning according to Islam:

Our original state, that which is "remembered" as the "context" for all memories	**Fitrah**	True, pure original nature
Memory	**Dhikr**	Rememberance of God, of Reality, of Context and Meaning
"striving to open up completely to the memory of Fitrah." The attempt to regain total spontaneous awareness of Memory as the context of experiences	**Jihad**	Struggle, "war," to always remember & to regain pure spontaneity of our original nature (**Fitrah**)

3. In the modern West, because of our worship of Progress with a large P, we put **becoming** as more important than **being**. Science and technology deny or submerge Being and the soul and replace them with a **tabula rasa**—blank slate—a person becoming more and more "Progressive." But toward what goal do science and technology lead us? **What are we going to become**?

4. As the diagram suggests, in Islam (as in Hinduism), **Being**—our original nature—is more important than becoming. The whole Islamic enterprise is to **remember** the pure spontaneity of our original nature: **Fitrah**. How does one try to accomplish this goal of total memory?

   a. prayer: 5 times a day
   b. fasting, especially during month of Ramadan
   c. alms giving: 2 and 1/2 % of net worth
   d. Pilgrimage to Mecca (Hajj)

There is a tension between the outer and inner dimensions of Islam. This tension between external rules and inner commitment is the arena for the struggle of **Jihad**. The **Jihad** for our outer or social self is the seeking of social justice for all; the opposite of "greed is good." The **Jihad** for the inner self is the recognition that whatever one wants most, whatever one gives most of one's time to, is one's real god—what one truly worships. Most people worship success and wealth. Such people might give no time, a little time or some time to God. But such people are not fighting the inner **Jihad**. To the one fighting the inner **Jihad**, the pilgrimage into the heart, God is everything.

Conclusion

1. Modernization in Islamic societies must give primacy to Being over Becoming. But how?
2. Modernization, because it is Western in origin and values, worships Progress and will be regarded as atheist by Muslims.

3. There will be friction between Islam and the West until a truly Islamic modernization is developed and until the West stops imposing our values.

Adhita's plan is detailed, demonstrates an intense desire to answer her focusing questions, and gives a sense of her point of view. Although the Indian dimension of her identity involves a culture that has seen centuries of conflict between Hindu and Muslim, and in spite of her commitment to her own religion—Hinduism—Adhita demonstrates no prejudice toward Islam. Indeed she seems to identify with Islam. At one point in her outline ("Body," item 4), she expressly connects Islam and Hinduism. Her point of view seems to be that of an Easterner resenting the imposing of a technological modernization permeated with Western values. Although this outline does not use the strict format of a classical outline like the previous example, it does a much more thorough job of demonstrating the thought process Adhita has given to the topic and how she intends to communicate her conclusions when she begins drafting. As with Brian Jones, we revisit Adhita's work later as it plays out in her use of the Eddy Model to craft the drafts and subsequent revisions she wrote based on this outline.

Invention through Observation

In order for this method to be of the most use, students need to have a specific purpose behind their observation. This technique is not about voyeurism; to make this work the most effective it can be, students need to make some decisions. First, and perhaps most important, students must be taught about human-subjects permissions and the ethical gathering of data before they begin observing others. Second, they should decide what they hope their observation will demonstrate to them and then look just for that kind of evidence. For instance, if a student believes most college students cheat during exams, they must decide what cheating looks like first, such as glances toward another's work or leaving a textbook open. Only then can they focus their observation on just the behaviors that prove their claim. Third, they must choose the most unobtrusive methods by which these observations can be accomplished and recorded so they don't inadvertently influence their subjects, thereby skewing their findings.

Tools for Recording Observations

For most students, the easiest method of recording observations is just taking notes on what they see. This can be done in a word-processed document, a blog, a wiki, or a discussion thread located on the course LMS. Or some students still use a pen-and-paper journal. If students are assigned a group project involving observation, teachers can decide whether to include the entire classroom community in a thread or use smaller groups, thereby limiting the number of users contributing. Or these groups can reflect the membership of their regular peer-response teams. Moreover, since recording is an individual and often silent activity, it is an excellent way of beginning to analyze an audience, which is a crucial part of the writing process we revisit in later chapters of this book.

Another method for recording observations is a travelog, which is helpful to students in figuring out what happens in another culture and why and how. Unlike the previous example in which the observer remains detached, here your students should analyze their own behavior along with what they observe of others in order to determine what cultural values might be motivating their own behavior, as well as the behavior of those they watch. Tell them to avoid judging the behavior; they should just describe it, not draw conclusions yet. Everyone's culture is incredibly complex. Students will listen, talk, interact, and record observations and feelings in their potentially very significant travelogs. This will help your students avoid the easy way out of merely misunderstanding complicated behavior by falling back on stereotypical thinking.

Since we want students to become sufficiently engaged with collegiate life to reach whatever goals they set and to obtain passing to outstanding grades, your students may wish to begin their travelog by just noting the interactions taking place in one college setting, say your writing class. After a set amount of time, you might invite your students to share their observations about your writing class, if they are comfortable doing so, with one or more of their new classmates. They are all travelers and might appreciate each other's attempts to understand the shared new setting. You might further invite them to compare their perceptions and notes with you.

Since college communities are made up of many, often conflicting, spaces, students should not limit themselves to observing just one class or one space. That too could lead to stereotypical thinking. If a student observed athletes, for instance, and only watched the practices of the football team, how much would that tell them about the values and culture of the swim team? The crew? The softball team? Encourage your students to make observations of behavior, language, and customs all over campus in spaces such as a dining hall, a residence hall, the campus health center, a chapel, the fitness center, an art gallery, the student union, and, yes, party sites. They are really only limited by the size and availability of these spaces on your campus. How people interact with one another outside the confines of a rule-driven space where there is a clear authority, like a classroom, can reveal far more than can observations of controlled behavior.

In our digital age, it is tempting for most students to literally record via a camera, phone, or other device the interactions going on in these spaces instead of noting observations themselves. Or, they might want to use a search engine or library database to gather data on various cultural communities. However, you will want your students to avoid recording these conversations and using research at this stage for three reasons. First, in some states and on some campuses, recording others and then using those recordings without their written consent is illegal and unethical. Second, having a machine make observations defeats the purpose of the travelog. Third, simply skimming search engines or even scholarly journals defeats the purpose of this activity, namely that it allows students to be selective and make choices about what they notice. In order for students to become active observers of the cultures they are trying to understand, it is essential that they take their own notes. Later, chapter 9 of this text helps you open up the possibilities of library research for your students, which of course can be a powerful invention strategy in itself.

Travelogs can be very helpful to your students as they gather and formulate their conclusions about their formal writing assignments. The travelog journal becomes an invaluable resource as a seedbed of ideas and perceptions your students can turn to for writing topics, not just for your class but throughout college.

Dialogue as Observation

Sometimes the deepest observations result when a student conducts a turn-taking dialogue with another student or with several students. Again, there are many ways you could ask students to do this. A low-tech method requires that each participant take a page of their journal, draw a line down the center of it, then dialogue in two journals at the same time in sequence, with minimal speaking. Robert's students engage in this invention method quite often. A good way to start this dialogue is by beginning and ending every exchange with a question. That keeps things moving and focuses the conversation. Of course, this could easily be done using a word-processing document formatted into two columns as well. For instance, your students could use their initial travelog observations about your class to dialogue with a classmate about their first impressions of college or of your writing class. A broader observation might ask, What are a couple of behaviors gender-nonconforming students on campus exhibit that gender-conforming students might emulate? Robert has noticed in his classes that both he and some of his students often have a hard time stopping such dual dialogues. They are usually illuminating and significant. In fact, after the first month or so of classes, students often ask Robert to dialogue with them during workshop classes, and he keeps a journal for such purposes. He also shares this journal with students who want to reread later their contributions to previous dialogues.

Some students tell us it is easier to have such conversations by simply talking rather than in writing. Of course some people are more verbal than others, but the point is that when we do dialogue, be it via pen and paper or electronically, we create a written record to keep as long as we want. Experienced writers don't trust their short-term memory; they try to commit as much as possible to writing.

In your own teaching travelog journal, you might also find it helpful and interesting to explore how this text addresses you as both a teacher of writing and a student of pedagogy. This book is partly a map to your new culture of the intercultural writing classroom, and we are your guides. What are the characteristics of an excellent map? What are the characteristics of an excellent writing teacher? How does a guide get the most out of a map? How do critically engaged readers get the most out of texts? Explore these questions in your travelog journal. In the end, the teaching philosophy you adopt or adapt will become your map, influencing where your teaching leads both you and your students.

USING THE EDDY MODEL—THE PRELIMINARY STAGE: GROUP INVENTION STRATEGIES

Group-Inspired Invention

Another effective invention strategy was taught to Eddy by his students in England. English students tend to be much more group oriented than US students; individuality is the most privileged cultural value in the United States. Not so in England. Usually three to five of Robert's students would get together outside class, and, yes, often in pubs. The people doing this would have at least a tentative idea of what their topic might be. Robert discovered both at the University of Durham and at the University of Nottingham that these groups were always made up of more than two people but rarely more than five. In a group of two, one hears only one other viewpoint. In a group of more than five, "things get too messy," according to one of Eddy's students. All of the several dozen student groups Robert learned of used some variation of one single question: What do you need to know about my topic? The writer with the proposed topic listened as the other four students told him what they needed to know about his topic. Sometimes the writer asked follow-up questions to clarify what was being said. Usually the writer just listened and took notes. A large percentage of the finished essays eventually handed in during this course included footnoted acknowledgement of indebtedness for specific ideas to the students in these groups. Sometimes there was a general statement of indebtedness to the group members, who were also named.

In addition to inviting students in the United States to experiment with this group invention strategy outside class, Eddy gives time during workshop classes to use this method in class. This strategy of asking an audience what it needs to know about a topic can be introduced to students by taking one or two topics, in sequence, and asking the entire class to respond. This full-class experience is often a good technique to demonstrate the advantages of this strategy. This activity often shows not only what a specific audience needs to know but also demonstrates the stereotypes that exist and that must be analyzed or debunked. In addition, this activity highlights for students that their audience is at least dual: instructors and other students. To be effective, student writers need to understand and believe it is essential that they address both audiences in their assignments. They might find it interesting and helpful to discover that in the writing of this book, we had the same problem. We had to address multiple audiences: instructors, their students, our students, editors, our colleagues—essentially anyone who decided to read this book. In creating this book, we have had to accommodate other instructors' teaching methods and values, as well as our own.

Group-Inspired Invention from a Non-Western Culture: China

During Robert's last two years teaching at a Chinese university, he became aware of a group invention strategy that took time to recognize because of its novelty to him. The following method vividly illustrates for students the notion of how language and visual rhetoric shapes thinking in another culture. In his end-of-semester questionnaires on the course, his students in the United States name this Chinese method most often as their invention strategy of choice. In order to make it available for his students in the United States, Eddy first explains it to them and provides the following contextual background.

Robert explains that Chinese literature and criticism are often based on pictorial logic rather than the verbal logic of Western writing. The term for pictorial logic in romanized Chinese is *yijing*, whose character is 意 境. The constituent parts of Chinese characters are called radicals. The character for *yi*, or "mind or consciousness," is 意, which is composed of two radicals that help us understand the resonance of the words *yi* and *yijing*. The first radical of *yi* is *yin*, which looks like this: 音. *Yin* means "sound" or "voice." The second radical is *xin*, meaning "heart or mind." Its form is 心. Together, *yin* and *xin* give the word *yi* (consciousness), the connotative resonant sense of "the voice (sound) of your heart and mind." Thus, *yi* (mind or consciousness) with the connotation of "the voice of your heart" seems more auditory and abstract than visual and concrete. However, the second radical of *yijing*, *jing*, supplies the visual and the concrete. The character *jing*, 境, has at least four definitions: (1) boundary; (2) situation (good or bad situation in life); (3) environment, place; (4) stage or degree of consciousness (in the sense of conscious awareness, creativity, or meditation). Four radicals constitute the character *jing*. The first is *tu*, which is written as 土 and means "soil." The next is *li*, which has the form 立 and means to "stand up" or to "establish oneself." The third radical, 曰, *yue*, means "speak." The fourth radical, 儿, *er* or *ren*, means "child" or "people." Together, these four radicals give the connotation that *jing* is a concrete place where a person is bound by the good or bad situation they establish by standing up and speaking their personhood.

Putting the nuances of *yi* (mind) and *jing* (situation, place, level of consciousness) together suggests the full resonance of the term *yijing*: the mental place (image) and situation in which a person's level of consciousness is demonstrated by how they speak their heart. The quality of the *yijing* is dependent upon the clarity and concreteness of the images one creates and the verbal logic embedded in the mental images.

Robert first provides this background before using this invention technique with US students. Since the current generation is so visually oriented, this Chinese invention strategy can be attractive to students in the West. Outside class in China, five to eight students got together, often the same core group for the entire year. At first Robert, who was occasionally invited to these "writing sessions" as students called them, thought they were talking about images from movies. From the different sessions he attended involving various groups, the common features Robert observed were the following: a student announced their paper topic and ideas about how to approach the assignment. There was silence, sometimes for several minutes, and then someone started describing in a highly concrete and detailed way a mental picture. The would-be author visualized each image, while another student or two took notes that often included sketching each image. After every person finished describing their image, the second stage involved people trying to relate their image to the topic visually. Significantly, they did this by explaining the details of their image. The third stage of the process involved the author trying to construct a focus that encompassed and explained the connections of all the images. This was done by talking about the visual features common to all the images. The fourth and final stage involved the author, with help from anyone present, trying to translate the pictorial and concrete into verbal arguments based on what the students called "Western logic": the movement from the premises of an argument to its conclusion. For a fascinating example of pictorial logic in classical Chinese culture involving the symbolic meaning of flowers and their colors, see the work of An Lan Zhang (2015).

Group-Inspired Invention from a Non-Western Culture: Egypt

During his years as a university teacher in Egypt, Eddy learned to question whether what Americans call *digressions* are instead contextual thinking. Are we Americans too goal oriented even in our invention strategies? Robert's Egyptian students used a group invention strategy that, at the time, he labeled *going off on tangents*. Their sense of the development of ideas is through associations, often highly intuitive rather than logical. Everything connected through personal association with a subject, topic, or focus was considered a necessary part of the context of the paper. If any associations were left out, students felt they had falsely oversimplified a complex subject. Given the training of Egyptian students to try to see all the elements in the contexts of subjects, of course they thought it best to engage in group—rather than personal—invention strategies.

To engage in this activity, students got into groups of three to five, if possible. All the group members were invited to write down in the manner they preferred—diagrams, lists, or continuous sentences—all the ideas expressed or suggested by all members of the group. In this way, at the end of the activity, the would-be writer could see different ways of connecting all the ideas associated by the group. The would-be writer in an American academic setting, where focus is everything for most US professors, could decide to try to connect all the ideas, as Egyptian students do. Our American students, instead, can pick and choose what seems valuable rather than trying to connect everything, although trying to connect everything remains an option. US academic writing typically insists on clear focus, and your students should follow this basic characteristic when they enter the drafting stages of writing, unless they consciously decide to code mesh several cultures and languages. You should leave enough time during the group invention gatherings that the topics of each student are attended to by the whole group.

What Eddy learned in his years in Egypt was that what he thought were merely subjective personal associations were better understood as socially constructed associations that were widely held. While we are certainly not urging students in the United States to write in a way that would cause writing instructors to label their drafts as *unfocused and full of digressions*, we do recommend that students are regularly required to engage in group association of ideas as an invention strategy.

Invention as Cache

In our examples and methods outlined here, the techniques are intended to give students tools for culling what they think about the various cultures they encounter that may differ significantly from their home ones. The notations about these ideas and observations are, for the most part, going to remain private and unshared even with us, their instructors. Students need a private, and, most important, nonevaluated or nongraded space to explore the roots of their stereotypes, their fears, their attractions, their desires. Their brainstorming about cultures in these activities builds a cache of ideas that may never see the light of day in freewriting, much less shared drafts. We are willing to bet, however, that more than a few of the thoughts noted in their brainstorming will eventually surface in their collegiate writing career.

After your students have practiced multiple individual and group invention activities, ask them to consider which ones help them to best understand and evaluate their evolving metacultural awareness. For example, if any of the invention strategies were not productive, especially group activities, ask them to try to determine why. Did a given person dominate the activity? Look at the modality of relationships in the Kluckhohn Model and their corresponding value orientations. Were people holding back too much, perhaps afraid to offend others about tricky or sensitive topics or issues? How could the group improve communication? Did the members of the group have different learning styles that conflicted and caused an unproductive dispute to surface? For example, did some members insist on more focus than others? Why? Did some members want to adhere to time limits while others found pursuing ideas more important than time? Did some members prefer "chaotic" learning, going in several directions at once, while others were more systematic and habitual? How could your student become a spokesperson to help the group negotiate these issues rather than giving up on itself and dissolving? Certainly some groups should disband if differences in learning styles, interests, or perspectives are too great. But before breaking up happens, there should be real attempts at negotiating differences. The first way to try to avoid breaking up is by seeing differences as potential assets, as "natural" divisions of labor. Could the person who likes to proceed methodically be the recorder of the group, the one who interprets the chaotic associations of the person whose learning style mirrors the science of chaos? Second, if the new culture of the writing classroom is a crucial site for testing the proposition that the United States can be a successful and productive polycultural society, aren't peer groups more than a little symbolic of the future of the country? Aren't we worth the extra trouble of hard work toward constructing congruence and refusing to dissolve into conflict?

Charting and observing cultural values is difficult, exciting, and humbling. It is difficult because it is highly complex; it is exciting because it teaches us much about the cultures competing for our allegiance; it is humbling because we realize how profoundly we oversimplify the world by universalizing our values, that is, projecting our culture onto people and cultures that are different from theirs. Ultimately, all invention activities like cultural mapping, travelogs, and such help all our students, as Fan Shen puts it, "to reprogram [their minds], to redefine some of the basic concepts and values [they have] about [themselves], society, and about the universe, values that had been imprinted and reinforced in [their minds] by [their] cultural background, and that had been part of [them] all [of their lives]" (1989, 460). Students who can gauge the values and logic embedded in US academic discourse can learn when it best suits their purposes to use it. Standardized American English highly values individuality, as well as competition and verbal logic. Middle-class and above Americans, especially those benefiting from unearned white privilege, have learned individuality and competitiveness from the beginning of their lives. Most privileged students exhibit these characteristics without being aware of the values. They think it is the "natural" way of behaving. If such students engage in the cultural-awareness activities outlined in this chapter, they can see and learn that they are not behaving "naturally," not following a universal "human nature"; they are acting ideologically from the system of values they learned from their backgrounds. In learning to reconcile differing value systems, our students gain crucial awareness of how they might begin to balance their multiple amphibian identities. Likewise, our first-generation students, both of color and white, and certainly international students, have multiple amphibian identities of equal complexity and will be acknowledging to varying degrees the mainstream realities of white middle-class individuality. According to Kynard and Eddy, HWCUs are "competitive, independent and isolating, and HBCUs are typically noncompetitive, interpersonal and interactive" (2009, W27), which means students of color, international students, and first-gen students are negotiating and becoming more aware of not only their own racial, cultural, and class values but also of the particularities of white, middle-class ways in mainstream college language and culture. The code-meshing option becomes an evolving judgment on individuality and group life, competition and cooperation, being and becoming.

CONTEXT-BUILDING WRITING ACTIVITY 6

Who Are You? In-Class Exercise

Please get into groups of three people by choosing two class members you have not yet talked with. The goal is to find out as much as possible about the person being interviewed without asking inappropriately private questions. Instead, ask some good questions, like How do you want our class members to know and understand you?, How would you describe true racial equality, say in a class setting such as ours?, or As a future supervisor in a multiracial setting, how will you help monoracially provincial supervisees to start having substantial work relationships with people of races not their own? Try to ask unique questions that will require the interviewee to speak candidly about culture in all its forms; don't just keep asking the same questions of each other. Take five minutes to write down the questions you plan to ask whomever you wind up interviewing. Do not share them until you play the role of the interviewer.

Take thirty more minutes to complete this activity. Then, the three of you will take turns playing each role listed below for only ten minutes each: person interviewed, interviewer, and journalist. When you play the interviewer and person interviewed, try to answer as many questions as you can. When you play the journalist, note on a piece of paper or a screen the name of the interviewer and interviewee. The journalist is responsible for taking notes on the responses to the interviewer's questions. At the end of ten minutes of interviewing, the person who played the role of journalist will introduce the person interviewed by the interviewer to the other two. Then, switch roles until everyone has played each part.

Person interviewed_____

Interviewer_____

Journalist/Reporter/Mini-biographer _____

Notes: _____

_____

_____

_____

CONTEXT-BUILDING WRITING ACTIVITY 7

Information-Literacy Practice

View one dozen news stories about crime. How many reinforce racist beliefs about blacks and other people of color? Review "Negative Perception of Blacks Rises With More News Watching, Studies Say," *sciencedaily.com* (July 17, 2008). Find four additional academic sources, including at least one naysayer, and construct an argument about how open and pluralistic contemporary people need to critically evaluate the effects of white supremacy and white racialized stereotypes about crime and men of color. On white supremacy, consult "How History and Reality Means Many of Us Have to Fight to Not be a White Supremacist," http://www.alternet.org/culture/how-history-and-reality-means -many-of-us-have-fight-not-be-white-supremacist?akid=14283.2555710.cy8DGh &rd=1&src=newsletter1056948&t=12. (Write in a group with two coauthors and if possible with people who self-present as three different races).

CONTEXT-BUILDING WRITING ACTIVITY 8

Prewriting: Observing Others

Pick a group or person in your community and watch them without their discovering it. How much do you really know about this person or group? How does the individual or the group spend the day? For this essay I want you to gather observations, lots of them, about everything you notice about your subject's daily life. Write up your findings by explaining what you expected (your hypothesis) to learn or observe about them. Why did you choose to watch this person or group out of all those possible? What were your assumptions before you began your surveillance? Recreate the person's or group's behavior based on what you saw them do/say/and so forth. Finally, move from what you have noticed about your subject to drawing some conclusions about their personality based solely on your observations. Before conducting the observations, you should know very little or nothing about the person or group you observe.

CODE-MESHING ACTIVITY 3

What do you intend to mean, professor, in this syllabus? We need a nurturing language environment to be fully challenged to excel. Is that what you want? Nurture or control?

Write a code-meshed paragraph or poem or other genre you might deliver to your writing instructor now or in a revised form later. Reread the course syllabus and decide, especially focusing on the course outcomes statement, what the teacher cares about in education work and wants you to achieve in your writing. What does the teacher claim to want from you in terms of the actual *language* of your written texts, and is this what you want to give? What do you want the teacher to know about what your home language and your code meshing work in the course mean to you? Maybe you will deliver this and maybe it will remain writing just for yourself.

3

THE PRELIMINARY STAGE, PART 2
Prewriting Using the Eddy Method

SILENCING THE INTERNAL EDITOR: FREEWRITING

In using the Eddy Model of Intercultural Experience, your students may have some degree of fear of failure about exploring new subjects and cultures. As for collegiate culture, they will also hope they will learn a lot and do well in it. After all, they are enrolled in a class in which they will receive a final grade. They are not entirely certain how to do well in the new culture of higher education, so they may revert to old behaviors. In the past they might have been rewarded for second guessing their environment and teachers. As a result, they might have some vague ideas about approach. They will have positive or negative anticipation (or both), but little focus. What they need now is a strategy for getting their initial thinking and brainstorming into a more reader-friendly form. In order to become more effective writers, your students need to develop different strategies appropriate for different rhetorical situations and audiences. We encourage students to expand their original invention reflections further by engaging in freewriting.

Freewriting is automatic, stream-of-consciousness writing often framed by start and stop times. We've found that most students like five minutes best. Three minutes is too short and ten too long. But you should experiment with what your students like best, or what seems most productive. Students can often concentrate better when freewriting is a group event. Since it is often completed as a silent activity, freewriting is usually done during class. In order to obtain the most unedited writing possible, it is crucial that students understand that what they write will not be judged initially by either their instructor or their peers. Freewriting is automatic writing in that students write whatever comes to mind, no matter how strange or illogical. Freewriting can be wildly intuitive and associational. Encourage and allow time for your students to write all these random thoughts down. Now is not the time for them to edit themselves. Students should write nonstop and try to go just fast

DOI: 10.7330/9781607328742.c003

enough to stay ahead of their controlling, autocorrecting minds. The goal is not to go as fast as possible but to explore a topic without limitations. If they say, and ours often do, that they don't know what to write, ask them to use a set phrase with which to keep going. For example, have them literally write the phrases *I don't know what to say* or *this is silly* over and over on their paper or screen. Tell them to just keep putting down these or similar words, and a topic will spontaneously emerge. One always does.

Topic selection for freewriting is rarely an issue in Amanda's classes since topics are often assigned immediately following a class discussion, and freewriting always lasts three to five minutes. Freewriting regularly takes place during the last ten minutes of class, thereby enabling all her students to have a chance to share their opinions about the discussion topic directly with her, especially those who do not wish to or do not have the opportunity to speak with the whole group during class. Often these freewritings are produced on a sheet of paper or on a computer, and a printed copy is turned in before class has ended. Amanda rarely discusses or comments on them beyond making observations about the student's thoughts, with little concern about the content, surface errors, or length. She never assigns a grade to an individual freewrite, nor does she share any part of them with the rest of the class. She sees these freewrites as opportunities for students to express themselves without the a grade hanging over their heads or the peer pressure of a broad audience, namely their classmates. These activities compute into her students' in-class invention writing grade, which includes freewrites, feedback sheets, reading responses, brainstorming exercises, and the like and accounts for only a small percentage of the final course grade. Although freewrites often serve as a more formal invention technique than say, listing, as occurs in other activities, her FYW students regularly produce freewriting texts that unconsciously express racist, sexist, homophobic, classist, and other stereotypically narrow thinking and reasoning.

Robert, on the other hand, does believe freewrites can be commented on and most definitely should be if they seem to express threats of violence toward others. As we will see later in the chapter, he regularly discusses and shares the content of his students' freewritings with the entire class, which students understand in advance. He sometimes assigns freewrites that are a few minutes long, but just as often his students spend an entire class session completing a freewrite exercise. Some of Robert's students move directly from invention to drafting without freewriting at all, or, during a class-session-long freewrite, produce a text that serves them as a working draft. In subsequent chapters of this book, we examine the writings of two of Robert's students who did just that. Amanda and Robert agree, as most of their colleagues do, that only a small percentage of their FYW students can do this effectively since most novice writers benefit from the developmental direction that comes from moving from smaller to more complex writing activities. We don't dispute that some students can produce a coherent draft based on merely a list of few words. Most, however, need the security of taking smaller steps (first brainstorming, then freewriting, then drafting for a broad audience) toward constructing an argument.

As with the invention strategies in the previous chapter, you certainly should not feel you must teach your students both of the following free-writing strategies, nor should you suggest they use them every time they begin writing. Ask your students to try out any number of the strategies a sufficient number of times so they are genuinely familiar with them and can decide if and when they want to use one of them. Remind them of the value in having a large repertoire of writing processes that will help them respond to different audiences and subjects effectively and appropriately. Let's look at each of these types of freewriting, as well as student samples of them, in turn. The first example comes from Amanda's class after the completion of a class-long discussion, while the second strategy comes from Robert's class and asks students to apply the K Model to their cultural assumptions.

DISCUSSION-BASED, TIMED FREEWRITING

One of Amanda's thematic composition courses looked at the cultural ramifications of the concept of justice in a variety of arenas beyond the courtroom. For instance, students discussed whether the utilitarian concept of the greatest good for the greatest number was inherently just. They also examined how criminal justice is doled out and defined, and, by extension, can lead to dehumanization. On other occasions, the class discussed various examples of social, racial, and cultural injustices that have shaped US history. All these discussions helped her students examine the origins of their values, especially in regard to acts of dehumanization.

One of their many discussions of justice centered on the infamous shipwreck of the US whaler, the *Essex*, and her crew; only eight of the men survived. After many weeks at sea with no food or water, the men decided one of them had to die in order for the others to survive. Although lots were drawn, none of the men would kill the unlucky soul, at first. Within days, however, the men succumbed to murderousness and cannibalism. At the conclusion of the discussion of whether the actions of the *Essex*'s survivors were justified, Amanda invited her students to freewrite on these circumstances or another situation that might lead one to conclude that taking another's life was just or justifiable. Here is an example of a ten-minute associational freewrite written by one of Amanda's students during that class:

> I think the only time it would be ok to murder someone, If they have done something to a person that really affected them or someone in their family. For example If a little girl got raped or even just a random woman, and the father of that daughter murdered her rapist, or the grown woman murdered her rapist I would see that as moraly right. If some person murdered someone very close to you a friend or family member, I believe it would be morally correct to murder that person. I even think that it have a dog or any pet that you really love and someone kills them on Purpose, I believe it is morally right to murder that Person.

It is clear that this freewrite does discuss occasions when the writer believes murder would be justified in his mind and in his value system. It clearly has not been edited for surface errors, and Amanda believes commenting on those errors would be inappropriate and potentially damaging. Instead, Amanda's response is usually an observational, non-judgmental sentence or two that globally responds to the freewrite. In this instance she noted it is interesting that the taking of a life is equated with murder, which is seen by this student as reparation for a perceived wrong instead of, say, a premeditated action, especially given how US popular culture often depicts murder. She also observed the student's idea that harming animals is as significant as harming people, and how that in expressing that idea, the student made the parameters for justifiable murder more complex and less one dimensional.

When writing this book, Robert and Amanda had some extensive discussions about this freewriting sample and whether it is an appropriate example. Robert lobbied for its removal from the book, Amanda for keeping it. He thought it promoted the ease by which people do violence to one another. Pedagogically, the most important part of the exercise for Amanda is that students feel comfortable sharing their thoughts, warts and all. She saw the frank, though logically flawed, expression about murder as the first step toward her student's evolving an ethos that sees inhumanity in the thinking expressed in this freewrite, without her having to pontificate or highlight it herself. Because the freewrite is a classic example of the acceptance of dehumanization in action and promotes the idea of a privileged few holding power in a society, even if that society is made up of eight men in a lifeboat, the freewrite created an incredible teaching moment. Amanda believed that anything beyond observational commentary would violate the spirit of freewriting and potentially could silence the student from expressing any other ideas that could be interpreted as or considered verboten. Note also that a freewriting sample written by one of Robert's students that appears later in this chapter is much longer than the sample by Amanda's student; she tends to assign more of them but allows less time for completing them. Over the course of a semester, Amanda's students are able to produce as many as twenty freewritings for their portfolios. Although these freewrites could easily be expanded into working drafts and developed more, similar to Robert's examples, they rarely are, as was the case with the sample discussed above. Instead, they routinely serve in her students' portfolios as a reservoir of controlling ideas that merely *could be* returned to in later essays. Now, let's look at Robert's use of a class-long freewriting exercise.

EXTENDED FREEWRITING USING THE K MODEL

Earlier we affirmed that five minutes is our recommendation for the length of time for freewriting in classrooms or other learning spaces. We also advise teaching colleagues to experiment with their individual courses to see how much time their students find is most productive. Though we most often assign five minutes of continuous freewriting, Robert has found that a percentage of his students see class-long freewriting sessions as a productive way to turn off the editor in their minds and simply get their current ideas down on paper or screen. For example, Robert has used the following assignment, without change or adaptation, in the United States and in three international cultures. It remains unchanged because it so consistently occasions powerful and insightful student writing. Writing it enables his students to complete some preliminary thoughts regarding the topics of the essays they will write in their first-year writing class. It involves six steps and builds directly from the K Model prewriting his students complete that was discussed in the previous chapter. Students are set the task of using the entire class session as a long freewrite, in which case they get through all six items in the assignment, or if they rebel against such a long freewrite, they are free to choose to get through as many of the six steps as possible, as long as they stay active and productive for the entire class session.

CONTEXT-BUILDING WRITING ACTIVITY 9

The Preliminary Stage: The Key-Cultural-Assumptions Freewrite

1. Choose a key cultural assumption that is a fundamental aspect of your view of the world and of yourself. Common examples for mainstream Americans would be the ideas of progress, time is money, competition is healthy, and technology will eventually solve all problems. Remember that cultures often teach values and assumptions indirectly or unconsciously. Therefore, step one is often difficult, and it is a key decision you must make. Talk to your instructor, classmates, friends, and family members about this key decision. Go back to the brainstorming you created earlier for assumptions you want to explore in your freewriting.

2. What are the positive and negative influences on you of your key cultural assumption?

3. Where does your key cultural assumption fit in the Kluckhohn Model?

4. Using the K Model as a guide and aid, write about what other directly related values your key assumption is firmly associated with.

5. Having done steps one through four, how do you think you should try to modify or eliminate the cultural assumption? If you try to modify or eliminate it, how and why will you do so? If you think you should keep your cultural assumption unmodified, why do you want to do so even though you examined its negative influences in step two? If you choose to modify your cultural assumption by trying to retain its positive influences but eliminate the negatives, rephrase the cultural assumption as you think it should be in order for it to create only positive results.

6. Explain what you have learned about your cultural assumption in this freewrite.

Because freewriting isn't polished writing, some students just address each step as if they are answering questions, while others may compose coherent paragraphs that tie the concepts together. Robert's students eventually go through at least three drafts in composing this difficult and important assignment; however, we focus our analysis here on only their initial freewrites because, like Amanda's students' freewrites, none of these samples was revised to demonstrate the other stages of the Eddy Model. In the case of freewritings taken through multiple drafts, Eddy suggests that by the final draft, each step could easily form at least a full page of analysis. He asks his students to try to see this as not so much a personal paper as an attempt at objective, scientific cultural analysis and critical thinking. A few students initially see this writing assignment as inviting very private diary-like narratives. Instead, it is an invitation for students to examine, in a public and formal manner, how their culture has composed one of their key values. In a sense, freewriting is the culmination of the Preliminary Stage because it requires students to provide a structure or framework for their brainstorming. Let's look at one prewriting sample that was written by a student who used this assignment during a class-long writing session. To help direct these writings, Robert asked his students to write about one of the following three cultural assumptions: individuality and economic independence as an ultimate goal; in God we trust; or friendship as being essential to personal happiness.

STUDENT SAMPLE OF THE PRELIMINARY STAGE—THE KEY-CULTURAL-ASSUMPTIONS FREEWRITE

The key-cultural-assumptions writing assignment is central to later chapters of this book and to elucidating the Eddy Model of Intercultural Experience. The following freewrite, however, demonstrates how one first-year college student responded initially to this assignment given the three assumptions listed above. Notice how the writer, Taka, struggles to even accept that "American culture can be adequately encapsulated by three assumptions or that these assumptions are in fact at all distinct." On the one hand, Taka literally follows most of the directions in each of the six steps, but on the other hand, he takes the assignment and makes it his own by questioning his having anything interesting to say about the assumptions and replacing them with the assumption that United States culture is narcissistic and suffers from megalomania. Although he rejects the assigned prompt choices for analyzing the Kluckhohn Model, he does use it to examine his own assumption of US superiority, which is much more than he was asked to do. He also makes the assignment his own by not following the steps mechanically but by weaving the analysis into a unified examination of superiority as it affects the cultural assumptions Robert assigned. Here is Taka's freewrite:

American Exceptionalism: European Conceit
Taka W.

It has been theorized that the United States is qualitatively different from other nations; a nation founded upon principles of liberty, equality, individuality, and democracy. Over time, this theory has been co-opted by American neoconservatives to imply a natural, inevitable superiority over all nations. Nonetheless, both these schools of thought are in fact marks of traditional European philosophy, one which is centered on the self as an element of the divine. It is this fundamental belief, that we are each fundamentally unique and uniquely superior to one another, that underlies contemporary Western and particularly American culture. It is no surprise that America has inherited this trait from its European parents, after all, it has come to pass that the first "true" Americans were Europeans.

This assignment, and my response to it, is further indicative of the principle that Americans are not only fundamentally self-centered, but entirely self-obsessed. This assignment, after all, has the gall to suggest that American culture can be adequately encapsulated by three assumptions or that these assumptions are in fact at all distinct (or that I would have anything interesting to say about how these assumptions relate to the Kluckhohn model). At the same time, I have the temerity to outwardly reject this prompt, professing its innate invalidity and instead giving my own assumption, defining American culture as one of narcissism and megalomania.

I regard the three given assumptions—individuality and economic independence as the ultimate goals, the importance of faith in God, and the essentiality of friendship—not as profound insights, but as painfully obvious symptoms. These each result from the quintessential American (and Western) belief that we, as a nation and as individuals, are uniquely, rightfully, and naturally superior to all others. We believe that because we are so unique, we are entitled to independence (both as individuals and as a nation). We cannot imagine being contained by a foreign (or a foreign domestic) government, though we believe others ought to be governed by us. We believe that economic independence must be earned—of course, no one can be reasonably expected to maintain a belief which is actively detrimental to their wellbeing. The reason we value economic independence is that, as Senator Marco Rubio so ineloquently put it, "we are a nation of haves and soon-to-haves." That is, we are so fundamentally convinced of our own superiority that we believe (even when faced with overwhelming evidence to the contrary) we can and inevitably will overcome any struggle to achieve economic success. Quantity and quality of friendship are both ultimately measures of popularity. Family is given, friendship is earned. We value friendship because obtaining it satisfies our need to manifest our key assumption: that we are superior. God is the oldest of the supposed triad. Belief in God is twofold: we believe our superiority is God-given, divine in nature, and we distinguish ourselves from those who lack our God, viewing them as lesser beings, living a lie. Thus, the three given assumptions are really all indications of personal superiority: material wealth, social wealth, and moral wealth.

The belief in superiority is materialistically valuable, and may very well be biological in origin. Belief in superiority gave rise to manifest destiny. And say what you will, but as it manifested, manifest destiny proved very valuable to the United States. Of course, it was a similar line of thinking which drove Pax Britannica, Nazism, the Crusades, and all the other European endeavors of nationalism and imperialism. Each of these strove for conquest and hegemony. Not so much out of malice or sadism (though this undoubtedly occurred in each case), but out of a profound belief that each was so superior that it was obligated to share its superiority with the world. Contemporary Pax Americana and its imperialism are merely continuations of this tradition. Of course, the West's conquests have at times improved the lives of both the conquerer and the conquered. But, more often than not, it has manifested as racism, bigotry, prejudice, hate, and destruction.

The assumption of superiority also manifests itself on a personal level. There is no doubt that a sense of superiority can lead to a sense of self-actualization and happiness. However, it can also lead to discontent and shame when we fail to live up to our proclaimed superiority.

Moreover, it drives us to act immorally. We take as much as we can, more than we need, under the belief that we deserve it. When we approach the poor or disenfranchised, we validate our sense of superiority, rather than feel pity for our fellow human and appreciation for our own privileges (and when we do feel pity, our attempts to rectify their situation tend to be either pitiful or imperial in nature). When we approach foreign societies, we assume that the best and only option is for them to adopt our culture. We are so driven to avoid insecurity, to live up to our own assumptions, that we prefer greed and destruction to humility and humanity.

In the Kluckhohn model, the assumption of individual and national superiority fits in at least two categories: social relations and man-nature relationship. In terms of social relations, this assumption leads to the hierarchical organization, that there ought to be a natural order to relationships within an organization, with leaders and followers. However, there is a twist. So great is the rapacity of American narcissism that, both internally and internationally, we each believe that we should be the leaders, and all others our subordinates. While Americans would rarely admit their valuation of greed, it is nonetheless one of tacit approval. However, it is not inherently a greed for materialistic wealth. It is a greed for power. With an assumption of superiority comes an assumption of deserved dominance, and money is but one form of power.

In terms of the man-nature relationship, this assumption leads to dominance over nature. As Americans, we envision ourselves as unique, removed from and atop nature. We believe nature can and should be conquered, just like our fellow human.

It is common to mistake sense of superiority as a human—rather than American—trait.

Indeed, greed, conquest, pride, and prejudice seem to be constants throughout global human history. America is unique, however, in the way in which it has codified superiority in its culture and philosophy. The origin of the difference is existential in nature, a matter of Heideggerian ontotheology. In the Western tradition, we believe the self to be an element of the divine, with man as an image of the divine. The Eastern traditions focus on cosmological unity and discovering one's true identity (or lack thereof). In the West, we believe in our natural superiority. In the East, one is not distinct from nature. If Eastern cultures are ones of shame then American culture is one of pride. The difference is that Eastern cultures avoid shame through humility, whereas American culture strives for pride through domination.

Perhaps the greatest sin of self-importance is not really its effects, but that it is itself a delusion. Of course, it is likely an emotionally, nationalistically, economically, and thus biologically valuable delusion, so whether or not it is worth eliminating is a matter of perspective: should one favor happiness or truth? More to the point, eliminating this national superiority complex would ultimately be a matter of eliminating self-deception. We cannot truly remove our spectacles and examine the lenses, for we need the glasses to see. We cannot ever fully divorce ourselves of experience, irrationality, bias, and emotion. The best we can hope to do is examine the glasses of those around us and the simulacra which are reflected back to us. And, after all, if I am so superior, why would I ever change?

This freewrite begins with a sophisticated title, unlike most students' formulaic titles, like "K Model Response." Even a cursory reading shows that this student comes to the exercise with historical, philosophical, linguistic, and political awareness (conceit, Rubio, Nazism, Crusades, self-actualization, Heideggerian ontotheology) uncommon to most FYW classes. His syntax and tone suggest someone who is comfortable expressing his thoughts and who has little need for sentence-level feedback. Robert was initially impressed with Taka's complete engagement with his values, so much so that Robert noted how Taka's argument resists or fights back for historical equality; clearly the piece serves as a critique of white privilege that both surprised and delighted Robert. Taka is clearly engaged in a level of rhetorical analysis remarkable for a traditionally aged FYW student.

The piece creates interest by suggesting that US superiority is universally assumed in all arenas. Taka boldly examines how this cultural assumption influences his values and behavior vis a vis friendship and faith, showing how each serves as a vehicle for unearned US exceptionalism. When applying this value to the K Model, he only devotes about a paragraph to it; he limits it to social relations ("hierarchical organization, that there ought to be a natural order to relationships within an organization, with leaders and followers") and human-nature relations ("dominance over nature. As Americans, we envision ourselves as unique, removed from and atop nature. We believe nature can and should be conquered, just like our fellow human"). Regardless of its effect on his reader, Taka routinely uses pejoratives and generalizations to describe US exceptionalism ("self-centered," "self-obsessed," "nationalistic," "imperialistic," "bigot[ed]," "racist," "immoral," "greedy," "dominant") without awareness or acknowledgement of the paradox that he too is a United States citizen. At no time does he qualify his claims or attempt to show any positive aspects of the assumption, as step three of the K Model asks. Nor does he attempt a discussion of the final step of modifying or eliminating the cultural assumption. He was not required to complete each step and may even have lacked the time to develop the freewrite in these ways. His piece remains rooted in discussing the negative qualities of the assumptions he sees as "painfully obvious symptoms" of US superiority and entitlement. Thus, his desire to shock overcomes his ability to develop an intercultural ethos or ever fully engage the K Model here. Ultimately, Taka's strong freewrite could have been more effective if he had considered how the claimed superiority of the United States relates to other values and why it lacks positives (if it does at all).

When Robert discusses successful freewrites like Taka's in class, most students regard them as excellent and deserving of an A grade. Then he has to remind students that he uses portfolio assessment with no grading until the end of the course, when students' final grades are based on the best work they produced in the course. But in response to this freewrite, Taka's classmates commented on its sophisticated references and that they were unnerved by it. Some were made uncomfortable by the tone, feeling personally attacked by Taka's critique of privilege. What do you think? How convincing is his argument? Do you think he believes all he claims, even as it applies to himself? His family? His home culture? How would you outline his argument?

FREEWRITING BEYOND THE K MODEL

In the previous section we looked at how one of Robert's students used the K Model to write a lengthy freewrite about their key cultural assumptions, so lengthy it could serve as a working draft. However, the next writing task our students face may not work well with the K Model, or even at all. Students need skills they can use regardless of topic, course, or instructor. So, we need to move students entirely away from the K Model for this next set of freewrites. In the K Model exercises, the students are in the passive state of **I was composed**; in consideration of their new college culture, they should now be urged to achieve the active state of **I compose**.

The value of freewriting is that we often find gems amidst all the verbiage or the center of gravity in our thinking-feeling about a topic. The following example of a five-minute freewrite comes from a British student of Robert's who attended the Egyptian university where Robert taught. The students were required to analyze a pre-Islamic environment in Egypt. A number of Egyptian students used the topic to attack the Great Pyramid as a symbol of the oppression of their ancestors by tyrannical pharaohs. The British student, however, like many westerners, fell in love with the Great Pyramid. But he was a Muslim and did not want to offend his Egyptian classmates. He was blocked and couldn't write. Freewriting was a perfect way to set him "free." Robert told him to think back to his first visit to the Great Pyramid and to write whatever came to mind, reminding him that he didn't have to show it to anyone else and that freewriting is a time when writers don't have to be afraid of making overstatements. Here is what the student wrote:

> God it takes my breath—wow—a beautiful pointer to the world of spirit—God it's beautiful—shocking to have a bit of the spiritual world here—wow—too much—how can one describe this?—my breath, my breath—this has my soul in magnetic tow—wow, too much—how can any human creation be so beautiful—it is reality—I wish I could live here all the time—if I saw it every day, what would it be like?—I'm getting closer and closer—it reaches heaven somehow—it seems a million times bigger and taller than the highest skyscraper, yet it is lean and the mother of elegance—I love it—it stuns me—wow, wow—how can we know reality except by seeing this?—I need to be lifted out of myself like this—the beauty of this sets me free—I'm alive here—it is Beauty, not beautiful—the motorway leads to the pyramid—how can we look at the pyramid and say there's been technological progress?—we need this to see and open us up—it couldn't have been built by slave labour—it is an act of group human love—it is Beauty, Joy and Identity—I begin to know who I am—

The British student was embarrassed by the exuberance of his freewriting; Robert told him there was no reason to be. It was, after all, personal and "free" writing. He was surprised at the depth and direction of the student's thinking-feeling. Notice how in the final paper that eventually grew out of this freewriting, the student's distinctive response to the Great Pyramid gives focus and unity to a draft as academically formal and balanced as the student could be on this subject. Here is the opening paragraph:

> The Great Pyramid is located on the Giza Plateau, close to the heart of Egypt's modern capital. It is dramatically juxtaposed to the bleak ugliness of the Western skyscrapers of central Cairo. To reach the unique environment of the pyramids, one leaves downtown Cairo heading west, into the desert on a well-kept divided roadway. Suddenly the modern city disappears around a bend and hills of sand, and one is in a new world which is ancient. The Great Pyramid dwarfs the skyscrapers. It seems, because of the unique geometry of its shape, to reach heaven. Yet, in scientific terms, it is much shorter than the tallest of modern buildings. It is 482 feet high. How does it create a sense of dwarfing the modern works of contemporary humankind?

Clearly, freewriting is a fundamental tool that allows students to move beyond the disjointed invention techniques of the earliest part of the Preliminary Stage and toward the false starts and oversimplifications that exemplify the working drafts they will be creating while immersed in the Spectator Stage.

PROGRESSING TOWARD THE NEXT STAGE(S)

You should develop assignments for your own students. Essays are like tickets to an unknown destination. You will give students directions in the assignment, but directions to what precise location? And what are the characteristics of this new culture they are supposed to enter in their papers? We said earlier that academic writing has the characteristics of being skeptical, analytical, and critical. These are the qualities most instructors expect to find in their students' writing. One could argue that all college writing, in the first year certainly, is writing across cultures because there are many departments, many teaching methods, many specialized languages and behaviors on a campus. While they surely won't enter them all, your students will enter quite a few of these cultures by participating in academic and social activities, taking classes in certain departments, and declaring a major. Entry into a new culture often also comes out of effectively or closely observing the culture one is trying to join. To be accepted as a successful college writer of intercultural experiences, your students need to demonstrate the three characteristics of skepticism, systematic analysis, and critical mindedness in all their writing, regardless of who assigns it.

All they know is that they have been given a writing assignment and a deadline. But, they do not know what they are going to write about much less what they think about the topic. This is where the power of the Preliminary Stage, especially freewriting, comes into play. Let's say their instructor has designed a sequence of essay assignments discussing Islamic culture. Let's imagine this sequence of assignments on Islamic culture will finish with a summary paper called "The Face of Islam in a Multicultural America." The sequence involves Islam as an international culture. Islam is the second largest of the world's religions, with more than a billion believers. In exploring Islam in its international aspects, for example, students might look at the Palestinian-Israeli conflict, or at Islam as practiced in Egypt, or at coeducational classes at Egyptian universities. Perhaps they will read and write about the large Islamic minority in China that numbers more than twenty million. Or they might study Islam in the world's most populous Islamic state, which is not in the Middle East but is Indonesia.

So, a student must write a number of papers about Islamic culture. Perhaps they have no interest in this subject, or maybe they have negative connotations of Islam because of the military actions in the Middle East going as far back as the Gulf War, past the 9/11 attacks and on to the other armed conflicts in Afghanistan and so on. Perhaps they are an American Muslim, whether immigrant or native. Maybe they simply want to learn more about a major religion of the world struggling to decide how to respond to technological modernization in a way that does not lead to cultural suicide. Maybe they hope to have business relations in the future with the Islamic communities abroad and want to better understand the cultural basis of those communities' business orientations. Maybe the student wants to create their own e-space for informing other first-year students about a specific aspect of Islamic culture: the literature, the music, the philosophies, the laws, the food, the language, the celebrations, the customs.

The assignment sequence looks at Islam as an international culture but also as a domestic culture. In this phase of the sequence, perhaps the student will study how Islam came to the Americas in the person of African slaves, some of whom, it is reported, memorized the holy book of Islam, the Quran (which is about the length of the New Testament), so as to retain their essential identity. Perhaps the student will read and write about the Nation of Islam, and about Malcolm X. They might study the movie directed by Spike Lee and then study other cinematic images of Islam in the United States. Perhaps they will read about Muslim immigration to the United States. They might want to look at Islam in American sports. Perhaps they are interested in sports history, and in such figures as Kareem Abdul-Jabbar and Muhammad Ali. They might want to read about how, for example, the charismatic three-time heavyweight champion of the world, Muhammad Ali, polarized US public opinion about the Vietnam War by refusing to step forward to be drafted into the Army on April 28, 1967. This action of Ali's, which he said was solely based on his religious convictions, and with which, ultimately, the United States Supreme Court concurred on June 28, 1971, by unanimously reversing his conviction, was a key event in the social history of the United States in the 1960s. Regardless of their eventual choice of topic, an assignment sequence of this nature gives students the opportunity to write about how their personal cultural values influence the way they react to another culture, like Islam. Whatever their initial point of view, students must decide which aspect of the subject they will write about for all the assignments in the sequence. Using a variety of the invention techniques of the Preliminary Stage of the Eddy Model, namely brainstorming, outlining, and, most important, freewriting will help them determine their focus and subject for the extended writing tasks of the sequence.

Writing assignments, then—tickets to unknown destinations—provide students with several useful problems. First, they need to begin by figuring out what they think and feel about the topic and where their thinking is stereotypical. The Preliminary Stage of the Eddy Model is essential here because this figuring out, of course, happens as your students make use of various invention techniques and brainstorming. Second, they must get their ideas down in a format ready to share with others. Initially, these ideas might appear in the form of a freewrite only their instructor might read or comment on. Only after students decide to take their work beyond an audience of one do they move from the Preliminary Stage to the next step, entering the Spectator Stage. Usually this move translates into students writing a working or initial draft in which they consider the needs and characteristics of an audience, often for the first time. Although instructors are a crucial part of the audience—the new culture—students too often mistakenly believe instructors are the whole audience. In the Spectator Stage, we help students realize they have at least a dual audience: instructors and other students, individually and as a group. They gradually discover how different people can be when talking with them one on one or in a group. Soon your students will even notice that your class might behave differently when certain students are present or absent. They should notice, study, and analyze these classroom dynamics to continue understanding audience. Finally, students should revisit and rework their writings based on the interplay of their ideas, your evaluation, outside information (like research), and peer review; in tandem, these forces will influence what actually remains in the final version they have time to produce before the deadline. So far, we have examined the steps in the Preliminary Stage; the next few chapters examine the Spectator and Increasing-Participation Stages in which drafting and revising take center stage, and we begin looking at how audience increasingly affects our students' attempts at writing about culture.

4

THE SPECTATOR STAGE
First Draft

DOI: 10.7330/9781607328742.c004

QUESTIONING WHAT ONE BELIEVES: FALSE STARTS, OVERSIMPLIFICATIONS AND MISUNDERSTANDINGS

At this point, your students will have completed invention techniques that enabled them to grasp some aspects of their home culture(s) and their often-uncritical thinking about home and excessively critical thinking about other cultures. During the Preliminary Stage of the Eddy Model, our students begin leaving their home cultures to arrive in a new, mostly academic one. They leave the old securities of their home culture and are only just beginning to make real contact with the new setting. As we have stated, it is during that first stage that students have hopes and fears about what the experience will be. In terms of a college writing course, there are significant hopes that they will get better at writing and overcome procrastination and not knowing what to say. But there are real and operational fears that their previous experiences with writing, procrastination, not knowing what to say, and fearing they really have nothing to say will haunt them pretty intensely. These fears are also why that first stage is exemplified by vague ideas of approach, or first thoughts, vague questions, and vague senses of what to argue.

We ask you to review the Eddy Model of Intercultural Experience located in the first chapter of this book. The Spectator Stage is the next we cover, and it is the first that engages the left column, Stages of Behavior. At this juncture, students naturally misunderstand and oversimplify the new culture and likely stereotype it as well. Oversimplification results not just from failing to engage a subject but also from never moving past one's initial attitudes and opinions. In essence, this is the level of engagement the freewrites from the previous chapter demonstrate. For some of your students, entering this stage may result in their having considerably more mood swings than usual; these will be positive more often than negative because students usually come to the new culture by choice and expect an overall constructive, or at least professionally useful, experience. In this stage, students are still largely passive yet careful observers of their intensely new scene. These behaviors have led some sociologists to refer to this developmental stage as the *tourist* or *exotic* phase; some of your students may try on the new culture but repeatedly remind and/or convince themselves it isn't a permanent adaptation. If you have traveled, you have experienced the excitement and anticipation that comes from exposure to new foods, smells, sights, languages, and behaviors in a foreign setting. Our method in this text depends on moving your students past this metacultural level of inter-action toward an active, polycultural engagement of new cultures and peoples. The Spectator Stage eventually ends when the fundamental passivity ends, that is, when one begins substantial intercultural inter-action with the people and societal structures of a host culture. This overcoming of passivity is, it should be noted, the beginning of the end of that special sense of newness or stereotypical "exoticness" or "bor-ingly familiar" uninterrupted white privilege of many American college spaces and personnel.

Perhaps the most important characteristic of this stage of intercultural experience is that our passivity and alertness to the new culture makes us so other-directed that we lose our usual degree of self-reflection, and being other-directed is the source of that awkwardness so common to the newly arrived. We forget that as we gaze intently at the external spectacle, we are ourselves quite a spectacle. Contextual knowledge has largely ended, and we have no place to stand as we try to respond in a balanced way to our new setting. Our construction of a new and appro-priate contextual landscape is our first and ongoing essential task.

During college your students must construct a new contextual land-scape in terms of how to interact with other students, individually and collectively, and with their instructors. Since these interactions occur very early in most courses, we suggest discussions about what is observ-able take place in groups or as posts on the LMS. These comments should not critique since critical comments can shut down insecure writ-ers and your students will not have had the chance to learn how to give any kind of substantive feedback yet. In terms of the Stages of Behavior in class, the Eddy Model identifies the Spectator Stage as the time when your students **must interact with others in class**. In a writing setting this means that, ideally, all class members help each other with the more or less inevitable false starts, misunderstandings, and oversimplifications of the writing to learn of a first draft. What exactly is a false start in an FYW course? For Robert, a false start in a first draft has two character-istics: it (1) misunderstands the complexity of the topic being pursued and (2) oversimplifies the topic by not recognizing the monocultural provincialism of the writer's unnoticed point of view in their false start. The writer is being monological, talking to the self about a matter that has many sides rather than just one. For Amanda, a false start doesn't have to be this complex; it is usually as simple as realizing a change of topic, thesis, source, or example is needed. For example, false starts occur in Amanda's classes after students find a source but after a close reading discover it contains no useful passages that support their claims; the source itself is a false start, and the student must search again for a more appropriate one.

False starts are to be expected in this phase of the writing process. False starts are much better than no starts. Certainly there are differences in learning styles; some writers won't begin until they think they know exactly where their writing will take them. They like elaborate outlines and will not begin the first draft until a clear scheme for the whole paper exists. If such writers can be productive and effective, fine. But do not let your students think all experienced writers take this approach, or that something is wrong if they don't. Such writers are the exception, not the rule. Moreover, we have seen no evidence that the final drafts of such elaborate planners are stronger than those of writers who **discover** in their first draft what their real focus is.

If students wait until they have sufficient background knowledge so they will make no mistakes, they will delay or postpone engagement in the new culture or paper, perhaps permanently. It is better to expect mistakes as evidence of active engagement and to model for students how to be as gracious as possible about being corrected by others now, or by themselves later. Caution them against paralyzing themselves through fear of errors or of false starts and "wasted" beginnings.

On the other hand, do not think we are arguing against planning. We are arguing against overplanning, which is often a strategy to avoid writing a draft and engaging significantly in the new culture. It is one of the best excuses for procrastination. The line between proper planning and overplanning is individual and is dependent upon the writer's audience and purpose for a given piece of writing and their current knowledge of the subject.

So what is proper planning for the first draft? There are those who like to enter a new culture with maps, guidebooks, guides, and as much support as possible. They do not like being "lost"; indeed, they want to know where they are at every moment. Others do minimum planning and believe they can learn best by jumping into the new culture and experiencing the rhythms of everyday life. They think that getting lost is the best way of finding yourself in the new setting. Such people want to experience the culture without carrying too many intellectual expectations into their view of the new setting. They fear stereotypes and other forms of control over their thinking. Each of these two modes of experiencing the new culture or paper has positive and negative dimensions. Actually, they are the opposite ends of the continuum in answer to one question, How much planning should I do? Let's look at the two ends of the continuum.

PLANNING THE DRAFT

We all need to draw common-sense lines between these two approaches so as to obtain the benefits of each mode of experiencing a new culture and a first draft. Most writers don't delay writing by continuing to plan until they know 100 percent of what their first draft will say. Likewise, most writers don't jump into a draft with zero sense of where they will go and what they will argue. So where do we draw the line? Your students must understand that the answer is partly personal—how much planning do they **like** to do, partly rhetorical—how much planning do they **need** to do to be effective, and partly a matter of deadlines—how much planning does the syllabus allow them **time** to do?

One of the positive dimensions of elaborate planning is that it acknowledges the vast complexity of a new-culture paper. Elaborate planners would say that oversimplifications are inevitable unless they plan carefully and thus admit the complexity of their subjects. Elaborate planning is a form of **respect** for the topic and the needs of the intended reader to understand the issues involved in the topic or the values embedded in the new culture. These are all significant positive points.

The negative dimensions of elaborate planning are also significant. The first negative is that elaborate planning postpones the writing of the first draft. Second, elaborate planning can give a false sense of expertise, or of significant understanding of the topic culture—when, in fact, one is still at the introductory stages of contact with one's topic and focus. Finally, an elaborate plan tends to become an end, not a means, a structure unto itself, which the excessive planner is reluctant to change substantially or to discard when appropriate.

The positive side of minimum planning continues the line of reasoning developed in the previous paragraph. Seeing the first draft as a discovery draft demonstrates a desire to engage the topic and its give and take. Students acknowledge that they will oversimplify and misunderstand but also that they will be open to correction and improvement.

They will have immersed themselves in the paper and so are ceasing to be spectators. When your students finish their first draft, they will be ready to enter the Increasing Participation Stage. Spectatorhood will have largely ended. Your students will begin to be truly "in" the new culture and paper topic because they will be internalizing new values.

The negative side of minimum planning continues the line of reasoning begun in the discussion of the positive side of elaborate planning. It is presumptuous to travel to a new culture with zero planning. This lack of preparation shows no respect for the culture or topic. Zero planning also implies that all cultures are pretty much the same in the important details and that one can understand the new culture by applying the knowledge and values of one's home culture. To argue that we should go to a new culture with no advance planning so we can avoid stereotyping ignores the giant point that we will unavoidably respond to the new culture through the cultural conceptions of our existing identity anyway. Or, put another way, arguing that zero planning helps avoid stereotyping is a line of thought that ends up defending ignorance in the name of openness, a serious and humorous contradiction.

Careful and appropriate planning is better than no planning because it helps students see the different cultural conceptions and values of the target culture, however imperfectly and tentatively. Careful planning also helps students to see their own values more clearly. This gets them thinking about the issues to be faced in their sojourn or paper.

What is an appropriate degree of planning, avoiding both no planning and overplanning? We said earlier that the answer depends on how much planning **your students like** to do, how much they **need** to do, and how much **time** you allow them. But as a general rule, the minimum amount of planning for a first draft allows your students to go through, in a serious and substantial way, at least one of the invention strategies from the previous chapters. If because of time constraints or personal preference, your students limit their planning to the invention strategies introduced in the previous chapters, it is best to choose a group strategy. A group strategy is best because it will be more interactive and detailed and will be much more likely to help your students see beyond their current and merely personal viewpoint as they begin listening to the other members of the group converse with them and with each other.

If one of the group invention strategies from the previous chapters should be regarded as the minimum amount of planning for a first draft, on the one hand, and on the other hand you want your students to avoid overplanning, then what additional planning is appropriate? The answer is best understood by introducing another question: What is the **purpose** or **goal** in the draft? This question could be answered in the negative: to avoid misunderstandings or oversimplifications. Or one could answer the question of purpose in general terms: to get a grade of A. But these two answers are too general and obvious. We need an answer that is specific to the topic and to the sense of audience, one that depends upon the point of view the writer will argue or on the strongest question they have in response to their topic.

A first or discovery draft can appropriately have as its purpose the pursuit of an answer to an authentic question, **your student's** question about the subject of their draft. Be certain they choose an authentic question, which means a question they do not know the answer to. Your student's search for an answer to a real question of theirs can give life, focus, and a ready-made structure to their discovery drafts. These questions should address a key issue or dimension of the subject they will write about.

CONTEXT-BUILDING WRITING ACTIVITY 10

Planning the First Draft

To help you decide whether you want, need, or have time to do additional planning beyond the group invention strategy you have already used, answer questions like these:

What is the main idea I want to communicate in this paper, or for what authentic question will I pursue an answer?

What will my readers already know about this subject? What do they need to know, and what stereotypes might they hold that I must disarm?

What do I think and feel about my topic? What do I need to know, and what stereotypes might I hold and need to address?

How should I organize my draft to communicate my focus most persuasively to my readers?

How much time do I have before the final draft is due? Given the nature of my specific topic and focus, will further planning save me time in the long run?

If the answers to these questions help them decide they need—and have the time—to do additional planning, remember that effective plans come in many forms: quick or more elaborate notes, diagrams, or outlines.

The Eddy Model says the Spectator Stage of the writing process involves not just false starts, but, more important, misunderstandings, oversimplifications, and writing to learn. This stage ends with the completion of a draft. In the previous chapter, we also note that the brainstorming that results from the invention activities may never see the light of day again. In the rest of this chapter, we discuss drafts two of Robert's students wrote based on some of the invention techniques they completed. Before we can do so, however, it is essential that we take a moment to reflect on how we got stuck in the Spectator Stage ourselves, and how writing to learn helped us move to the next stage.

A ROSE BY ANY OTHER NAME . . .

As we worked on this chapter, we experienced repeated false starts and misunderstandings of our own that nearly threatened the success of this book, notably about a seemingly inoffensive term in our profession: *draft*. Robert wrote the first draft of this chapter and Amanda wrote the second; these were false starts by design as we found our collaborative rhythm. While jointly revising the third draft, we realized we had oversimplified the term *draft* to the point of misunderstanding how the other used and understood that term. We agreed that most writing teachers use the terms *rough* or *first* to describe initial writing assignments. We also discovered that neither of us use *rough draft* in classes because it discourages students from doing their best work, and it produces something akin to a haphazard, rushed, last-minute attempt at writing. Amanda even avoids using ordinals at all when referring to drafts because they imply that the writing is only one of many attempts, suggesting that sloppy thinking and writing will be acceptable until the next version. Amanda's students complete a discovery draft and then a final draft for each major writing assignment in her classes, with only the last receiving an individual grade. Students are then allowed to revise a set number of these essays, and only those become finished pieces that are placed into a portfolio that determines 75 percent of the final course grade. For short response essays, she only collects their "final" drafts; these are not allowed revision, and their grades make up part of a student's discussion grade. In her classes, Amanda often refers to freewrites as the source for a working draft but, as stated before, they are not graded. Robert also uses freewriting that is not graded, but his students regularly produce first drafts while freewriting. Robert does not distinguish between types of first drafts; as the Eddy Model shows, he uses *first, working,* and *final* to describe the major writings his students produce. These pedagogical differences initially left us unable to come to agreement on many fundamental concepts of drafting, including what kind of assignment actually results in or produces a draft, what the shape and content of a draft consists of, who the audience is for a draft, whether drafts are graded, whether they are shared and how, and what they are called at various stages of the writing process.

So how did we ever resolve these misunderstandings and oversimplifications? First, we noted the areas that held agreement for us: we both reject the concept and values in calling a draft *rough* and acknowledge the necessity of final drafts in determining final course grades. Second, we agreed that using *discovery* and *first* interchangeably would not confuse the readers of this text if we contextualized their use, and using both honors each of our classroom dynamics and styles. Third, we agreed that regardless of terminology, we both believe the most important aspect of the Spectator Stage is the concept that in writing to learn, our students discover what it is they believe about a subject, what they do or do not know about it, what more they need to know, and most important, what they are not considering in terms of the needs of their readers. These were the very same challenges we faced while negotiating terminology, and they made us question long-held teaching philosophies and pedagogical practices. It was after more false starts and numerous intense conversations that we asked ourselves whether we were holding on to our values because we still believed them or out of complacency. We had to name the unspoken assumptions about pedagogy we both had brought to our working on this book. In the end we agreed that neither of our practices is more or less valuable than the other's. In order to be successful, we had to work our way through these misunderstandings and naturalized practices and create a revitalized way of teaching and defining drafting for our students and ourselves. Let's now analyze the discovery drafts produced by our student authors, Adhita and Brian, and see how they, like us, resolved their challenges with engaging in the Spectator Stage.

STUDENT SAMPLES OF WORKING DRAFTS ABOUT CULTURE

The next section of this chapter takes us through the journeys of two of Robert's students' as they prewrote and composed their first drafts. As a reminder, these drafts are works in progress that exhibit contradictions, errors, and uncertainty. They don't serve us as perfect examples, just two samples that demonstrate the concepts being discovered by their authors. In addition, while both authors chose culture as an overriding theme, they attempted two different writing assignments and used different prewriting activities before composing their drafts. Remember that effective plans serve two purposes: to get your students to the writing of their first draft and to help them construct a more detailed, organized, and persuasive first draft. Plans are disposable and should not become ends in themselves.

The first example is the more elaborate plan of the two and utilizes observation, journal entries, note taking, and formal outlining as its methods of prewriting. The plan and draft were composed by Adhita Sharma, whom we introduced in chapter 2. Sharma explored these questions in her brainstorming:

1. What does Islam teach about memory?
2. What does Islam try to remember (or forget)?
3. How do these questions relate to modernization?

These three questions constituted what she most wanted to learn about Islam and provided her a plan and draft. The structure of her plan evolved through attempts to understand and answer her questions.

Let's examine how her elaborate plan influenced the degree to which she oversimplified her subject or misunderstood it in the first draft. We said earlier in this chapter that the first draft can be considered as an occasion to uncover the inevitable oversimplifications and misunderstandings of our topic and focus. We should not be depressed or made insecure when we uncover oversimplifications and misunderstandings in a first draft. Instead of being upset, we should be pleased that we've progressed in our analysis of our subject so that we now **understand** the limitations of our current knowledge. Such understanding of the limits of our current knowledge, whether pointed out by readers or realized by ourselves, represents substantial progress in the writing process. Here is Adhita's first working draft.

Modernity in the Islamic Countries?
Adhita Sharma

Modernization of the Islamic countries is a process entirely separate of the processes of modernity involved in the evolution of Western civilization. This difference is due to the basis of these eastern lands, which rest upon a contingent of nowness. one is. Things are. Western thought stresses the ideas of striving and becoming. Modernity of the two entities cannot be compared to each other; the same ideas of progress cannot be applied to both. Oftentimes because of this, misunderstandings arise between the two, and friction and disunity are the results.

Islamic culture and the Muslim religion stress ideas of being. As above stated, one **is**. This concept of being begins with **Fitrah**, which is the true, original nature of all people. People are inherently good, and the soul is pure. Fitrah expresses the soul with characteristics of heavenlyness. The soul is paradise. It is childlike, joyous, and with spontaneity. The nature of all reality is within Fitrah, and this nature is one of purity. Reality. Words such as paradise and heavenly are, in the Western world, words which describe things beyond the phenomenal world.

Yet, in Islam, these words are those of the world around the being, and what is within the being. They are almost tangible. Because the soul is born pure, the memory can serve as a guide or framework for the future and past memories and experiences. **Dhikr**. This is reality, and it is memory. **Jihad** is strife, but not the type of strife associated with the West. This is the strife to balance the internal purity with the external world. It is the strife to open oneself to Fitrah, and to gain a total awareness of reality. A goal of Islam is to fully perceive reality as it is, now, in the state of reality and in its state of being. This state of awareness recognizes the world which God has created. God's world was created out of beauty and functionalism, between there is no division. The world of God was created with no recognition of the sacred or of the profane; both concepts are blended into one. Every single one of God's creations, no matter how minute, is an expression of beauty and of purity. Redemption comes from the soul, which is the framework. There is no reason to change reality in its state of being, as it was created to sustain the beauty and purity of all people. The unbearable beauty of the full perception of reality in a state of being is the basis of thought in Islamic culture.

Western culture is based upon Judeo-Christian thought, which revolves around the Bible. In this school of thought, the soul is born impure, and mankind has fallen from the grace of God. The first book of the Bible, Genesis, tells of man's actions which led him to his fall. Western civilization relies on striving, or becoming pure. It is a battle between the impure soul and the fight to become pure. The fallen soul cannot be relied upon as a context for any memories or for the making of a future. The human in the Western world is constantly searching to better himself in the eyes of himself, society, and in the eyes of God. Redemption must penetrate from the outside. The strive for heavenlyness on the earth is important. To be Godlike is primary. The phenomenal world around the human is nothing so wonderful, being is wonderful only after becoming pure in the eyes of God and reaching heaven. The phenomenal world needs progress. All things can be improved by man, even the smallest of God's creatures. Even the intangible soul can be fixed. There is no beauty in reality, and this reality was created and is still being created by man, and not by God.

The Islamic view on modernity is greatly affected by their basis of purity of the soul and of the beauty of reality. It is affected by the concept of being in God's world now, and perceiving its reality. If all and everything are pure creations of God, then where is the need to change? The intangible soul, present from birth, is pure. Reality is pure. Scientific and technological advances interfere with the balance of the world as it was first created. It ruins the theories of absolute reality and the beauty of God's world. Large, obtrusive, Western buildings defeat the purpose of beauty and functionalism, which is present in Islamic architecture. If the Islamic nations are to modernize with the consent of the population at large, than it must modernize internally. The process must work within the realms of God's absolute reality. It can not be penetrated from the outside, as many of the

Western nations are trying to do, as the Western ideas on modernity differ too greatly from those of Islam. It is impossible to expect a Western way to work in an Eastern culture.

As the West leads in science and technology now, it believes that their way is the "right" way, and that it will work for any culture. Unfortunately, this leads to more instability, as it oftentimes seems that the Western super-powers cannot respect a culture so different. Friction between the West and the Islamic nations arises from a basic conflict within the Self, which projects itself in the societies, the architecture, and in politics. The differences are not respected, and one being stronger than the other physically leads to the attempt of domination. The Western nations do not have the time or the resources to explore the fields of thought within the East, and realize that modernization must happen from within.

Adhita has fastened onto several ideas but ignored the rest of her outline. The points she focuses on are key ideas, and she tends to repeat them more than develop them. This is, certainly, a productive first or discovery draft because it is now clear what the writer wishes to focus on and confront. Let's go over each of these three points.

The first point—that Adhita ignored part of her outline—is not a complaint or criticism. Some writers would say that by not "trying out" all of her outline, Adhita in effect wasted part of the time she gave to her planning work. But always remember that plans serve first drafts, not vice versa. Some teachers argue that in a first draft especially, a writer should behave a bit like someone doing freewriting. Those teachers tell their students that if they are drawn in a certain direction, they should follow that center of gravity and overwrite rather than not fully explore the idea or emotion that draws or impels them forward. We agree. **In a first draft, your students must be more interested in getting ideas down on paper or on the screen than in judging those ideas**. They must learn to leave the judging of ideas for second and later drafts.

The second point—that Adhita tends to repeat her main ideas rather than developing them—is not a bad thing in a first draft. She is repeating the ideas to see how true they seem, to discover to what degree they ring true. She is "trying on" the ideas. She wants to see how far she can extend them. This strategy is an appropriate use of a discovery draft.

The third point—that this draft is productive because it makes clear what the writer's main interest and focus are—is the most important point of all. When students have found which dimension of their subject they are most committed to better understanding, their first draft has been successful. These drafts have a direction and purpose not based on mere supposition—the planning stage—but on firsthand experience in the new culture of a first draft.

Before we move to the second example of a discovery draft, let's revisit its purpose: to expose misunderstandings and oversimplifications. Let's continue our analysis of Adhita's draft by examining its oversimplifications.

Adhita emphasizes the decisive differences between the Judeo-Christian doctrines of the Fall and Original Sin and the fact that Islam teaches that people are born with "pure" souls and that the Creation is pristine. Her outline (Body section, number 2) states that according to Islam, people have "forgotten their original nature." Adhita says nothing directly about this **forgetting**, which Christians could rightly claim is not so different from the Christian doctrine of the Fall. Adhita is also less than fair when she overstates what she sees as the Christian position that there "is no beauty in reality." Yes, Christianity teaches that the Creation partakes of the ruin created by the Fall, but it is also the arena of redemption and reflects—imperfectly but truly nevertheless—the beauty of God's work.

Adhita's paper is highly abstract and philosophical, and yet her subject (modernization) is concrete and technological. She is comfortable in the realm of spiritual theorizing but seems to demonstrate a fear, or a rejection, of technology. She insists that she is rejecting what she considers the oppression involved in forcing "Western" technology on Islamic societies, but one wonders if she wants to reject technology as a whole. Consider these two sentences: "Science and technological advances interfere with the balance of the world as it was first created. It ruins the theories of absolute reality and the beauty of God's world." In her second draft she will need some balance and critical questioning of her intense position in favor of what she sees as the Islamic position on the soul, creation, and the world of technology, a technology that is indeed a human creation.

Adhita's identification with the Islamic position in this draft is so strong and uncritical that one wonders if she was really thinking of her own Eastern religion—Hinduism—as she was decrying the invasion of Western technology. We will see how she considered this interpretation in her subsequent revisions. The final draft appears in a later chapter.

HOW DO I KNOW WHAT I THINK I KNOW UNTIL I WRITE ABOUT IT?

The second sample of planning beyond an invention strategy, and the first draft it produces, is a powerful and troubling example of the culture of violence in our society. We must not try to hide from this violence, but as a society we must face it and try to disarm it with justice.

Especially given the focuses of this chapter, we must not misunderstand or oversimplify this violence. Although still about culture, the assignment to which the student was responding invited writers to introduce their home culture and to illuminate its central values by narrating an experience in which a key decision was faced. The key decision had to be one that pulled the writer in several directions, any one of which might have been followed. Students had to complete the draft by analyzing the cultural values embedded in the decision that was finally made.

This disturbing draft was written by another student whose brainstorming work we examined earlier, Brian Jones. He was a twenty-four-year-old ex-convict who had left the streets to attend college. The goal of his education was to become an electrical engineer with his own small company. He wanted to employ ex-convicts and give them a real alternative to a life of crime. He had been very successful in his college career to date.

Another Night in the Hood
Brian Jones

It looked like just another friday night in the hood. I quickly walked around the corner to the game room. As I walk I pass the same old routine people. I was in a hurry to meet my partner at the spot. When Sean and I were in juvenile detention together we decided when we got out we were going to get paid. We are both sixteen now so the law considera us as adults. So a far as we see it we are not taking no shorts and no shit! When we are on the corner one of us holds the other one sells the drugs. This night it was my turn to hold the gun and watch Sean's back. We were already told by some kids out there to watch out for a blue 4 door Chevette. They said it was some stick up kids from Brooklyn. About two hours later things were going as normal. We had been doing good this night. There had been no police and definitely no sign of any stick up kids. But I guess our good luck was due to end. Before I knew it there was the blue Chevette. Two kids had jumped out and grabbed my partner Sean. They had not noticed me off to the side of the game room. In my mind I knew I had to make a decission and do it fast. I could just stay quiet and let them get the money. I could run half way down the block and get some more of our homies. Or just come from around the corner shooting at them.

If I decide to go get help I have a better chance of having the odds in our favor. Plus if I get the homies we can run these kids off our corner for good. But this could take to long and they could be gone by the time I get the homies and back. Even worse by the time we get back Sean could be dead. And if Sean gets shot he would be wondering were I was at. And if he was shot I would have to put up with all the homies in the hood.

I thought about just not saying a thing and let them get what they came for. This way both of us would be alive to see tomorrow. And as they were leaving I could come out from the side and surprise them. But if so this means they would already have our money and have a good chance of getting away. I might hit one of them, but what if he is not the one with the money. The thought of just coming out shooting was a choice too. This way I would catch them off guard before they got the money. If I hit first then most likely Sean and I would not get shot. I would also let them know that we are not two little punks on the corner just waiting to be robbed. We already decided that we were going to be serious about getting money when we are out there on the corner. But this will mean I would have to take a chance at killing someone. Since I am sixteen the law would deal with me as an adult. As of now the going rate on murder is about 20 years!

Its funny how fast your mind moves when you are under pressure or just press for time. I don't know if I really made a decission or if my actions were just forced out of me due to my tight situation. If I could compare my actions to someone I guess it would be a person by the name O-Dog from the movie Menace 2 Society. The charcter in this movie was just buck wild. He never really thought to much about anything he did. He really used to just do things by the speare of the moment. Nothig mattered to him. He was the kind of person you could be cool with, but at the same time he was capable of causing trouble. He was nothing but a real product of his environment. Since his living conditions were bad he too was bad. Plus the fact that this person really nevers thinks about the things he is about to do. He pretty much does it by the moment. And since his personality is always wild whenever something is about to happend he will always be the aggressive one.

All I remember is stepping out and hearing rounds of gun shots. The next thing I knew I was dragged in the game room and my partner kept asking for the gun. All I could remember is the pain that ran all up and down my leg. I knew I had been shot but it did not seem as important to me at the time. My mind was really on the money. I wanted to know if the money was still ours. I kept wondering if I had hit one of them. I had already been known in the hood to have a gun. And I was also known to have the heart to pull it out and shoot. But this was my first time getting shot and my first time being in a shootout so close. Most of the time when I had to use my gun I would have them fools running once I began shooting. But this time I was right there in the middle of the whole thing. My eyes were open the whole time the shooting was going on, but it all seemed to be a blurr.

I never feared for my life as I think about it. See when you play the game in the concrete jungle death is one of your chances. I knew that I was subjecting my self to either getting caught by the police or I could be shot and killed. I never would think about it when I was at work. But after hanging out some late nights and someone either got shot it would make me think. I just would rather get shot for a reason than for nothing. I was looked upon by the kids in the hood as I tough guy or some kind of hero. See I stood up for our hood or our corner. Thats what one needs out here in the streets. In the streets your name and your reputation takes you a long way. My man Sean until this day says he owes me his life. I feel I did the thing I had to do. I really don't think my choice was thought out it just happend that way. The way I see it is if I'm going to go out from this world I'm going out fighting. I'll never let it be said that I was afraid of anything not even death itself!

With the completion of this draft, Brian ceased to be a spectator in the very new culture, for him, of the college writing classroom. This draft moves back and forth between the present and the past tenses. Brian presents his consciousness at the time of the event and uses the present tense to do so. When the twenty-four-year-old reflects on the values he held at an earlier age, we see the past tense. But his use of tense is more problematic than this. We teach writers not to change tense unless there is a compelling reason. Certainly changing of tense can only be justified if it is done with control and for a specific rhetorical purpose. Brian's shifting of tense made some of his peer readers wonder if his past was really over. Did he use the present tense to talk about the past because it is not really the past?

During discussions about this draft, Brian said that by writing this first draft he discovered what he called two "amazing lessons" he did not previously understand. First, that being an ex-convict is like being an alcoholic: one is never "cured." Instead of calling himself "cured," he had to work hard, set viable goals, develop a support structure, and avoid alcohol. Brian said that the "excitement, danger, and reward" of drug dealing and the status of neighborhood "hero" continue to be "narcotic temptations." He was able to withstand these "temptations" because he came to regard them as a form of individual and group suicide.

The second "amazing lesson" Brian said he learned by writing his first complete draft of a college paper was that he didn't know what he thought until he tried to put it down on paper. He said that by struggling to finish this draft, he learned he was **making decisions** all during his life of crime, whereas at the time he thought of himself as being "pushed along by fate." The writing of this draft confirmed his taking full control of his life and refusing to be "pushed around" by his environment. Here's the way he put it:

> With this paper I am rewriting my self and my world. I never realized on the streets that writing contains such power, but even then one of my secret dreams was to be a writer. I never thought it would come true. I will never give away power over myself again.

In the chapters to come, we revisit Brian's other drafts of this paper and more of the feedback he wrestled with to rewrite it.

THE NEXT STAGE: BECOMING RECEPTIVE TO READER RESPONSES

If, by now, your students have finished their first drafts, it is time to congratulate them on their progress. The completion of the first draft is a crucial achievement. They have left the spectator phase behind; they are beginning to belong in a substantial way to their new culture of college and its distinctive language of critical thinking called *academic discourse.* They are gaining a sense of the choices that, as Brian put it, "rewriting [your] self and [your] world" opens up for real writers. If your students gave the group invention strategies from the previous chapters several attempts, they will have begun to learn in substantial ways what the others in the classroom are like. They will have begun feeling more comfortable with some people than others. Such preference for certain writers over others, while inevitable, should be thoughtfully considered. Ultimately, we want our students to be thinking of classroom interactions as a process, an intellectual, polycultural conversation. If they see interaction as a process, they won't be as readily "imprisoned" by first impressions, especially negative ones. Encourage them to avoid staying focused on their first contact with the other people in the classroom, just as they would not expect a conversation to end after the first exchange. Careful, skeptical thinking, the kind appropriate to an academic setting, requires that we do not accept or trust our own opinions and judgments but test them as vigorously and systematically as possible. Encourage your students to be especially open to the people they first respond to negatively. Remind them that they should stay open to students to whom they respond to negatively not only because first impressions are often wrong but also because even if they don't change their negative response to them, those students can become valuable audiences to help them see people and issues from different perspectives. Your students may even find these rhetorical confrontations helping them overcome stereotypical thinking, a trap they will very likely fall into during this stage.

The peers your students respond to negatively probably possess key pieces of the intellectual puzzles and contextual landscape the students need to work with. They need each other, in the manner of a conversational dance. Your students need to understand and appreciate their readers' perspectives in order to better define their own. One of the most misunderstood and poorly taught elements of writing is audience awareness. The first step in helping students build this crucial skill is helping them understand that conversations with students who largely agree with them are often of little value in getting them to deepen and broaden their understanding of their audience and of their own thinking. Begin thinking of ways you can encourage or even devise a reward structure for your students who seek out the student-readers who have ideas or behaviors they find dissonant or unpleasant. The more accomplished we become as writers, the more we seek out those we think can thoughtfully but strongly disagree with us. The reader who says of a draft "this is beautiful; this is great" does less for your student's growth than the one who says "I completely disagree with you on this point for these reasons . . ." We argue you especially have an obligation to help your students by modeling this behavior. Interact, if nothing else, in the name of democracy and equality. Part of developing an intercultural ethos depends on our understanding that we don't have to like everyone in order to work with them constructively and with respect, whether in the classroom or in the world of work beyond college. The next three chapters ask you to revise everything you currently practice and believe about peer response, feedback, and writing workshops.

5

THE INCREASING-
PARTICIPATION STAGE
Working Drafts and Revision

COMPOSING A WORKING DRAFT DEPENDS
ON AUTHENTIC AUDIENCE RESPONSE

Michelle Johnson helps us understand that writing across race, what she calls "racial literacy work," yes, takes commitment and care, but we need to reflect frequently on our purpose. Johnson puts intention this way: "My purpose here is not to judge . . . writing centers in general, directors, staff, or my students, but to complicate our discussions of literacy, race, teaching, and tutoring in an effort to push us, including myself, to risk and to reveal more" (2011, 213). In the same book chapter, Johnson shares her writing center consultation questions for her students, which are part of the required work in her racial literacy course. Among the required postconsultation questions is the following: "How much do you think your consultant understood about race and writing? Explain" (219). What Robert admires most about Johnson's argument here is the invitation "to risk and to reveal more." In end-of-course evaluations, students have repeatedly shared that what is best for them about the racism and writing work they do in Robert's class, and what is worst for them about it, is Eddy's "endless invitation to reveal and question more and more of our own racialization, his racialization as we experience it, and the racialization of our peers and everyone else who reads our papers" (end-of-course anonymous student-evaluation comment). Robert requires his students to respond as thoughtfully as they wish to these two questions when they ask someone to read their first drafts, whether classmates, tutors, or anyone else, including family members: (1) How did your racial identity and comfort level, especially if the reader is of a race not your own, influence the dialogue about your paper? (2) How did the reader's racial identity and comfort level, especially if the reader is of a race not your own, influence the dialogue about your paper? Perhaps Robert's deepest regret about this book,

DOI: 10.7330/9781607328742.c005

especially relevant in the current chapter, is that neither student whose work we explore so closely—Adhita Sharma and Brian Jones—would give permission to share any of their written responses to these two questions as they thought about the experience of getting feedback on their first draft from family, friends, classmates, tutors, and their teacher. All Robert can share here is that Adhita allowed him to say that her very light skin and phenotype allow her to pass as white before people know her name, and that her writing in response to those two questions for the five groups of readers was "embarrassingly revealing about [her] own racial identity and issues." Brian would not give permission, he said, because he did not want Robert to publish his "endless cussing" in those writing tasks, tasks he did not like doing because they were, in his opinion, "confession time." In Code-Meshing Activity 4, at the end of this chapter, notice how Robert sets up the use of those required two questions so as to honor home language and code meshing.

So how do we invite the most authentic audience responses to first drafts? After finishing the activities in the previous chapter, your students might have just started to interact with others in class in earnest by asking you and possibly their classmates to speak to the oversimplifications and misunderstandings left unresolved in their first drafts. The focus now shifts to talking with students about critical reading, evaluation, feedback, and revising those first drafts into working drafts. Effective revision is tied to the concept that as changes occur in the writer, they are reflected back in what and how they write. While most composition textbooks look at revision as exclusively a linguistic exercise—moving ideas, cutting paragraphs, adding more detail, and so forth—this chapter suggests that authentic change happens organically. As the author interacts with more and more people in the new culture, these interactions primarily engage writers to fully comprehend what compels their readers and to modify their discourse accordingly. We suggest that genuine revision can only occur when writers are so fully engaged with their new culture that they actively solicit meaningful feedback from those readers. One needs to become a dual ambassador, knowing when to talk and share and when to listen (even if only politely) and keep silent. Ultimately, revision is viewed as openness to change and not just moving text around or cutting sentences. This process begins to create polycultural authors who can navigate their way between and among their home culture and others with ever-growing understanding of the contingent quality of cultural work and life.

Students must be repeatedly reminded that the audience for their writing includes more readers than just their instructor. Eventually their finished essays must provide unbiased information about their topics so their readers can draw their own conclusions. If an objective for your composition courses includes helping your students become the best and most effective writers and communicators they can be, you must encourage them to keep the lines of communication open with as many other writers as possible. This interaction involves peer review, which can and should be an important mutually supportive activity for writers and readers. During the Increasing-Participation Stage, your students will move from merely interacting with you and their classmates to actually understanding those dynamic collaborations enough to be able to achieve conceptualization and develop their first drafts further and more fully into working drafts.

These class interactions must help your students understand what they are doing, or should be doing, as they compose a response to classmate work. It also includes helping each student reviewer understand how their peers responded to the reviews the student reviewer completed on their peers' drafts, and how you as their teacher responded to those responses. In other words, as instructors we need to train our students to perform authentic response, and we can do this by introducing a metacognitive element to the process of evaluating another writer's work. Too often students are merely asked to fill in worksheets and read aloud as a means of responding to another's writing. We have watched novice instructors and bloated textbooks use these methods for years with little success and have watched students struggle to find the point of such busywork. Similarly, we have observed students who, upon receiving feedback from their instructor, have been unable to decipher it or apply it to a revision. The Increasing-Participation Stage requires clear conceptualization and engaging dynamic peer settings. When instructors succeed in coconstructing engaged peer responding, including whole-class responses, such work regularly leads to better feedback and therefore to more confidence for each writer in the class, especially as each student writer begins to dialogically engage other course members and wider audiences.

Metacognitive feedback requires students to respond to the feedback they receive on their own writing with the same attention. In Amanda's classes, metacognitive self-feedback occurs after her students engage in revision workshops. After her students read the responses they receive from their peers, Amanda asks them to write down for themselves, on the same feedback sheets or essay, the specific things they should have included or will include when they rewrite the essay. She borrows and adapts this technique directly from her years spent training writing center tutors. Instead of telling students what to do next, Amanda's tutors are trained to end their sessions by having their clients verbalize or write out what they will do next to rework their assignments. By verbalizing their next steps, writers not only remember better what needs to be worked on but also conceptualize the work to be done. This self-critical feedback can focus on local issues, like the need for more quotes, but more often it reveals the global issues yet to be developed, such as organization or clarification of concepts and coherence.

These interactions should not be regarded as of minor importance. They involve not just your students' learning the craft of academic writing and reading but also concern their deeper engagement in the collaborative character of writing. In the world of business, government, and activism, writing is a team sport. Literally, groups or committees do much of the writing. Such writing depends on various types of feedback to be successful.

In the Increasing-Participation Stage of Intercultural Experience, your students can gain self-confidence, a sense of connection to their environment, and a feeling of power over their thinking and selves. These changes can happen because with revision, writers cease being spectators of the cultural values they unconsciously exhibited in their discovery drafts. Your students will likely have exhibited unconscious cultural values in the way they oversimplified or misunderstood the subject of their first draft. As explained in the previous chapter, such oversimplifications and misunderstandings are inevitable. Remind your students that they should not be embarrassed or insecure about such limits to their knowledge or understanding of a topic. You should, however, encourage them to want to grow beyond such oversimplifications because they represent stereotypical thinking or monocultural provincialism. By helping students become more than spectators, revision enables students to become active participants in the new culture of college writing.

Revision means students must begin exhibiting the key features of American academic writing: being skeptical, analytical, and critical. Revision as applied skepticism is certainly not easy. Yet when your students accept the challenge of rewriting, they begin to rewrite themselves and their world as they wish them to be. This is a difficult and complex activity but tremendously rewarding when they begin to gain more control of their thinking. They should try to be flexible and open as they revise what they think and feel. Help them understand that as they begin to adapt to the required skepticism, they begin to internalize these values. As they revise their writing, they are revising themselves, ever so slightly, but truly nonetheless. How can this experience not be exciting, indeed liberating, so long as the student is in control and is being consciously intentional? Since rewriting is perhaps the most intense form of thinking, how can conscious study of their intellectual faculties as manifested in revision not be difficult, frustrating, and exciting for your students?

As they keep practicing the revision process in their college papers, your students are going get better at it. And getting better at revision depends on getting better at critically reading and *responding to their own* writing, not just that of their peers. This point is crucial. Too often, composition teachers only have their students think about the feedback they are providing on others' writing but not so much on their own writing. Key to becoming a critical reader and responder is understanding that one must go into these activities with purpose. Students should never set off in response groups without any direction; perhaps they should even first watch their teachers modeling the act of responding. Effective revision only happens after authors internalize a critical evaluation of their work and put constructive feedback to use. Students want to engage in authentic response. As they do this difficult, intense work, often for the first time in their academic lives, remind them that they're making operative the skeptical college mindset and culture. Their growing cultural identity as a college student will influence more than the revision of papers. It will begin to influence their whole life. Your students' increasing internalization of this new skeptical culture will eventually lead toward a crisis of identity that may be intense or not so conscious. But it will happen.

As they become increasingly bicultural, and begin to function effectively in the new college culture, your students will start to notice they have at least two sets of values and behaviors: those of their home culture and those of their college culture. This awareness constitutes a profound change in your students' lives. Don't underestimate it. Your students will begin to use the critical resources of both cultures to question certainties in either culture as they discover they can look at the world and themselves through the focusing lenses of either their home culture *or* their college culture. Similarly, they will question whether they are in control of the changes that are happening or if they are being controlled. These are difficult but necessary transformations to question. The general answer to these questions is both. To construct any answers to these thoughts about the changes they are experiencing, your students need to answer two questions:

1. Can you describe in detail the changes that are happening to you?

2. Which values of your home culture are affirmed and which are challenged by your new college identity?

If your students can answer these questions in detail, and if they keep periodically revisiting these questions in their journals and in conversation with friends, instructors, and family, they will be exercising control over the changes they are experiencing. Many writers have said we can't know who we are until we can articulate our values and beliefs in writing. Concept formation is key to this stage of your students' thinking, writing, and cultural identity, and concepts are something *they* construct in response to cultural influences, but this construction is much easier to accomplish in conversation with others. Your job as your students engage in the activities in this chapter is to guide your students in responding to others' writing and in revising their own in a substantial way from their first drafts. Most experienced writers are sensitive to their audiences and want many responses to a draft in progress so they can use the most effective feedback for constructing their revised draft. In the rest of this chapter, we provide methods for obtaining multiple responses from a variety of audiences, and we demonstrate how our student authors, Brian and Adhita, went about obtaining the dynamic feedback they used to revise their drafts.

HOW AUTHENTIC RESPONSE FOSTERS CONCEPTUALIZATION AND REVISION

As we stated above, conceptualization is the key to revising not just one's writing but one's world. What does it mean to produce a concept? Remember that a concept is something we *make* in an attempt to understand and gain control of our thinking by structuring and restructuring our understanding. Think of the situation this way. Your students will likely be first-year college students for nine months. If they lived in a foreign country for nine months, after a month or so in the new setting, they would probably tend to become increasingly a participant and begin to feel less foreign and more aware. If your students had their family and friends with them in the new culture, the students would naturally talk about their experiences and their meaning and significance. It would be almost impossible *not* to talk to family and friends about their experiences. Nothing could be more natural than such comparing of experience and the attempt to understand and make sense of the exciting but challenging new world. You want your students to think of getting responses to their discovery drafts in much the same way.

Having the opportunity during their nine-month sojourn in the new culture to talk with more people than just family and friends would be a good experience for your students. If they could talk with other travelers (classmates) and more experienced travelers (tutors), your students would have the benefit of different perspectives from those shared with family and friends. Your students can worry later about which perspectives are most useful and realistic. For now, they should simply want to look at the new culture and their responses to it in as many different ways as possible. Also remind them to develop or foster relationships with the locals in the new culture, such as current and/or former instructors, who are, after all, actually long-term immigrants since professors were originally students themselves in their then-new culture of college work and life.

There are five types of audiences your students might consult and engage with in collaborative conversation as they begin to rethink their first draft:

1. Family
2. Friends
3. Classmates
4. Tutors
5. Instructors

In Amanda's classes, she regularly asks her students to engage only classmates, tutors, and herself. As noted above, Amanda's students are generally trained with the same techniques she provides to her tutors for soliciting feedback (see Context-Building Writing Activity 15 toward the end of this chapter). Robert encourages his students to collaborate with each of these types of readers, as is demonstrated in the feedback examples located later in this chapter. Of these five groups, your students should remember that the first group—family—represents their original culture. The second group—friends—depending upon whether they are friends from home or college friends, represent either home or college cultures (and a few may even represent both). The third group—classmates—represents fellow students who are also negotiating the relationship of their home and college cultures. The fourth group—tutors—belongs substantially to the world of college culture since tutors have already learned how to negotiate the college culture well enough to support other students in writing projects. The fifth group—instructors—belongs fully to college culture; it is the culture through which instructors publicly, or at least professionally, are measured or measure themselves and the world. Your students should remember the perspectives of these five groups so they can interpret and get the most out of the responses each provides. Try to allow your students ample time and energy to talk with and consult all five groups since each will tend to offer very different responses. Such varied responses from varied audiences will reinforce the real variety of approaches and choices available to your students when revising their drafts.

CONTEXT-BUILDING WRITING ACTIVITY 11

General Advice for Writers Soliciting Feedback

1. Give the reader/responder a typed copy of your draft.
2. Give the responder a specific deadline. It is neither polite nor realistic to assume your responder(s) can get back to you immediately. Likewise, the feedback will not prove helpful if you don't receive it with time to actually incorporate it into your writing process.
3. State the specific questions you want answered. Avoid yes or no questions.
4. As you compose the questions, don't consider simply the person responding and how they can help you. Also consider which of the five groups they belong to: family, friends, classmates, tutors, or instructors.
5. Remember that *revision* does not merely involve correcting grammar, spelling, usage, mechanics, and looking at word choice. This more accurately describes proofreading and should be done at the end of the writing process before you hand in the final draft of your paper (see chapter 7 for proofreading advice). *Revision* involves looking at the major ideas, argument, and structure in your draft and conceptualizing them more fully, more insightfully, and more convincingly.

THE FIVE AUDIENCES: EXTENDED EXAMPLES
OF THE FIVE TYPES OF FEEDBACK

Here we outline questions and methods for obtaining a critical reading from each of the types of readers in the five feedback groups and follow each with extended examples from our student authors. Remember that any questions or directions for reading the draft should be *specific* to the purpose of the writing. If your students ask vague and general questions, they will get vague answers. In order to dynamically revise the draft, your students need suggestions on how to achieve greater *conceptualization* of major ideas, arguments, and organization. Conceptualization requires students to understand the nature, significance, and relationship of the ideas they have structured as an argument or claim in their essay. All writing is an attempt to persuade the reader of something, at the very least that the draft itself is worth reading. Your students must decide what it is they want to persuade their readers to think and/or do before they can ever draft a genuinely authentic revision.

The rest of this chapter looks at extended examples of feedback our student authors received from each of the five groups. We will examine the feedback received first by Adhita Sharma and then by Brian Jones. Just as occurred with the drafts in the previous chapter, the feedback here is presented unedited. We reproduce it here faithfully to demonstrate the feedback provided by the members of each type of feedback group. You may wish to revisit those discovery drafts (in the previous chapter) to better understand the feedback from each audience. Ask yourself, Would my feedback be similar to the feedback that follows here? Why? How would it be different? Why?

FEEDBACK FROM FAMILY

Although we live in an increasingly mobile world, our students may not be able to consult their families in person for feedback on their writing. Even if they are able to, your students must realize that positive family feedback might make them feel good, and may even aid in their level of confidence, but it might not help them build a stronger revised draft. Remind your students that their families tend to see the completed draft and be pleased with it rather than primarily focusing on what has not been finished or where the essay is not convincing.

To generate the best feedback from family members, your students should take some simple steps. Before they begin reading, students must show their family members the instructor's written assignment that goes along with the draft. The student should inform the family member that when they discuss the draft, whether in person or not, at the very least the student will take notes about what is said but preferably will ask permission to record the conversation, if it won't make the responder too uncomfortable, so the details can be listened to over and over. This recording could be done with any technology. Our students can help family understand that by giving permission to record these exchanges, their conversations will be less impeded by the process of taking notes. Before they begin reading the essay, your students should talk with the family member about what they believe the assignment requires. Next, your students should share questions they have written, which will direct their family members toward focusing their comments on how best to substantially revise the major ideas in the draft. After they read the entire draft, your students should have each family member describe in their own words what the major focus is in the essay. If the family member describes the essay's focus as substantially different from the author's, or doesn't see or understand the focus, the author should try to explain it and ask what can be added or deleted to clarify things. Later, students can revisit the parts of the discussion in which they explain what they are trying to do and in which the responder explains why those attempts failed or succeeded.

Next, since family members are experts in the home culture, but may or may not be experts in college culture, students should ask readers which ideas in the draft they found interesting, unusual, or upsetting. Students should ask family to talk frankly and informally about why and how they reacted as they did. Again, discussions about these changes and their possible results, as well as what to do when home and college cultures are in disagreement, should be recorded. This can be a wonderful chance for students to better understand the cultural changes they are beginning to undergo or face and help both family and the student appreciate the growing complexity of their bicultural emerging identities.

Adhita's Example of Feedback from Family

Adhita asked her father for a response to her first draft. He has a college education, works in banking, and must compose many reports. He's an experienced business writer. She showed him the instructor's written assignment and asked him to read her draft just once. She was interested in first impressions. He agreed to let her tape their conversation so she would have the exact wording of all comments. She asked him to talk about what he thought was the major focus of her first draft.

Her father made the following comments on the tape regarding his initial response to her essay:

> O.K. This is interesting, but not the kind of stuff I read every day. This is very abstract, very philosophical. I never saw you as a philosopher before. I always thought of you as hardnosed and practical. But I guess that's me more than you. O.K. let me get to the point here. You're looking at "East" and "West." You see the East as spiritual and natural; you see the West as technology-based and not very religious. Aren't these stereotypes? Doesn't the East yearn for or crave technology, wealth and consumerism? Aren't there many religious people in the West? You see the East as "natural" but I think the West is much more environmentally conscious. I never met a tree-hugger in India. When I'm home in India every summer I see an educated class that wants to be as westernized as possible. Everyone else just wants to find their next meal. When you revise this paper you really need to get beyond these stereotypes. The "East" is a creation, I mean the **idea** of the "East" is a creation of the western mind. The "East" in the mind of the West is a fairy tale to escape to when we feel our life is too fast, too burdened with work and competition, and too artificial. Please don't get hurt

or insulted or cross, honey; you asked me to be honest. Your first draft is sort of a fairy tale. I think there really is no East. There are India, China, Japan, etc., and they are so different from each other. I don't know anyone who thinks of himself as an "Easterner." If there are no Easterners, then there is no East! Gee. You're turning me into a philosopher! The college years really are an exciting time: exploring everything.

Adhita's father recognized the oversimplifications she made without having to label them as such. By asking his questions, he points them out as well as suggests that alternate views may exist that Adhita hasn't considered. Following this response from her father, which she found to be clear and helpful, Adhita followed up by asking him if there were any ideas in her first draft that he considered upsetting to him. He responded,

> The idea or viewpoint that did upset me in your first draft was your attack on technology. I know it was sort of indirect, but it was there. When you attack technology you attack business, and when you attack business you are attacking me! If you want me to be totally frank, my first thought was "where did I go wrong as a parent?" How could you hate business? It's fed you, entertained you and sent you to a college to teach you how to attack it! The only thing that keeps me from getting too upset is that I don't think you really mean it. Are you willing to go hungry in a non-technological society? I don't think so. You enjoy summer vacations in India, living the "natural," non-technological life, but would you like to spend the whole year there? Would you like to spend only summer vacations in America? Adhita, you need to appreciate that you will be judged by what you say and write. Please consider more carefully what you are writing. Be sure you mean it completely.

The level of questioning in this response asks Adhita to take seriously the claims she has made and whether she has considered audiences outside herself. We see in the coming chapters how Adhita revised her draft using this feedback.

FEEDBACK FROM FRIENDS AT COLLEGE AND AT HOME

Before your students solicit feedback from their friends, they should divide them into home or college friends. Home friends often react much like family members: seeing what our students have achieved rather than what they haven't. College friends, depending on their year of study and degree of commitment to their major, will already be exhibiting the critical-mindedness of college culture. Each class of friend can help with understanding home or college cultures. For feedback from home friends, your students should follow the same guidelines offered above for family members: show them the instructor's assignment; ask them the main idea of the draft; talk about what ideas they found interesting, unusual, or upsetting; and have a frank conversation about how they think the author's ideas are changing because of the new college culture. For college friends, your students should show their friend(s) the assignment and ask them to read the draft aloud while the author notices where the reader stumbles or seems confused or lost. Then before asking their friend(s) to read the paper a second time, silently to themselves, your students should ask their friend(s) to look for the following things:

> What is my main focus or interest or question in the draft?
> Where is the draft convincing to you personally? WHY?
> Where is the draft *not* convincing to you? WHY?
> What do I have to do to make my next draft more convincing to you?

Your students may even want to personalize or annotate these questions with additional comments like "Please be specific, detailed and honest" or "Don't spare my feelings."

Adhita's Examples of Feedback from College Friends

Adhita's college friend, Preston, a computer science major in his junior year, responded to her first draft after he first read the instructor's written assignment. She chose him as someone whose commitment and future career mark him as a defender of US technological civilization. She wanted a constructive critic to argue against her draft so she might be able to write a more persuasive second draft. He agreed to let her record their conversation.

Preston first read the draft out loud. Adhita made notes about where in the text he stumbled or seemed confused or lost. After he finished, she asked him about those places in the draft where his natural reading rhythm was interrupted, presumably by problems with understanding. After Preston's second (and silent) reading, Adhita asked him to respond to the questions above.

Preston responded to the first question as follows:

> The question mark in your title makes me wonder if you are really sure of your focus. I don't think you are. I think your emotions are stronger than your thinking in this draft. I see the comparison and contrast you are making between the East and West, but I really don't see where you are going with this. The East can't or shouldn't be a copy of the West when it comes to technology is what you seem to be saying. But are you sure that technology is really so Western?

Preston put his response to the second and third questions—discussing where the draft is convincing for him and where it is not—together.

> Actually I do think this paper is pretty good for a first draft. I like the way you label the West as progressive, yet you don't call the Islamic lands backward, which I must confess, without having thought about it a lot, was what I thought. I do appreciate the way you help me see what a stereotype I have about ways of looking at another major civilization. The more I thought about it the more I started to appreciate what you say is their emphasis on *being*. I started to see their *being* emphasis in terms of music, fun, concerts, pleasure, entertainment, and things like that. These things are very important in life too. Is this sort of what you mean?
>
> Still, though, there are important ways in which your paper is not convincing to me. I question the areas in your paper where you compare the meaning of key words between two different cultures. Sure there are going to be differences. But does that mean there is only one definition of the words in each culture? I don't really know anything at all about Islamic countries, but are you sure there aren't other interpretations of *being, becoming* and even *technology*? I sort of feel like you are oversimplifying. What about the groups in America, like certain environmentalists, who seem to hate technology? Don't they matter? I think you make everything too black and white. I see passion for "honor" of old cultures in your paper, but I don't see any balance and objectivity in your paper. Are you sure that the Islamic people, at least secretly, don't want to be just like us technologically? I admit that I bet they do. Am I just another over-proud American?

The last of Adhita's questions prompted this response:

> On the bottom of your third page you write: "If the Islamic nations are to modernize . . ." The Muslims are very religious people (so I hear) and who says they have to change or "modernize"? You *assume* that they have to modernize. Aren't you showing your American prejudice here? I mean, things that I hold dear I do not want to change unless they are harmful or will cause harm later on down the road. In your next draft I think you need to explain to students why the Islamic nations need to modernize. By the way, the photos I've seen of Saudi Arabia make that country look more modern than us. So which Islamic countries are you talking about?
>
> I am also unclear and need further explanation about this key comment on your final page: "Western superpowers cannot respect a culture so different." It is not clear to me what your exact point is here. Please help me out here. I don't want to think that either I am not smart enough to get your point or that your paper is unfocused! We badly need a couple of good examples.

It is interesting to note the tone and depth of commentary Preston gives to Adhita's work. He points out items like her emotions getting the better of her thinking. He questions her assumptions about Eastern views toward technology, modernization, and culture when he calls them oversimplifications. He also questions her conclusions and lack of balance. Preston even suggests that it might be his need for further explanation that is making the essay unconvincing to him. Although he says it is a pretty good first draft, he clearly needs more as a reader than the essay provides. Adhita went on to ask two classmates for additional feedback. We will see how Preston's response compares to theirs in a moment. First, let's look at an example of feedback from Brian's college friend.

Brian's Examples of Feedback from College Friends

Brian wanted feedback from a college friend. He chose Rahsaan, who, briefly and less seriously than Brian, had sold drugs. He also asked Rahsaan because Brian wanted to compare their processes of critical consciousness and how self-critique led them away from the street and toward college. Brian asked Rahsaan to respond to four questions:

What is my main point in this story?
Where do you believe my story? WHY?
Where do you not believe me? WHY?
What do I have to do to make YOU believe me?

To the first question, Rahsaan responded, "Your main point is that shooting at somebody supposedly made you a 'hero,' and you protected your friend and your investment. But the whole issue should have been to protect your friend, not your friend and the money, or as it seemed to me, mainly the money!" Brian's second question about his believability elicited an important response from Rahsaan.

The part of your draft where you said it was your first time in a serious shootout shows real insight into the street mentality. You mentioned that at earlier times, you had basically used your gun to shoot in the air and scare people off, at least that's what I thought you meant. This time you were in the middle of the real thing, and your eyes were wide open, but *everything was still blurred!* That's the key point. This is completely convincing to me.

You know that a gun can cause deathly fear in opponents, self-esteem and confidence in holders. But when the holder gets into a real situation where he might have to use the gun for the first time, he will find out his real state of mind. This crisis will show whether the person is a gun faker or a gun user. It shows if the person really has that needed street mentality of do or die, and when he does it because his street mentality tells him he has to, everything just happens and happens quickly. The fear that every person really has but hides deep inside, comes out in the form of blindness or blurred vision *so that he cannot see what he really feared.*

Rahsaan responded to Brian's third question with the kind of candor that bespeaks real friendship.

> I don't believe you at all on page two of your paper where you say this: "I thought about just not saying a thing and let them get what they came for. . . . I might hit one of them, but what if he is not the one with the money?" You say that if you let them get the money and then you came out shooting that both of you would live to see the next day. But this doesn't make any sense. Both of you could have been shot in the crossfire after they got your money just as well as before they got the money. This waiting until they got the money would only display cowardice on your part. According to the hustler's code, it was your responsibility after all to watch your partner's "back." This is completely unconvincing to me.

Rahsaan's answer to the last question was intriguing to Brian.

> You need to better develop this crucial part of the analysis on page two of your paper: "It's funny how fast your mind moves when you are under pressure or just press for time." You need to think about the process of this "decision." Was this a "decision" or just animal instinct? Did you simply notice that you were shooting or did you decide to shoot? What are the affects of having to make this very important decision so quickly? Do you think if you had more time that you would have made a different decision? This is a critical idea that needs complete examination.

Rahsaan asks questions of Brian about his choices as a writer. The questions he asks can only serve to make Brian question those choices and consider how the answers might result in a re-visioning of the essay.

Composing pointed questions elicits genuine feedback for several reasons. First, the questions give the reader a way to see the assignment itself and what was required of the writer. By giving this basic information prior to asking for feedback, the author provides a road map for the reader's response. Many student authors make their first writing misstep in how they read the assignment for requirements. Sometimes just clarifying or going over those with someone outside the course can make all the difference in understanding how to rewrite an essay. Next, these questions elicit constructive feedback because they only ask for global feedback. Again, since most global issues are tied to the actual requirements of an assignment, these questions keep the focus there. Similarly, by only asking for this global level of response, the reader is not asked to speak to aspects of composition with which they aren't comfortable, such as grammar and mechanics. These questions are also broad enough that they can be applied to any genre of writing. Whether a student is drafting a lab report, a narrative, or an argument, these questions ask readers to comment about the viability of the main concepts in the writing. Just as a narrative must convince the reader of the credibility of the dialogue or plot, an argument must provide compelling evidence to support a claim. While the questions are particularly helpful for those responders from outside class, in many ways they also mirror the questions we have our students ask of their classmates, tutors, and even their teachers.

Feedback from Classmates: Dialogues and Journals Instead of Worksheets

The revision of a draft, the production of a concept to organize a writer's thinking, requires the writer to open up and at least indirectly examine their cultural values. Since classmates are in the same position, they can provide your students with the most important feedback for their writing. Urge them to resist thinking of their classmates' responses as poor substitutes for instructor feedback and of their relationships with their instructors as more than temporary and artificial. In their future professional work world there will be no teachers per se, and peer relationships will be much more important to their success and productiveness than their relationship with any other group. To get the most out of their classmate responses, your students must work hard to understand classmate interactions in class. Remind your students that their classmates are cotravelers. In their writing, classmates are also constantly negotiating the relationship of their home and college cultures. This process of constructing an intercultural space is sometimes pursued consciously, but more often it occurs with too little conscious awareness of what is happening to one's self and the world. With time, your students can help each other become more aware of, and thus more in control of, these momentous changes.

When they are ready to get a peer response from a classmate, and to provide one in return, try this activity. After two students have read each other's first draft once or twice, have them begin a dialogue in both their journals simultaneously, beginning with this question: What are the strongest beliefs and values that influenced the author's thinking in the draft? This question can begin extremely valuable simultaneous dialogues if the reader and responder can be open and nonjudgmental. Most of us tend to take for granted, hide from, or not significantly understand our sustaining cultural values. Your students' job in the dialogue is to resist this inertia against cultural analysis by defining, articulating, and thus **performing** their cultural values so they can better understand the real context of their drafts. The context of the first draft is the sustaining cultural values through which, like focusing lenses, your students perceive "reality." Remember, you are having your students write in each other's journals at the same time.

When Adhita, author of the student paper on Islam and moderniza-tion, finished a particularly revealing dialogue with a classmate, it was strikingly clear to both that Adhita only saw the negative dimension of Western technology. She hadn't previously accepted how negative her attitude was, even when it was pointed out by her father in his response. Moreover, Adhita's presentation of Islam was one sided, idealistic, and therefore uncritical. In her dialogues, Adhita noticed she conflated Islam with her own religion—Hinduism—and was defending both reli-gions against what she called "Western scientific-atheist values." It was good for Adhita to see how her own values conditioned her response to her topic. In this way, she could aim at being more balanced, fair, and direct in her next draft.

When simultaneous dialogues in the journals begin to uncover for classmates how their sustaining cultural values largely determine their approach to drafts, it is time to explore these follow-up questions:

Why do you believe your cultural values?

What evidence in their favor do you find compelling? Why?

What is the counterevidence? How do you respond to it?

In order to clarify your thinking, and to expose the evidence and argu-ments for and against your cultural assumptions, produce a justifica-tion of your belief based solely on evidence and argument.

A written response to such difficult, fundamental questions helps your students realize that writing is their answer to the world and that build-ing a convincing theoretical foundation for their cultural commitments is a powerful form of action. By constructing a believable theory in sup-port of their cultural commitments, your students begin to observe the power of consciously intentional language. When your students engage in dialogue with their classmates about such important questions, they learn words are two-sided acts, territory shared. Your students learn that the same words might create different responses between dialoguing classmates. When Adhita was dialoguing about technology, she was at first unaware that the word itself has negative connotations for her. Yet most of her dialogue partners had as unthinking a positive association with the word as Adhita did a negative one. Thus they were not demon-strating the use of **consciously intentional language**. They were talking to themselves.

Dialoguing about such fundamental issues, since it has the expressed purpose of aiding classmates in constructing more powerful second drafts, tends to occasion a constructive and collaborative relationship. The students can be a significant resource for each other: a two-person team. For example, the classmates who dialogued with Adhita naturally played the devil's advocate and presented the positive side of technology. They asked her why she hated technology. One student, Karen, said, "You suffer from a severe case of technophobia! You need a cure! Get real. Do you really want to give up on medical technology?" Adhita responded that if she was guilty of technophobia, Karen was demonstrating "technophilia," a worship of machines. Adhita asked in Karen's dialogue journal,

> Why do you love technology? When I think of technology I see vivid images of the nuclear disasters at Three Mile Island and Chernobyl. I see the atomic bombs at Hiroshima and Nagasaki. I see the bodies of thousands of people in India killed at Bhopal, where I lost several loved ones. I could go on and on. Do you pretend these things never happened, or are unimportant, Karen?

Karen responded,

> I do not blink at these tragedies. I think every human life is precious and irreplaceable. I'm sorry to learn of your loss of loved ones at Bhopal. Please accept my sincere condolences. This terrible negative side of technology is real and we need to try to do something to stop it. But what about the other side of the story? I have an uncle who is kept alive by a dialysis machine. My father is still alive four years after a triple bypass operation. Where would they be without technology? They would be dead. I'll agree with you—I'm pushing to be fair—that I and most of our society are too one-sidedly pro technology; we might even, as you say, be guilty of worshipping it. If you and I could combine our views, it would be a balanced attitude toward technology, that all our society could live with. I think you and I are both right, but incomplete.

Adhita replied,

> Thanks for being so direct and kind. I really will think about what you said. I hope your uncle and dad live to be 100. You're right about medical technology, O.K.?

As Adhita prepared to write her next draft, she needed to think seriously about her uncritical negative attitude toward technology in her first. So, she sought out another response from a classmate, Naomi. Because Adhita, like so many other writers, found it useful to ask respondents to read her draft out loud to her so she could see where they had trouble understanding her text, she asked Naomi to do that as well. As often happens, Naomi stumbled at many of the same points where Preston had trouble. When Adhita recognized that the two readers were having similar problems with her text, she learned where she had to clarify and deepen her thinking.

In Naomi's written response, Adhita wanted Naomi to respond to the same questions Preston had. Naomi responded to the first question,

> Adhita, I'm sorry, but your specific interest in the first draft is not clear to me. After reading your draft several times, it seems like the question mark in your title might represent your own confusion? You stress the subject of economic modernization in the West and Islam; you present the two cultures as opposites, or at least very different from each other, in religious terms. You seem to say or imply that religion should determine the shape of technology in traditional (or every?) society. I think this is a great idea, but not very realistic. Also, I don't think you've thought about Islam in the USA; I read somewhere (sorry I can't remember where) that it is the fastest growing religion in America. Hell, even the great singer Cat Stevens became a Muslim. His Muslim name is Yusuf Islam. My point is that maybe you shouldn't present the West and Islam as utter opposites.

As we saw with previous responses, here is another audience who asks Adhita to question whether it is she who is uncertain about her claims. Adhita is being asked to question her simplifications by yet another reader, especially in terms of religion, technology, and culture. In responding to the second question, Naomi said, "Your draft becomes convincing in this statement: 'If the Islamic nations are to modernize with the consent of the population at large, then it must modernize internally.' This is convincing to me because sometimes change is good. Surely we all know this. People of all classes, races and groups should be allowed to change, in order to grow, as long as it is for the benefit of everyone, not just some privileged group." Naomi answered question three—about where the draft is unconvincing for her—in this way:

> The first paragraph of the paper is strongly unconvincing for me. You need to offer some at least hint of proof in support of your accusations. You make broad generalizations about the two cultures without any hint of verification. It's like you want us to believe you on faith or blindly. We're being taught as college students to fairly judge evidence, but all you do is make claims with little or no evidence. What am I to judge? Please give me something to judge. I want to believe you, but not blindly!

For the first time, Adhita is pointedly criticized for her lack of evidence to support her claims. While the previous responders made comments that danced around this, Naomi makes an issue of how the lack of evidence correlates to the essay being unconvincing, which directly affects the success of Adhita's claims. It is no wonder, then, that the final question—about how to make the second draft more convincing—elicited this response:

> As mentioned in question 3 above, you really need to supply some convincing evidence in support of your claims. Please try to be balanced and fair to both sides; It seems like every mention of the West is an attack.

Haven't we done anything right? But I also think you should also try to create some theories about how to structure your evidence. Wouldn't it be good to add two or three theories about possible solutions to the problems you present, for both cultures? Shouldn't you have some quotations from the Koran and the Bible? Thanks for letting me read this. You gave me some very new ideas to think about.

Adhita is left with some powerful, and repeated, feedback that asks her to consider that her presentation of Islam is one-sidedly positive and too negative in her references to Christianity. Her first draft did not create a sense in any of the readers who gave her feedback that it was balanced and fair. In seeking feedback from classmates, it is important that your students remember they share the same instructor, assignment, and culture of that individual writing class. For this reason, they can be the most insightful commentators on first drafts. Their feedback should be received by your students as supportive and constructive criticism.

CONTEXT-BUILDING WRITING ACTIVITY 12

Soliciting Feedback from Classmates

To give (and get) the best classmate feedback:

1. Provide a typed copy of your first draft to each student.
2. Formulate the questions for classmates. Your questions can be general ones about your rhetorical situation: Who is my audience? What is my purpose? But include some detailed, text-specific questions that inquire about key ideas, arguments, and structure.
3. Remember that just as your classmates will be reading your first draft closely and critically, you should read their responses critically as well. Obviously, you shouldn't try to follow everyone's advice. Often you won't be able to follow everyone's advice because responses will vary greatly and will frequently be mutually contradicting. This variety of response should not upset you. Such variety does not necessarily indicate that you've been unclear or inconsistent. Readers are people; people see things differently. Try in your questions to get classmates to distinguish between what they think you have said and their **reaction** to what you have said.
4. When evaluating a classmate's draft, be sure to answer the questions asked. Try to make your response as detailed and concrete as possible.

Brian's Example of Feedback from Classmates

Brian's intense draft produced a number of peer responses that were too observational to be of much help to re-vision his writing. His first attempt at peer response used the same broad questions that were asked of Rashaan. The first peer response he received, from Dorothy, stated, "In this draft, Brian is speaking personally and morally. He is express-ing his true self and he finds the means to solve the problems he faces. Morally, he believes it is OK to take risks in life. He feels he can't be a 'man' if he is thought of or seen as a coward. So basically, he is trying to be accepted by his peers or society." The second, from Stephanie, noted, "The writer has taken a very personal situation and composed a very eye-opening reality to himself. He has shown me that the ideas or requirements for this paper were understood and met. He has placed the situation into an analytical point of view for himself and the reader. It is almost as if there is no bias, just instinct and reaction." The final peer review was by Kim: "This draft makes me realize that everyone has a story to tell, a personal conflict to reflect upon, and lesson from his life experience. It is possible to produce powerful expression through multiple drafts that have real meaning to the writer himself. Brian wrote a quality analysis paper without being given some arbitrary assignment on analysis. (These types of assignments are given all the time in schools today and I feel students rarely benefit from them.) With this assign-ment, however, the student not only learned a great deal about himself, but he also learned about effective writing." None of these responses is particularly effective, although the praise is polite. The first is merely a summary, and the second never makes clear where or how the essay met which of the specified requirements. The third is a bit more developed but is mostly observational praise. All three responses fail to adequately provide advice for how to rewrite or even what deserves reconsideration in his essay. We argue that this is the type of feedback typical of most students who have not been trained to respond purposefully to drafts.

After revising his response questions, Brian asked for feedback and "complete honesty" from Elisa. Notice how her response to the first question—about the main focus of the draft—is much more critical as well as observational.

> The main issue is exactly as you state it in your title: "Another Night in the Hood," where violence becomes routine. The conveying message that comes through the story is that of self-conviction. Your language, lifestyle, personality, and identity portrays one who has become a product of soci-ety's pain, lost self-esteem, and longing to belong.
>
> Overall, you are attempting to justify and prove to the reader, as well as to yourself, how tough you are. You want us to believe that your mind does not have a conscience. Yet you do not fully convince me of this.

Elisa responded to question two—Where is the draft convincing to her and why?—in this way:

You state that if you were to compare your actions to those of someone else, you would choose the character O-Dog. Accordingly, O-Dog is the ultimate hero to you in terms of survival. O-Dog has survived the catalyst of his environment, which is in constant war with society as a whole. This comparison is the convincing aspect of your paper for me personally. Your details about your feelings for the gun, standing on the corner, passing, not just the same people, but the same types of people every night, and not having any fear of dying are all very realistic. I have known individuals who have, and still are involved in this type of lifestyle. I use the term "lifestyle" because this life becomes a choice after living it for numerous years. Somehow they know there is another way of living that does not include sliding down a double bladed razor.

Elisa's response to the question about where is the draft not convincing requires her to confront the turbulent subject of "street" or "gang ethics."

I am ready to accept that the tough street image and never fearing death were all possibly true about you, but you were even then still seeking out and beginning to try to understand that there might be another meaning to this perpetual life style. Your conscience was beginning to emerge when you thought "I might hit one of them, but what if he is not the one with the money?" I bet you will tell me that what you meant was that if you hit the wrong one, the money might get away. But I don't think that's the whole story. I ask you if this is a form of street justice, or is this an ever so slight opening of compassion? I am also not convinced that even at the height of your criminal stage, that you were all bad, as you try to portray in this draft. Sorry. I don't believe you. When you step in front of your friend Mike, to take a bullet meant for him, it is more than "street ethics:" watching your buddy's back. It is human friendship, pure and beautiful: dying for a friend (and also for your reputation; O.K.?).

Again, we have a high level of observation, but she uses it to question the easy conclusions Brian comes to. For instance, by offering Brian an alternate way to view his taking the bullet ("not just for street ethics") for his friend, Elisa shows him he has a choice about how he wants to analyze the affect these events have had. In answer to Brian's final question—about how to make the next draft more convincing—Elisa wrote,

To be more convincing, I feel you should change your title and focus to acknowledge that even in your criminal era you were not pure bad. You should admit that even then a part of you wanted to get out of hell. If that is not so, then how is it that you have changed? In his autobiography, Malcolm X tells us he changed from a life of crime because of God's will, and the help of a person in prison named Bimbi, who convinced Malcolm of his own intelligence and his responsibilities to help the oppressed black race, especially the ghetto poor. What influenced you to change? Who or what was your Bimbi? Who or what caused you to re-invent yourself? What about titling the second draft something like this: "Another Night in the

Hood: How I got Out" Or "Why I got Out" Or "How to Leave the Street"
Or "Advice to Fellow Criminals on Going Straight"?

By trading his generalized questions for specific ones, and after seeing
how little constructive criticism they produced, Brian learned how to
craft pointed response questions for his feedback workshops. Brian finally received some tangible feedback he could consider for rewriting
his essay. In the following chapters, we see how much of this feedback
made its way into his final draft, but first we look at the response both he
and Adhita received when they sought response from the writing center
consultants.

FEEDBACK FROM TUTORS

Have you stayed in a hotel with a concierge? These folks are employed
by high-end hotels to help travelers with information ranging from
directions to landmarks to suggestions of where to eat, which neighborhoods to avoid, and where the best shopping can be found. The
key trait of a good concierge is that they give you many options and
leave the choices up to you. In many ways, this role is similar to that
of the tutors or consultants working in most college writing centers.
Remember to think of peer tutors as experienced travelers in college culture. They are not teachers, although one can certainly learn
a great deal from them. They cannot be coauthors, composing the
subsequent drafts of an essay with writers, nor proofreaders, correcting grammar and spelling. They are experienced travelers who can
help your students make their own choices and make sense of their
experience of college culture, especially of their first drafts, just as a
concierge does for travelers.

The main benefit of working with peer tutors is that they can give your
students more detailed, objective responses than most classmates can
because they have more writing experience and, moreover, peer tutors
have been trained to give detached responses. They are peers: equals.
They do not pretend to be substitute teachers. Thus, they do not "grade"
or judge your students' papers. Also, remember peer tutors have read
and responded to more student papers than have most classmates. Peer
tutors tend to be hired because they are good listeners and good at asking
questions that will engage your students about their writing choices given
the constraints of the assignment. Because they like working with other
student-writers, tutors are usually friendly and good communicators. It
is best for our students to try to consult at least one tutor for each draft.

CONTEXT-BUILDING WRITING ACTIVITY 13

Soliciting Feedback from Tutors

To give (and get) the best tutor feedback:

1. Bring a typed copy of your draft and the assignment to your meeting.

2. Since most tutoring sessions last as few as fifteen minutes, you must maximize your time. The first few minutes will be spent reviewing the assignment requirements, and the next few will be spent reading what you wrote. Write out your three most important questions and show them to your tutor before they begin reading the draft. This will help them focus their feedback, and you won't waste time trying to think of what to ask.

    A good question, for example, is to ask the tutor what they think is the most important requirement on the assignment sheet and where your essay completes it. As you compose the questions you want the peer tutor to respond to, try to incorporate the goals you have for the draft. For example, Adhita asked one of her peer tutors, "As I try to achieve a more balanced response to Western technology in my second draft, where in my first draft are such possibilities presented?" As with all feedback, its usefulness is directly tied to the type and complexity of the questions you ask.

3. Although you can ask for a written response to your questions, don't assume there will be enough time for the tutor to do this. Instead be prepared to take notes and make corrections to your essay. Tutors are often trained to not mark on student drafts to prevent any accidental appropriation of a student's text.

4. You may be tempted during your tutoring session to ask the consultant for help with sentence-level errors (spelling, grammar, punctuation), but try to use the time to focus on global issues with the assignment requirements and save the other kind of questions for a follow-up tutoring session. Avoid asking yes/no questions.

Adhita's Example of Feedback from a Peer Tutor

Adhita received a useful reply from a peer tutor named Jim Givens. She chose him because her friends described Jim as honest, to the point, and fair to all points of view. The peer tutor's response to question one, about focus, is brief, with no elaboration: "The main focus is whether Eastern or Islamic countries should change their lifestyles to conform or be similar to their Western counterparts." The tutor's response to the second question, about where the draft is convincing, is also rather brief. It is clear the tutor is searching for something positive to say. "You probably have solid points through your knowledge of Eastern civilizations. Probably some good on the Western way, such as the attitude of constant advancement, and how man in the West does play the role of what's supposedly 'right' in Western civilization in God's eyes." The peer tutor gave a full answer to question three, about where the draft is not convincing to him. Adhita asked him to be completely honest: "Please hold back nothing," she insisted. His response:

> Are you sure that it is not the case that the only reason why it is impossible for the Western way of technology to work in the East is because they've never given it a fair chance? Western ideas can't all be that bad or the West wouldn't have flourished such as we have. I interpreted your paper as presenting as "fact" that the Western world revolves around the Bible. No matter what "mask" you call religion, all nations wear this mask in one form or another. I'm sure the East bases a lot of their behavior strongly on religion. I think you should never try to identify which religion or religious practices are right or wrong unless you are balanced and list both positives and negatives. Your first draft states or implies that one side of the comparison is all good and the other—the West—is all bad. Try to be a little fairer.

As with the previous feedback she received, Jim points out the ways and places where her essay oversimplifies things. The fourth question—about how the next draft can be made more convincing—produced a strong reply.

> This draft is well written, but it is difficult in certain parts because it is so abstract. For me it reads like a religious class on Eastern beliefs. Is this what you intended? Who is your audience and what is your purpose? For me your first draft is well focused. In fact I would say it is over focused because you didn't stand back enough from your topic to see what those who disagree with you would do or say.

A clear pattern of response emerges from the various readers of Adhita's essay. To a person, each notes the same kind of issues. Being a student, however, Adhita waited to receive her instructor's comments before really learning to trust in the feedback she received from these other readers. It is important that we regularly examine and affirm the feedback our students receive from other readers. Sharing our authority to evaluate their essays often is the only way students begin to realize their instructor's opinion is not the only opinion that matters and that other readers will question or notice the same things an instructor does.

Example of Brian's Feedback from Peer Tutors

Brian also asked Jim Givens to respond to his essay because, like Adhita, he learned that Jim is straight and to the point, although also diplomatic. Jim responded to the first question—What is the main focus of

the first draft?—in one sentence: "Your focus was on one specific incident where you had to make a tremendous decision which could have
cost your or Mike's life." Jim's answer to question two—about where is
the draft convincing and why—elicited this observational reply:

> Your story was convincing at this point: "It's funny how fast your mind
> moves when you are under pressure or just pressed for time. I don't
> know if I really made a decision or if my actions were just forced out
> of me due to my tight situation." I believe this happens to the major-
> ity of people. I mean that sometimes we all have to make split-second
> decisions, not necessarily under your circumstances of course, but in
> everyday life crisis decisions or instinctual responses may cause major
> effects in our lives.

In response to question three—Where is the draft unconvincing and
why?—Jim wrote,

> First, this is not a paper for a general audience. The sentence structuring
> and the use of slang, such as "the spot" or "shorts" or "homies," should
> have been explained. The slang and all was off-setting to this reader due
> to the time it took to decipher the meanings for someone who lives in a
> world of different slang! (Brian, do you think this is what multicultural-
> ism comes down to? Slang across cultures? I'm only half joking!) A basic
> vocabulary to these slang words would help tremendously.

The focus on local issues here seems a bit odd, especially given that it is
not connected to whether Brian's essay was convincing, and it is ques-
tionable whether the definitions Jim suggests would add much to the
paper at all. The peer tutor's response to Brian's final question—about
how to make the next draft more convincing—introduces a much more
detailed and thoughtful analysis.

> As the first draft stands, you the writer present shooting people and selling
> drugs as acceptable behavior in your world. You badly need to show the
> other side of the story. Don't you? The entire paper shows young readers
> that your behavior is "cool." In effect you say, "Oh well, forget that I got
> shot because I became a hero." Your carrying a gun, and not hesitating
> to use it, will cause some young people to look up to you. Maybe I'm just
> looking at this from a thirty year-old's point of view. (I started college after
> ten years in the military).
> When you say you're not afraid of anything, even death itself, that to
> me sends the wrong message, even if the facts are hauntingly true. Your
> draft does obviously deal with a very powerful situation. However, this one
> side of the story, or glorification of violence, is not the only visible way a
> reader should see "the concrete jungle." What you should include are the
> points you made invisible, such as the physical and emotional scars that
> such events play in your life. You need to talk about how you made your
> lifestyle turn around, to help people who are now in your old position to

change and save their lives. Finally, what I ask as a reader is what have you learned from this ordeal?

As we saw with Adhita's feedback, Brian repeatedly received comments that question his lack of reflection, his oversimplification of the effect these events had on his life then and now, and, possibly, his misunderstanding of audience. Brian is called to task about the assumptions his essay makes about how well his readers would relate to or even understand or sympathize with the events he recreates. Like Adhita, Brian soon discovered that these responses very much mirrored the comments his professor had to share about his essay.

Feedback from Instructors in End Comments

If peer tutors are experienced travelers in the college culture of reading and writing analytical papers, instructors are "locals" of the place. They are personifications of the cultural conversations that go on in scholarly books, academic journals, professional conferences, and classrooms. Substantial interactions with locals of the culture they're trying to participate in more fully are crucial to students' development of cultural consciousness. Remember that locals do have most of the advantages in conversations with newcomers. They know the rules and often administer them. They communicate spontaneously and apparently without effort. They don't worry about being judged. Your students, on the other hand, need to make a real effort to understand the locals and their initially "inscrutable" ways. However, as your students begin to make themselves understood, they gain the satisfaction of becoming contributors in conversations that might have seemed over their heads when they first arrived.

One of these conversations is the interaction your students have with any end comments or marginalia you place on their drafts. Too often students put too much stock in their instructor's comments, privileging them over all others. Whenever possible, professors should examine the other responses their students receive and find areas of agreement with those responses. Students will begin to realize just how useful these other responses can be, and they will begin to understand that faculty responses are not the only valid ones. When she examines peer responses, Amanda writes on them "I agree with X" or "I had the same question that Y asks of you." Validating other feedback also provides teachers with evaluative allies and prevents students from declaring that any response is just one person's opinion.

Example of Adhita's Feedback from Her Professor

After Adhita submitted her paper to her professor, she received the following end comments:

> The good news for me in this draft—as a first draft—is that you have focused on several related key ideas. You have found what interests you—Western technological modernization in Islamic countries and the cultural resistance it sets up—and this focus is clearly important to our modern world. I'm anxious to see how you develop this focus in your working and final drafts. You have repeated main ideas rather than developed them, but that is O.K. in a first draft because you seem to be trying them on for size. In other words, you are writing to discover what you think.
>
> As mentioned in a number of class discussions, we all need in first drafts to uncover our misunderstandings and oversimplifications. First your oversimplifications. You emphasize the difference between Judeo-Christian doctrines of the Fall and Original Sin, and the Islamic teaching that people are born sinless. But Fitrah—forgetting our original nature—could be considered by Christians as pretty much the same as the Fall theoretically and behaviorally. How would you respond to this reply? You also seriously oversimplify when you state that because of the doctrine of the Fall, the Christian position is that there "is no beauty in reality." Christianity sees this world as the arena of redemption, and as imperfectly reflecting the beauty of God's work. You cannot get Christians to be more open to Islam by writing in a manner that could be considered attacking Christianity or stereotyping it. Both religions are immensely complex and should not be oversimplified. You must give some clear sense that you are aware of these complexities, even though you are writing a short paper.
>
> Now let's look at misunderstandings. You claim in this draft that you are rejecting Western technological oppression of Islamic culture. But you seem to be repudiating technology as a whole. Also, you don't mention that even the most conservative Islamic societies do not reject Western technology totally. They wish to import Western technology selectively. What cultural and/or Islamic values condition this selection process?

Adhita's professor uses the terminology of *oversimplification* and *misunderstanding* in his analysis, but close examination reveals he is essentially giving the same feedback, in kind if not in language, as the other responders. In our classes we often invite students to confer with us at this stage as a sort of debriefing session. We ask our students to come with questions and prepared to look at all of responses with an eye toward revision.

Before Adhita scheduled a one-to-one meeting with her instructor, she reread the assignment, her draft, and the professor's comments several times. She reviewed feedback from family, friends, classmates, and peer tutors and decided what responses and advice she should return to. She wanted to get the instructor's opinion about her plans before beginning her second draft. She composed goals for her second draft and printed a copy for her instructor to read during their meeting. Finally, she planned to ask the instructor, and she put this in writing, how she could be open to feedback without relinquishing her authority as a writer. Adhita's goals for her revision looked like this:

Goals for my Second Draft
1. A comparison of the Christian Fall and the Islamic Fitrah.
2. Two contemporary Western views of self and memory:
    a. scientific, atheist, no core self view.
    b. The Christian position: self as expression of the soul, and influenced by socialization.
3. Self and memory in Islam.
4. Becoming (the myth of Progress) and Being (eternal values).
5. Technology and modernization in Islam: Western cultural imperialism or Islamic selectivity?

Having students write out goals is similar to Amanda's requiring students to write out on response sheets what they will do next. In the coming chapters, we see how many of these goals were achieved in Adhita's revision.

Example of Brian's Feedback from His Professor

After Brian submitted his paper to his professor, he received the following end comments:

> This draft is overwhelming in its presentation of your values at this time, your sense of choices, and your vivid demonstration of the desperateness of your situation. This is a deeply troubling draft, in part because of the clearmindedness you attribute to yourself, at least in your memory of this event as presented by you now. Were you really so thoroughly clearminded at the time? How have your memory and depiction of this event been selective? What principles did you use to select? What aspects of the event did your selection process make invisible or less visible? For example, in the opening paragraph you write that when "Mike and I were in juvenile detention together we decided when we got out we were going to get paid." Who was going to pay you? For what debt? What was the payment you imagined, exactly? How, why and when did you regard the "debt" as paid, so that you could stop criminal activities, enter college and become a productive member of society?

Brian's professor responds in much the same way as the others, not using terms like *oversimplification* but still making it clear that the events as presented are too selective. The questions that come at the end of the comment suggest Brian has not considered his audience enough in the selection of those events and activities. At this point it was time for Brian to meet with his professor and put together his own set of revision goals. As with Adhita, we will see later whether Brian chose to consider the recurring responses he received or rewrite his paper some other way.

Before Brian scheduled a meeting, he too reread the assignment, his draft, the professor's comments, and feedback from family, friends, classmates, and peer tutors and decided what responses to ignore and what replies he felt would help him think through the meaning of his experience. He wanted to get the instructor's opinion about his plans before beginning the second draft. Brian created these goals for his second draft:

Goals For the Second Draft
1. How did this event change me?
2. Why did it change me?
3. When did it change me?
4. What did I leave out in the writing of this story?
5. Why did I leave it out, or how did I select what to include?
6. How do I feel now about the person I was before? Is part of me still a criminal? If so, what "part"?
7. How can my experience help others go straight?

In the coming chapters, we see how Brian revised, incorporating some of the feedback he received, and how he achieved his revision goals for his second draft.

Feedback from Instructors via Office Hours

To become fluent in a culture and its language, a person needs to converse with locals often and as meaningfully as possible. There are many methods for students to achieve this fluency. One way is to use the office hours of all their instructors. A fifteen-minute visit to each instructor once a week substantially speeds up the process of gaining academic literacy. They should try speaking with their instructors about the most interesting, unusual, or troubling ideas mentioned or covered in class that week. They should try to direct such conversations toward assignments planned or in progress. During such encounters they might ask, How could I develop such an idea in a paper? or How could I pursue such a question in an effective way? Such questions would be appropriate to ask all their instructors, not simply you, their writing teacher. After you have provided your students with some form of feedback, whether oral or written, you should help your students make the best use of that response by scheduling a one-on-one meeting with each of them.

CONTEXT-BUILDING WRITING ACTIVITY 14

Student/Teacher Conferences

Prepare for and conduct your meeting with your instructor using these guidelines:

1. Review the assignment, draft, and teacher comments several times. Note any not understood.
2. In the meeting with the instructor, begin by asking about the instructor's written comments you want clarified or restated.
3. Analyze the instructor's comments. What is the instructor's major point? How can you relate the instructor's key response to your goals for the next draft?
4. Repeat in your own words the instructor's major response. Ask the instructor if you have correctly paraphrased their commentary.
5. Compose goals for the next draft and how to reach them. Type these to show to the instructor.
6. Share any interesting feedback with the instructor and ask for comments. If you feel particularly influenced by a response, ask whether the instructor thinks it constitutes good advice.
7. Ask for instructor advice about how to be open to responses received without relinquishing authority as the writer. Ask how the instructor responds to feedback so as to maintain authority.

REVISION: IT'S SHOCKING

At this time we'd like you to refocus on the chart of the Eddy Model of Intercultural Experience presented in the first chapter. Stage four, the Shock Stage, is the most troubling and difficult stage of the writing process and of intercultural experience because this is the point at which serious resistance to the new culture kicks in. But it is also the most potentially creative and insightful stage. Notice how our students now must create a role acceptable to the class. Culture shock is a fundamental disharmony with one's new culture. If the Shock Stage is permanent, and it is for some people, one must leave the new culture. Think about the considerable number of people who leave college by the end of their first year. We suggest that in many cases the reason for dropping out has little to do with intelligence and a lot to do with the inability to create a role acceptable to the college classroom. To create a role acceptable to the first-year writing classroom, one must take on the clearly logical habit of mind of academic discourse. One is asked to become skeptical, analytical, and critical. It is often difficult if not impossible for many first-year students to become skeptical and critical of their home cultures, so they wind up returning to the life and values they have always known. One experiences writer's block, like culture shock, because one fears the clear need for reconceptualization in order to fit in with the critical-minded college culture. One instinctively asks the questions (and fears the openness of the possible answers), Where will reconceptualization lead? What will I become? Most students fear and resist choice; when their teachers allow them to choose their own topics, own deadlines, own assignments for grading via a portfolio, they balk and plead for someone else to make those choices for them. It is quite the shock when they encounter a teacher who asks them to make these types of choices, to take agency and be more accountable for their own education.

But the uncertainty of the Shock Stage creates a real potential for growth and creativity. Fu Chun, one of Robert's students in China, wrote, "If a writing course doesn't produce times of deep writer's block and if a foreign experience doesn't produce a period of intense culture shocks then one has retreated to the surface of things, to comfortable stereotypes and deadly familiar dogma." If students accept the inherent challenge in the Shock Stage to introduce them to the new culture of college discourse, they will write with more power and conviction because they will have become explorers with the keen senses of someone in a foreign land, a place just beginning to become familiar and to feel like another "home." But we must emphasize that what makes the first-year writing classroom most foreign is the perpetual invitation to analyze and criticize all cultures, including academic discourse itself, endlessly, and to act on the critique. Academic discourse is more than playing with ideas; it is an invitation to change self and society individually, collectively, and democratically. Our experiences of teaching college writing courses in the United States, England, China, and Egypt have confirmed again and again that the students who turn the Shock Stage into a creative experience are those writers who accept the feeling of conceptual disharmony between their home and academic cultures. Moreover, they take their analysis seriously enough to consider changing their sense of self and society. They jump in the direction of a personal declaration of independence and interdependence and take their thinking, writing, and feeling seriously.

Before we leave this chapter, please remind students that revision is openness to change. It requires writers to be more interactive with other readers by in turn reacting to and being acted upon by the feedback they receive. All writers need to be able to let go of their first drafts and not try to save as much of the first draft as possible as they compose subsequent ones. The first draft exists only to get writers to a more clearly conceptualized revised one. Revising the draft of a first-year writing paper, if it is to be substantial and meaningful, requires students—even if only in the slightest sense—to let go of their current concept of self and to open their minds to change. This openness to change is no small feat because between the realization of change and their openness to it stands fear of change. This fear is directly connected to culture shock and to writer's block. How we understand and deal with this fear of and inertia against revision is the subject of chapter 6.

CONTEXT-BUILDING WRITING ACTIVITY 15

Steps for Tutors Giving Feedback to Writers

Ask the author to take out their own copy of the assignment and a pencil to take notes.

Take turns doing the following:

> Read over the assignment sheet with the writer, asking what they think the requirements are. Restate these so each student knows they will be responding based on those. If you need to, especially if the student doesn't bring in a copy of the assignment, write notes of what the requirements are on top of the essay.

> Read the assignment out loud to the student, sitting side by side so both of you can follow along and see where the reader puts questioning check marks.

As you read the assignment, the author should listen attentively for the following: places where the reader stumbles, sentences that do not make sense, use of quotes, and where the major requirements are fulfilled. Meanwhile, the reader of the essay should put light check marks in the margins of the essay so they can come back to them after reading the assignment.

One check mark is for mechanics and usage problems.

Two are for structural and organizational problems.

Three are for major, global problems like not completing a requirement, straying from the topic, illogical thinking, and lack of development of an issue or idea.

Other than check marks, avoid writing on the draft. Only the author should be responsible for making changes.

Begin your response by discussing how much of the assignment has been completed and where. Next, go back over the assignment with the student, explaining what you observed where the triple checks are located. These are the major issues, and most of your time should be spent here. It is much better to clear up these problems than to "clean up" an assignment that doesn't even complete its requirements. If there are so many triple-check problems that you won't have time for them all, focus on the most important two or three and go from there.

When going over usage and mechanics, you might need to be more direc-tive. That's okay. If you can explain usage errors without jargon, do so. There's no point telling students they commit dangling modifiers if they don't know what they are. Point one out, explain why it is a problem, and make many suggestions about how to revise those sentences. Have the author find the next one and revise it.

AT NO TIME MAKE A VALUE JUDGEMENT ABOUT THE ASSIGNMENT. DON'T SAY IT COMPLETES THE ASSIGNMENT WELL, IS GOOD, BAD, ETC. It is all right to give praise. Just make sure it is focused on specific things the student did well (i.e., "This is a really nice metaphor here. You may want to incorporate more since the assignment asks you for strong descriptions.")

Don't hesitate to use handbooks, dictionaries, and other reference materi-als. If you aren't sure about something, try to look it up, or tell the student you don't know.

Ask the student for any questions or whether they want to go back over something.

Be sure to deal with one problem and one essay at a time. If you don't have time to work on everything, suggest that the writer visit the writing center.

Before each student leaves, have them write a list of some things they will do to revise the essay. Don't assume they will remember. If they write it down, they will.

CODE-MESHING ACTIVITY 4

Required Two Questions for Everyone Who Reads the
First Drafts of Your Required Formal Papers

Here are the two questions I require you to write in response to anyone who reads and responds to first drafts of formal papers in this course, please, wheth-er family, friends, classmates, tutors, or your writing teacher: (1) How did your racial identity and comfort level, especially if the reader is of a race not your own, influence the dialogue about your paper? (2) How did the reader's racial identity and comfort level, especially if the reader is of a race not your own, influence the dialogue about your paper? You are required to answer these questions and send them to me, please, but consider answering in either your home language or as code meshing. Consider showing family members what you wrote in your two answers before you send it to me, as a courtesy and to show respect to and for them.

6

THE SHOCK STAGE
Writer's Block and Fear of Change

HOW CULTURE SHOCK CREATES WRITER'S BLOCK

In the previous chapter, we looked at questions and methods for eliciting responses to discovery drafts from family, friends, classmates, peer tutors, and instructors. Experienced instructors know most novice writers resist changing initial drafts. As with Adhita and Brian, most students ignore or reject these responses for a number of reasons. The first is usually because the comments did not come from their professor, who is ultimately going to grade the student's work. Sometimes responses are rejected because our students think their essays are good enough as they are and that making changes will only hurt their grade. A smaller number of students don't want to change their discovery drafts at all, nor do they actually believe they need to since their views on the topic have not changed. Some students never seriously read feedback in the first place, so they don't know how to implement any of it. Eventually, this fear of changing their drafts causes students to experience writer's block. We argue that writer's block is a by-product of engaging the Shock Stage of the Eddy Model, which is the most important stage student writers go through. Students in this stage experience culture shock after receiving feedback because that is when they begin realizing that what worked in the past, in high-school culture, does not work in college culture. Having one's writing, and thus values, challenged through feedback is threatening. Our epistemology and ontology do not take kindly to being shaken or challenged. After discovering old coping mechanisms are not enough to navigate collegiate discourse, first-year students often wind up with writer's block, a fear of self-exposure. How do we help students overcome fear of change and make up their minds for themselves? How do we teach them that since they remain in control, they have nothing to fear from change? Put another way, to master the art of crossing cultures, our students must acknowledge and accept both their natural fear of change and the potentially exciting openness to what might occur, to the real possibilities revision affords them.

DOI: 10.7330/9781607328742.c006

Resistance to change in a writing situation initially creates writer's block because our students are afraid of how change will affect their grades, but in the long term they fear the effects of change on their self-worth, their values, and their existing cultural norms. Like experienced travelers, our students will enjoy their time in and adapt to the new culture in selective ways and to the degree they choose only after they become as comfortable in it as they are in their home culture.

Culture shock is an emotional and epistemological challenge of dissonance with one's new culture in some significant aspects and perhaps in many. If the dissonance is too intense or too long lasting, the person might return home. We writers have a primal or existential fear of real questions because if answers to real questions are open, honest, and risky, very quickly, and inevitably, we come face to face with conceptual dissonance. Yes, we can flip the script and say such dissonance is the excitement of a dynamic college education, and that is true, but the dread and discomfort remain and are central to us, even if we want to be open. The thing about conceptual dissonance is that it absolutely requires reconceptualization. We all fear reconceptualization, even though educated people know it is the heart of educational work. When we have lost or have had to give up the safety of an existing (maybe long-standing) conception of the world and of self and others, especially of Othered individuals and groups that in educational settings can no longer be dismissed but must be seen as fully and complexly human and more like us than we realized, in these challenging moments, which truly are exciting but demanding, a deep part asks, What will become of my existing beliefs if I explore new ones?

If the Shock Stage is permanent, and it is for some, one must leave the new culture. Think about the considerable number who leave college by the end of the first year. In many cases the reason for dropping out has little or nothing to do with intelligence and a lot to do with the inability to adapt and to create a role acceptable to the college classroom.

One of the chief characteristics of culture shock and writer's block is an inward turning to escape the conflict between the old and safe and the new and perhaps dangerous. For the person with writer's block, this turning inward to escape the unknown means the writing, the revision, stops or never happens. This outcome is of course most serious. Everything seems to be at stake. Everything is up for grabs and nothing is safe except abandoning the new college culture and dropping out. The part of us that wants to return to the safety of the old and familiar presses vigorously—during culture shock and writer's block—for nothing to happen so the old ways will prevail and not be displaced or modified by the new. That's why we turn inward at such a time. It's not just procrastination or avoidance behavior we are facing. Some students say "I don't want to do the revision"; "I don't want to write"; "I don't want to continue with this boring or stupid topic." But the fact is that sometimes, and probably most of the time, what's really going on is that we are facing an entirely unknown future we are not ready to fashion and embrace. This is fear of self-exposure; fear of real questions with as yet unknown answers. If we persist in this condition of not writing, not revising, not thinking, not continuing to engage the new culture just at this point at which we are in fact beginning substantial adaptation, we will fail; we will drop out; we will go home. Nationwide, about half the students who begin college never finish. There are many reasons for their not finishing, of course, often economic, but a substantial reason is often just the condition of writer's block we are talking about right now.

When we ask friends, colleagues, and students about experiences with writer's block, they tend to respond in one of two ways. Most writers define it as a procedural block in their process and engage in avoidance behavior. Some get stuck deciding what to delete; some get stuck before they even begin because they have difficulty choosing or narrowing a topic; others never begin because they worry they have nothing important to say. Of course, a majority of students experience anxiety-based writer's block that results from having to meet deadlines at work, home, and school in a short space of time. Amanda has worked with her share of student athletes whose commitments to training create similar results. Many novice writers procrastinate by making excuses or engaging in superstitious routines and avoidance behaviors—until I start the wash; until I put on music; until I clean my desk; until I walk the dog; until I reach the next level on my videogame; until I go to the library. A different group of writers experience a conceptual block. This chapter examines conceptual blocks. Unlike the other forms, conceptual blocks come from within.

Fear of revision and change creates writer's block, which is the fear of a newer reality: fear of conceptual dissonance between the safe and familiar and the unknown implications of taking on any new positions, ideas, values, beliefs. To some extent, all writers, but especially student writers, worry that taking on a new point of view in a substantial revision constitutes a serious challenge to their existing values and beliefs. Many first-year students feel or think they didn't come to college to change or evolve their thinking but only to gain the skills they need for future economic success. But if someone is not open to changing their mind, their mind is tightly closed. How could we learn, grow, and improve under such confining conditions? Progress does not come from closing ourselves to change. We saw in the previous chapter that genuine revision requires reconceptualization. But to face change in our drafts and lives, we must consider once again these two most fundamental and essential questions if we are to try to maintain some control over our revision processes:

> Where will change (revision) lead?
> What or who will I become?

It is important to remember that culture shock doesn't happen at the beginning of our contact with a foreign culture. It starts to develop just at the point when the new culture begins having a substantial effect on our old culture. Why then? Why do we resist change just at the point at which our old views are changing? Because often, not fully consciously, we become aware that our old world-view is slipping away, and with it all our old certainties and timeless values. This experience is unnerving. We begin to develop an intercultural sense that identities, values, and world-views are arbitrary since they are cultural constructions that can change. Is my "self" a sociocultural construction that is endlessly malleable or changeable? Thus, the two questions are essential: Where will change (revision) lead? What or who will I become?

Students experience writer's block, like culture shock, because they fear the clear need for reconceptualization in order to fit in with the critical-minded college culture. A student instinctively asks the questions (and fears the openness of the possible answers), Where will reconceptualization lead? What will I become? To create a role acceptable to the first-year college classroom, a student must take the shape of a multiple amphibian, being at home in several environments. By this we mean we must become aware of when to adapt ourselves to a new culture for survival in it and when to remain in the environment we currently inhabit. The choice is partly audience dependent; we change based on those with whom we have interactions and the locale of those relations. If an instructor accepts the inherent challenge in the Shock Stage of introducing students to the new culture of college discourse, the students will write with more power and conviction because they will have become explorers with the keen senses of someone in a foreign land, a place just beginning to become familiar and to feel like a "home." But we must emphasize that what makes the first-year college classroom most foreign is the perpetual invitation to analyze and criticize all cultures, including academic discourse itself, endlessly, and to act on the critique. Academic discourse is more than playing with ideas; it is an invitation to change self and society individually, collectively, and democratically.

WORKING THROUGH THE SHOCK STAGE

What should you do when your students are experiencing writer's block? Some of our students at that moment are thinking about going home, especially first-generation students of color. They are asking themselves questions like, Do I really want to fit in tightly with a white middle-class place? Do I really want to try to fit in with a place that will never really accept me no matter what? Do I have to give up any of my identity to satisfy a white teacher? Do I have to "act white" to win in college? What do I have to give up to make it in college? When Robert has first-generation students, especially of color, or working-class students in general, or students from any oppressed groups who ask him some version of one of these questions in private in his office or after class, he says some version of this response:

> If you want to be here and succeed, your success will help other folks who feel like they don't belong also have a better chance to succeed by seeing your success. Yes, white dominance is violent and hard to challenge, and most white folks don't see or admit their unearned privilege, but it is unearned and has to be taken down and put back into fair human circulation, earned by labor, not gifted by unearned privilege. We both need you to become who you want to be with your eyes and mind 100 percent open, going where you want and being who you want, in spite of white dominance. Take EAE and mesh your languages and identity and flavor, and let's together work to create fully representative language choices for all of us. But—a democratized and egalitarian EAE is, until the ending of systemic racism, an impossible ideal but a useful fiction. Your producing perfect spoken "Standard English" and perfect written rhetorical persuasion in flawless EAE will not end how your body and being are marked in a violent white-supremacist system. But as you endlessly (a college and lifetime task) increase your linguistic repertoire, your rhetorical repertoire, and sharpen and widen your critical consciousness of how language and power operate in a racist system, the—for now—useful fiction of a democratized and egalitarian EAE can garner contested power for you individually and in coalition work as you position yourself in your location along the political-economic continuum of resistance, separation, and pluralism. As you prepare to position yourself in work you value, resist oppression in this country as necessary to build a multiracial democracy of real pluralism or separate and go to the country or continent that will welcome your work and your personhood.

Hard conversations but honest dual mentoring or multidirectional mentoring are essential to the teaching-learning work we do.

As an example of the student as mentor and teacher as mentee, a black woman retiring from the army after a twenty-year career, after listening to a version of the above with total but relaxed attention, asked Robert, "Especially for you as a Muslim professor after 9/11, do you think the security apparatus, which has certainly bugged your environments, only is annoyed by such teaching of yours or is more than annoyed? Why are you encouraging me to behave in such a way as to come to the attention of the security apparatus? A little advice here, professor, with all due respect: consider your own well-being a little more and worry less about your students. We can take care of ourselves. You—a white Muslim professor—are far more vulnerable than I am—a black woman career army officer honorably retired—in post 9/11 USA. Sir, you need to watch your back. We can take care of ours." Robert thanked her for her mentoring and replied that he would think carefully about everything she said. Robert was silent and thought that the meeting was over. Then the student said, "Sir, could I please have a reaction or response to what I just said?" Robert was silent for a few seconds and then shared with her a matter-of-fact reality: "When I am interviewed by the FBI as a local Muslim leader, which has happened a number of times, I notice how good they are at noticing proxemic factors in me, which I take to be attentive judging of my honesty and/or fear or absence of fear. They are also really good being informal and apparently friendly. What I emphasize in such meetings is that I believe that I love the country and all its people more than they do and that I believe in the ideals of our democracy but admit freely that the country is relentlessly and violently racist and that this reality threatens our national survival and that I work for justice and peace." The student looked at Robert with no proxemics of her own and said, "So you really do mean what you say, I see. But aren't you afraid of the security apparatus?" Robert replied, "I am a normal human being in terms of survival instincts, but all we humans have is our personal commitments and each other and what we might be able to build or rebuild together." The student ended the conversation in this office meeting with her first smile and said, "Thank you, sir, for seeing me and for having this real talk; I appreciate it. Salaam."

Successful adaptation to college on the student's own terms does not necessarily constitute an assimilation attempt. Students who choose to completely reject assimilation attempts and instead find their preferred place on the continuum of resistance, separation and pluralism also need to adapt selectively to college in order to get their credential and the training they want, then work to change the political economy of their country or choose separation and live and work in a different country or on a different continent. The coauthors of this book completely support adaptation and success in college for as many students as commit to that result. Neither of us privileges in theory or practice the attempt to assimilate to the existing violently racist system, which is in any event not possible for the vast majority of first-gen people, especially of color. Our commitment is to affirm students' rights to construct their own political-economic position wherever they believe it should be, but for ourselves, we commit to resistance and pluralism. We agree with Angela Davis in her recent reminder that we must support ever-widening coalitions for social justice that "resist the inevitable seductions of assimilation" (Johnson and Lubin 2017, 246).

One simple yet effective activity in helping students work through the Shock Stage of the Eddy Model is having them reimagine writing as another activity. For instance, one student in the midst of writer's block, who very nearly quit college, and who loves boating, told his instructor that, with a sudden sense of excitement, he decided "to ride the change required to revise his paper but control the throttle and wheel!" Another student, who acted in a lot of amateur rock musicals, overcame writer's block by imagining the new self he would become by revising as "just another role to play." A third student opened herself to the change by deciding she "didn't want to lose the metamorphosis college promises." This student added, "My grandmother was a stay-at-home type. My mother is a teacher and loves her career. Since I don't want to remain 'at home,' then I really need to do a substantial revision."

CONTEXT-BUILDING WRITING ACTIVITY 16

Role Playing for Revision

Often it is helpful for students who experience writer's block to reimagine writing as a different, and more enjoyable, activity. Instead of thinking of yourselves as student authors, imagine yourselves in an alternate role that requires change for success. For instance, a singer would not have much of a career if they could only perform one song.

The student who wrote the words about metamorphosis was Adhita, one of the students whose composing processes we've been examining throughout this book. In chapter 5, we see how she obtained responses to her first draft from a variety of audiences. After considering everyone's response, and after speaking with her instructor, Adhita developed a plan for revising her first draft. In spite of crafting a fairly clear statement of her revision goals, Adhita became seriously mired in writer's block and culture shock in part because the sheer amount of feedback made her uncertain where to begin. She said she wanted to revise, but if she did, she'd be writing. When writer's block—fear of revision—becomes a serious problem, and it does intermittently for nearly all writers, writing one's way through is needed. Adhita's friend Karen noticed Adhita withdrawing more and more and refusing to work on the revision. Karen offered to chat electronically with Adhita, which is what a friend or classmate should offer, to help with writer's block. She had to push to get Adhita to find the time to dialogue. But as is usually the case, the chat was well worth the time, for both people. Here's the exchange:

KAREN: What's wrong? Why don't you just write your revised draft?

ADHITA: I don't know? The subject has really gotten to me. I hate to admit it but some of the feedback I got really upset me. I told people to be completely honest, and I thought I was mature enough to take whatever they said. But I was really hurt and confused by what several people said. Even my father. Maybe especially my father. He had the nerve to say my paper was based on a fairytale! The more I think about it or try to forget it, the more it angers me.

KAREN: Could he be right?

ADHITA: What? Now you too? Get off my case!

KAREN: I don't know about you, but when I can't forget something even when I try and get angry when I think about it, it just about always means I don't want to face whatever degree of truth it has. Maybe you're upset because you think your father is partly right. Just partly right. Is it possible?

ADHITA: If my father is right, even partly right, then my view of myself, my values, my view of the world, all of these are based on a fairytale! I don't know whether to laugh or cry? I'm an adult woman. I'm eighteen years old! Not a child. God, what if he's right? It's so embarrassing!

KAREN: I'm sorry but I really think you're making a very big deal about this. Really! Just consider the possibility that your father is right. Think it through. Decide what you really think after taking what he said seriously, put down what you believe in your heart to be true, and why you think it's true; argue your case fairly; try to be fair to everyone. But you have to say what you really think.

ADHITA: Don't you get it? I don't know what I think anymore. Or maybe I'm afraid to think it through. Like the teacher said, maybe I'm afraid of where it will lead or what I will become. If my view of India and Islam is a fairytale, then my identity is a fairytale. India is part of me. If I'm doing fairytale thinking, then my self is a fairytale too. This is too ugly, too awful, really. God, I hate it when America and Americans and other Westerners colonize or trivialize India (or Islam, in this way all traditional societies are the same). They also intellectually colonize India and Islam by claiming to understand and represent it in their thinking and perhaps writing! The thing I really don't want to think about is. Forget it! This is stupid!

KAREN: What do you mean by "colonize" intellectually?

ADHITA: Intellectually colonizing to me means claiming to understand another culture, one which is technologically less developed than the West. But such thinking is "colonizing" in that the traditional culture is not understood in its own terms at all but is perceived really "recreated" in the mind of the Westerner in purely Western terms. This is a form of intellectual conquest which says in effect "I understand you! I know you! You are what I say you are, not what you think you are!"

KAREN: I see what you mean. If someone said that to me, I'd tell them where to get off. But what does "intellectual colonizing" have to do with your writer's block? You don't mean you think your father is doing that to you, do you?

ADHITA: Not exactly. I hope not, certainly. He calls himself "an American," even though he was born and raised in India, and went to college there. He did his MBA here. I was born in America but insist on being called "Indian-American," which we dispute sometimes. But not very far, because even though he thinks he is an American father, the main thing he wants from me, even though he would deny this, is blind obedience, like a traditional Indian father! So we're in a funny opposition. I was born in America but emphasize my Indianness; he was born in India and emphasizes his Americanness. The thing is—thank you Karen for asking me to do this—I never saw it this way before, what annoys me about him is it seems to me that he has taken on the American colonizing attitude toward India! And you know why? Because he's a bank president with a lot of money and he always says he owes it all to America, that it's the greatest country on earth. I told him he's a bank president because he's smart and works very hard. He refuses to see his Indianness! His core values—like who I should marry (an Indian! of course)—are pure Indian—and he refuses to see it! Yes, he and I are fighting over defining each other, just like the West and the so-called "Third World." He refuses to see his Indianness! That's the whole problem! What do you think, Karen. I really want to know, tell the truth.

KAREN: I wonder if you really want to hear what I think? I don't know your father. I don't know if what you say about him is reasonable. If your father refuses to see his Indianness, I think maybe your writer's block comes from your refusing to see how American you are.

ADHITA: What do you mean? I know I'm an Indian-American. End of story.

KAREN: Do you want me to write what I think, or should we stop? I don't want you to get too angry at me. Should we stop or go on?

ADHITA: Go ahead. Write whatever you think is true!

KAREN: I think that you are a 100% American who pretends to be Indian-American because it makes you feel "special," "cool," a kind of "star."

ADHITA: See! This is how intellectual colonizing works! You're trying to recreate me in your American image. I am not just an American! I'm more than that.

KAREN: I'm not trying to colonize you because I'm not sure. If I said I was sure, then maybe I'd be trying to colonize you. Your parents are probably the real Indian-Americans. They lived full-time in both countries; you only spent summers there. Maybe your father thinks you have a fairytale view of India because, ironically considering how interested you are in exposing the American colonizing mentality, you only see India through rose-colored American romanticizing perspectives. Could you have a positive stereotype of India, but a stereotype nonetheless? Could be what your father calls a fairytale? That's all I have to say. I don't know if I'm right. You're in charge of your own self and thinking. You have to decide. I take you seriously. Please take me seriously too. (And maybe your father too). I want to stay your friend. Don't get angry at me because I'm trying to be truthful with you. I know that what I say is not "the truth," just what I think might be the truth, or part of the truth. Wow, this travelog journal is a powerful thing. I think you have a great paper to write now. Or a great revision. Please help me like this when I'm blocked in the future.

ADHITA: O.K. I'll think about this. Thanks!

As a result of this dynamic exchange, Adhita decided to substantially change her plans for her revision. At first she wanted to write a personal paper analyzing her own Indian American identity and its relationship to the issues in her first draft. But she was afraid she might plunge from the personal to the truly private, so she decided to postpone this approach. Instead, she wanted to go after what most interested her at that point: the relationship of memory, identity, and modernization issues in Islamic societies. Notice in the following revision that Adhita never responded to Karen's perception that she might be 100 percent American and "playing" at being "Indian-American." Likewise, notice how, in her revised draft, Adhita never really looks at how westernized Islamic societies might be or might want to be. Though she insists on seeing biculturalism in herself, and that others see her dual identity, she wants to portray a culturally pure Islam that is monocultural and closed. As you read her revision, pay attention to where and how the essay changes from the first draft. Whose feedback does she incorporate into this new draft the most? Which advice does she ignore?

[Revised draft]

Islam, Memory and Modernization: Being Vs. Becoming
Adhita

The Islamic attitude toward modernization is greatly affected by their belief in the purity of the soul and the beauty of creation. It is affected by the concept of being in God's world now, and perceiving its reality. If all and everything are pure creations of God, then where is the need to change?

Western generated scientific and technological advances are impregnated with western cultural values, which interfere with the balance of nature and the relationship of people with the balance of the world as it was first created. For example, large, obtrusive western buildings defeat the purpose of the marriage of beauty and functionalism of traditional Islamic architecture and public planning. The humanly created landscape in Islam is suppose to mean something more than efficiency and cost-effectiveness. It has to show the culture's priorities. It has to be a form of worship.

If the Islamic nations are to modernize with the consent of their populations at large, then they must modernize Islamically. The process must work within the realms of God's absolute reality, or else modernization will lead to religious and cultural suicide. It is neo-colonial to expect western modernizations to work in Islamic cultures.

As the west leads in science and technology now, (just as Islam lead previously, during the Middle Ages), the west thinks that its way is the "right" way, and that it will work for every other culture. This cultural or technological arrogance leads to increased international instability, as it oftentimes seems that the western powers cannot respect a culture so different. The differences are not respected, and one being stronger than the other physically, leads to the attempt of domination. In the American media, the "arab" is reduced to one of two stereotypes, the imbecile or the terrorist, which the author of the medieval text The Song of Roland would recognize and approve. The Crusades still go on, but in ways that pretend not to be about religion.

So what are the key differences between Islam and the west when it comes to memory, being and becoming? Imagine for a minute if we could remember everything that we have experienced since our birth. It would be hyperintense, hyperactive, drowning in a sea of sensations and rushing thoughts which are unconnected. Insanity surely. Certainly there could be no "meaning" or relationships because we would see everything, but one at a time, chaotically. So, therefore memory must (1) be selective and it must involve (2) the making of meaning. The selectivity creates the meaning. I think our culture tells us what and how to select; what and how to "see." The west and Islam "see" different worlds.

What's the Islamic world look like?

In Islam there is no concept of Original Sin. No Fall. No corruption. This is a profound difference between Islam and the west. A giant difference. Thus, the core of human nature is pure and heavenly. According to Islam, we carry paradise at the Center of our Being. The key Arabic words are:

Fitrah [our true, pure original nature]
Dhikr [remembrance of God as context of all meaning (memory)]
Jihad [struggle, "war," striving to open up completely to the memory of fitrah]

The outline above suggests that Being, our original nature, fitrah, is more important than Becoming. In the west, Becoming, Progress, is more important than Being; Progress is more important than our original nature.

In my opinion western science and technology deny or submerge Being, the idea of a pure soul, and replace it with John Locke's tabula rasa, blank slate, a person becoming more and more progressive. But I ask one question, toward what ideal or utopia is scientific-technological "Progress" heading? What are we going to become? I think it is best for the reader to fill in the answer or answers. There are terribly negative possible answers: a nuclear holocaust, planetary death through environmental catastrophe, etc. But let's leave the negatives aside. What is the most positive "final" result we can imagine? By asking a half-dozen of my roommates, I discovered that I'm not the only person who has trouble answering this question of positive final outcomes of the scientific-technological religion of Progress.

Here I bow to the reader and ask for an answer.

Islam's sense of time is very different. Time has meaning as the unfolding of Being, not as becoming. Being, the eternal divine nowness, is all that matters. Fitrah, our original nature, is spontaneous joy and creativity. Paradise here and now.

Fitrah is the pure natural state of Islam. The word "Islam" is derived from the Arabic root "slm," which means peace, purity, submission to God's will. The whole Islamic enterprise is to remember the pure spontaneity of our original nature. How does one try to accomplish this goal of total memory, or return to fitrah? The answer is the five pillars of Islam in their outward and inward forms.

The five pillars of Islam are (1) the declaration of faith: "There is no god but God" and "Muhammad is the Prophet of God." (2) prayer five times per day; (3) fasting, especially during the month of Ramadan; (4) alms giving; (5) pilgrimage to Mecca. As in all religions I know of, there is a tension in Islam between its outer and inner dimensions. This tension between external rules and inner commitment is the arena for the struggle of jihad. The outer jihad is the defense of Islam, such as the Russian invasion of Afghanistan, which was an attempt to destroy an Islamic society. Fighting the Russians was a true jihad. But the outer jihad is also the seeking of social justice. Economic actions have to be sought in which remembrance of God is kept in mind and material welfare does not become an end in itself. Greed is not good in Islam, compared to certain American movies about the stock exchange!

The jihad for the inner self is the recognition that whatever one wants most, whatever one gives most of one's time to, is what one truly worships. Many people worship wealth as their only true god. They might give some time or a little time to Allah, but such people are not fighting an inner jihad. To the one who fights the inner jihad, God is everything. Such a Muslim tries to see Allah in every dimension of existence.

In Islam total memory is in theory possible. Jihad can lead, at least temporarily, to total recall, total fitrah. In the Islamic tradition, certain great poets like Rumi or Ibn 'Arabi, who are also spiritual teachers, report in their poetry, moments of total memory. I will give some examples of what the world looks like when one has "remembered" divine vision: when the "ordinary" is seen to be extraordinary: concrete, simple, beautiful, divine. Here are the quotes:

The intense, terrible beauty of perceiving everything as divinely
   beautiful—
a woman's spit
the pain of sexual desire
the unbearable nostalgia of memory
the fragrance of an oasis after a sudden rainstorm
the texture of bare flesh
the croak of a raven
the startling joy of lightning flashing over the desert
the ecstacies of the visionary, the poet, the scientist
the cool serenity of a shrine deserted by all pilgrims in the hour
   before dawn.

Such unbearable beauties are what matter in a perfect world—this
world when perceived correctly, openly and with the giving away of your
life to the experience of total recall of God, who is the beauty of ancient
days, forever new.

Total memory in Islam is possible because the core of our Being is divine, if we overcome the dream of forgetfulness, of thinking money, success, practicalities, being "special" are what really matter in life. The dream
of forgetfulness is a nightmare of materialism, selfishness, loneliness, violence and imprisonment of the human spirit.

Total memory in Islam is possible because the soul is pure, not corrupt,
as is taught in the Christian doctrine of the Fall, and thus provides the
context that organizes all of our memories since birth into an unbearably
beautiful perceptual tapestry of ordered experiences that turn out to be
a face of God, our deepest conceivable joy and connectedness with the
natural world, all other people and with Allah. The only response to such
beauty, to such total meaning, to such ordering and arranging of all of
our experiences and memories is the shout of joy, in Arabic: "El Hamdu
l'Allah: thanks be to God."

Notice that Adhita went back to her original outline, located in chapter
3 of this book, which she produced before the writing of her first draft.
She selected from her first outline clearly and effectively, especially her
use of memory as "selective" and as involved in the "making of meaning."
These ideas clarified things in this draft and allowed her to introduce
an interesting and appropriate question everyone can relate to: What
would it be like to suddenly remember everything? It would be pure
chaos because the multitude of unrelated memories would overwhelm
us. But, she says quite logically, if you accept for a moment that total
memory in Islam is possible, then it arranges perceptions into a kind of
joyous work of art in which our life is a text or play or video or tapestry or
what she calls a "face of God." According to her, we become a mirror in
which God self-reflects. Although these ideas are surely novel to Western
readers, her line of thought represents a logically consistent position. It

can be argued against or attacked, of course, but it is an argument that is consistent and logical if you accept its premises.

Because of the multiple negative responses Adhita got to her first draft that said it was marred by excessive negative references to Christianity, she eliminated all such references in her second draft. She chose to virtually omit any mention of Christianity at all in her revised draft. There is one very brief and fairly objective allusion to the Christian view of the soul as fallen. Unlike her diplomatic silences with reference to Christianity in her new draft, however, Adhita continues and broadens her attack against what she now calls "the scientific-technological religion of Progress." It's interesting and important that she now calls science and technology the "religion of Progress." In this way, she presents a dramatic continuation or renewal of what she considers the religious war of the Crusades, but now it's not between Islam and Christianity but between Islam and "the scientific-technological religion of Progress." This is an interesting and subtle argument that has explanatory power as an attempt to make sense of the turmoil in the relationship of Islam and the West.

This draft is much more focused and insightful than her first draft, and a large reason for this improvement was the dramatic chat with Karen. The exchange got her more emotionally and intellectually engaged in the topic, showed Adhita how central the topic was to her identity as a person, and inspired her to be as fair as possible to everyone. The revised draft is much more disciplined in thought and expression and more original in some details. It is more interesting and understandable, even though her topic became more demanding and complex than in her first draft. The revision demonstrates considerable background knowledge of Islam. Moreover, she establishes a certain authority on the subject without arrogance or boasting, a point first-year students often do not reach. Indeed, the ending of the paper achieves an eloquence and sensitive commentary about a religion and culture not her own, a sensitivity all too rare in the United States.

How much crossing of cultures does the revision demonstrate? Adhita is not Muslim herself, but Islam, as in her first draft, is the "Eastern" culture and religion that seems to stand in the place of her own religion—Hinduism—against the colonizing and racism of the Western imperial project. In what ways does this revision really show a change in what she has become or is becoming? Can she truly be said to have engaged a new culture when her essay speaks so deeply to defending her original one? As a proud woman of color, in response to her new culture of white academia, Adhita affirms her home culture of color as a dynamic equal of white academia by more effectively using the methods of white academia while arguing against white dominance. Adhita overcame her writer's block/culture shock by saying in her writing-as-action that she is both inside and outside white academia. She can use its methods without accepting assimilation as colonization. She is demonstrating resisting white academia as white privilege while she operates as a polyculturalist using key rhetorical elements of the repertoire of her new college culture.

To see a stark example of crossing cultures, let's look at another example of how a student worked to overcome his own writer's block and fear of change. In Brian's case, his ability to control writer's block had the real potential to determine whether he would completely withdraw from college and thus abandon the work of developing an intercultural ethos. Brian's first draft required telling a story about a key event in his life on the streets and analyzing his choices in a situation of life or death. But Brian's revision of the paper required much more of him: a searching and systematic cultural analysis of his life. This kind of analysis requires courage and commitment. The revision required analysis and reconceptualization of criminal behavior by answering the two questions about where revision would lead and who he would become. Brian felt he could only do the analysis of the shooting by first answering the two questions about how he was changing because of rejecting the criminal life.

The required analysis for the revised draft made Brian edgy. He wondered where the analysis would lead and what would be revealed. Brian told his writing instructor that he planned to get his degree without really thinking about it: "[I wanted to] sneak into college, get my degree, start my engineering company and never look back. But I also didn't want to look forward too much to see where I was at or where I might be going." Brian dialogued with two close friends but shared part of only one of those exchanges; "much too private," he explained. Although he never did quote extensively from their chat, Brian did share the following questions and answers with his instructor. Brian's close friend Rahsaan asked him what "secret questions" remained in Brian's mind about the differences between his criminal and college selves. Here is Brian's answer and a portion of their chat:

> BRIAN: Just how far would I go to gain success in college? Would I cheat on tests if I thought I could get away with it? Since I know how many others are cheating, does that force me to cheat to keep up? Isn't that what "insider trading" is in the stock market? Aren't we deep down inside the same people in the same jungle? Just different parts of the

one jungle of eat or be eaten? I don't want to be a victim or a loser. Would I trust any of them stock market people to watch my back? Would you? Let's get real! College has to be honest and tell the truth or I'm leaving. At least I know the game and the score on the streets. I'm not sure about the college game and scorecard? Are we doing the right thing Rahsaan, or should we go back to the streets, where things are clear and honest?

RAHSAAN: What do you mean that the streets are "honest"?

BRIAN: You know what I mean. The competition wants to drop you before you drop them. Everything's clear. In the non-criminal world of college and business most people at least seem to follow the law. But is it really true? Are we fools if we think it's any different? I don't want to be a fool and sucker.

RAHSAAN: O.K. I see what you mean, but what are your final questions?

BRIAN: So what are my final questions? Like the prof man says, if I revise my paper, my life and my career
   1. Where will change (revision) lead?
   2. What or who will I become?

One can see that Brian is grappling with real choices in how to use the feedback from family, friends, and colleagues not just to revise the paper but also in thinking about his future. For the essay he decided, "The dialogues did make things much clearer to me, and I just transferred whole sections of what I wrote in the dialogues right into my revised draft." Whether this choice is the most effective is, of course, open to debate since one could argue it leaves the draft lacking in unity. One could also question how much risk Brian takes in his essay by repeatedly going back to the home culture to collect more feedback. Is he really adapting to the new, collegiate culture or attempting to bring the home culture to college? For students wanting to code switch, attempting to bring the home culture to college is exactly the wrong thing to do, but for code-meshing intentions, it is exactly right because it affirms selective intentional mixing of the two cultures. Brian is in the midst of giant decisions. For some students, this use of portions of dialogues in their formal papers is common and a great resource and time saver. How successful is this revision?

[Revised draft]

Another Night in the Hood
   Brian

It looked like just another Friday night in the hood. I quickly walked around the corner to the game room. As I walk I pass the same old routine people. I was in a hurry to meet my partner at the spot. When Mike and I were in juvenile detention together we decided when we got out we were going to get paid. We are both sixteen now so the law considers us as adults. So as far as we see it we are not taking no shorts and no shit! When we are on the corner one of us holds the other one sells the drugs. This night it was my turn to hold the gun and watch Mike's back. We were already told by some kids out there to watch out for a blue 4 door Chevette. They said it was some stick up kids from Brooklyn. About two hours later things were going as normal. We had been doing good this night. There had been no police and definitely no sign of any stick up kids. But I guess our good luck was due to end. Before I knew it there was the blue Chevette. Two kids had jumped out and grabbed my partner Mike. They had not noticed me off to the side of the game room. In my mind I knew I had to make a decission and do it fast. I could just stay quiet and let them get the money. I could run half way down the block and get some more of our homies. Or just come from around the corner shooting at them.

If I decide to go get help I have a better chance of having the odds in our favor. Plus if I get the homies we can run these kids off our corner for good. But this could take to long and they could be gone by the time I get the homies and back. Even worse by the time we get back Mike could be dead. And if Mike gets shot he would be wondering were I was at. And if he was shot I would have to put up with all the homies in the hood.

I thought about just not saying a thing and let them get what they came for. This way both of us would be alive to see tommorow. And as they were leaving I could come out from the side and surprise them. But if so this means they would already have our money and have a good chance of getting away. I might hit one of them, but what if he is not the one with the money.

The thought of just coming out shooting was a choice too. This way I would catch them off guard before they got the money. If I hit first then most likely Mike and I would not get shot. I would also let them know that we are not two little punks on the corner just waiting to be robbed. We already decided that we were going to be serious about getting money when we are out there on the corner. But this will mean I would have to take a chance at killing someone. Since I am sixteen the law would deal with me as an adult. As of now the going rate on murder is about 20 years!

Its funny how fast your mind moves when you are under pressure or just press for time. I don't know if I really made a decission or if my actions were just forced out of me due to my tight situation. If I could compare my actions to someone I guess it would be a person by the name O-Dog from the movie Menace 2 Society. The charcter in this movie was just buck wild. He never really thought to much about anything he did. He really used to just do things by the speare of the moment. Nothig mattered to him. He was the kind of person you could be cool with, but at the same time he was capable of causing trouble. He was nothing but a real product of his environment. Since his living conditions were bad he too was bad. Plus the fact that this person really nevers thinks about the things he is about to do. He pretty much does it by the moment. And since his personality is always wild whenever something is about to happend he will always be the aggressive one.

All I remember is stepping out and hearing rounds of gun shots. The next thing I knew I was dragged in the game room and my partner kept asking for the gun. All I could remember is the pain that ran all up and down my leg. I knew I had been shot but it did not seem as important to me at the time. My mind was really on the money. I wanted to know if the money was still ours. I kept wondering if I had hit one of them. I had already been known in the hood to have a gun. And I was also known to have the heart to pull it out and shoot. But this was my first time getting shot and my first time being in a shootout so close. Most of the time when I had to use my gun I would have them fools running once I began shooting. But this time I was right there in the middle of the whole thing. My eyes were open the whole time the shooting was going on, but it all seemed to be a blurr.

I never feared for my life as I think about it. See when you play the game in the concrete jungle death is one of your chances. I knew that I was subjecting my self to either getting caught by the police or I could be shot and killed. I never would think about it when I was at work. But after hanging out some late nights and someone either got shot it would make me think. I just would rather get shot for a reason than for nothing. I was looked upon by the kids in the hood as I tough guy or some kind of hero. See I stood up for our hood or our corner. Thats what one needs out here in the streets. In the streets your name and your reputation takes you a long way. My man Mike until this day says he owes me his life. I feel I did the thing I had to do. I really don't think my choice was thought out it just happend that way. The way I see it is if I'm going to go out from this world I'm going out fighting. I'll never let it be said that I was afraid of anything not even death itself!

But how did this event of me getting shot change me? It made me realize at the time that this was no game. I was really that drug dealer that would kill if I had to protect my investment. This event put me to the test to see if I really was going to "take no shorts and no shit." I had already said that we were going to be serious about getting money, but this event made words into actions. I was now that criminal in the statistics of America. You can say that this event made me into an O.G. (original gangsta or veteran to the war of the streets). It was like when you pledge a fraternity. The delima of whether or not to come out shooting was the pledging part, and my decision was what determined whether I went over into the fraternity of the hood. You can say that I got my letters (O.G.). The event was like a trial of my manhood, like what the Indians, I hear, went through. Now I was looked upon as a man of the hood or a warrior. This event actually put me deeper into the game, because it earned me respect.

How this event changed me is not the same question as **why** it changed me. I was only 16 at this time and everybody looked up to me like I was some kind of tough guy or hero or something. I fell in love with my new found fame, and I wanted more fame, and to keep my reputation. To keep my reputation of not being afraid of anything, not even death, I had to not care about consequences at all.

When did this event change me? It was all at once and yet slowly too. They are both true, even though logic says its impossible. I was only 16 when this event happened, and it changed me in a negative way. Though I had the body of a man, I was only a child, and a child's mind is very easily manipulated. See, my mind was manipulated by money but also by fame and respect. The way people looked at me—fear, respect, envy—was an incredibly powerful drug for me. Man I didn't want to lose it at any cost. To keep this fame and respect, I had to not care about anything or at least act like I did not care, because you know that no one wants to die or go to jail. As I got older this event along with many others lead me to believe that my life would not last long the way that I was going. I had to change my mentality of not caring about consequences and only caring about self-advancement, to caring about my life along with the lives of others. Else I'd be a dead man.

What does memory include and what does it leave out? What did I leave out in the writing of this story? I didn't say much about my fears. I was afraid that if I didn't come out shooting it would really hurt my reputation and make me look like a punk to Mike and my homies. I didn't talk about how even if I ran to get my homies I would still look like a punk. I really felt at the time that I had no choice but to come out shooting. In the first draft I didn't emphasize that I was backed into a corner and had no real choice about what I could do and still live in the only world I knew at that time. I said that O-Dog, the movie character, was a product of his environment, but I didn't talk about how I too was a product of my environment. Notice that I didn't talk much about whether I hit one of them, and about how this whole kind of life is a form of group suicide.

Why did I omit the things I left out of the first draft? Now I think there were two main reasons why I omitted what I didn't want myself or my reader to see. First, I didn't want to look like a punk or coward. And more importantly, I left out some things so that it did not come back on me politically.

How do I feel now about the person I was before, and is part of me still a criminal? The person that I was before, some people would call an animal. When I was in prison I read Malcolm X's autobiography. Looking back from prison on his life of crime, Malcolm referred to his pre-Muslim self as "an animal." I don't know if I was an animal, but I do know that the life I lived before was a constant hustle and struggle. I did not care about anything, not even death. I was not looking out for our (me and Mike) well being when I came out shooting, because we both could have been shot. If I would've punked out and let them get what they wanted, I would have been looking out for our best interest. I hated living in fear of it all ending at anytime. I always had to watch my back and live with caution, like a wolf being hunted by men. This is how I made it so long, and I still live with caution even now. You can say that in some ways I am still a criminal. I'm still not comfortable sitting with my back to doors, even in college classrooms. There are a lot of people from my past that have a reason to get even with me, especially the children of the people who bought drugs from me. I have children of my own now. When I look at them I think too often about the children I hurt indirectly. That's when I do feel like an animal.

But in some ways I am still a criminal. I still want self-advancement and I'll do whatever I can to get it now, like the big people on Wall Street. Are they really so different from me or the old me? Before, I did whatever it took to get self-advancement. It took, at first, being the best hustler I could be, but now I do whatever I can, like going to college. Patience is needed in college to help me get through hard times, because college almost guarantees me in the future what criminology promised quickly (but at too high a cost). The only difference is the speed of my advancement, because I am going to advance. I also still have the desire for fame and respect. Doesn't everybody?

How can my experience help other criminals to go straight? It can show them that if they stay the way that they are anything can happen. They will be put in situations where they will have to make quick crucial decissions like life or death just to protect their name or reputation. At some point they have to get knocked off the hill. It's inevitable. It's actually a form of suicide. An ugly death must come. Its only a question of when.

Also, my life can show them that there are other ways to get the things they want. It only takes patience. If the dedication they put into their name and reputation was put into getting advancement in whatever, they would not have to put their lives at risk. For a criminal, the price of success on the streets is too high. You can never really enjoy what you get. You know in your heart that its not really yours. It's a price no one will want to pay if they really start to think about it. The problem is, how do we get them to think? Mike is very intelligent, but his thinking will only go in certain channels. How do we get Mike and other criminals to see the big picture? Our society has to find an answer or continue to build more prisons than any other "free" country in the world!

Notice that in his revised or second draft, Brian did not, like Adhita, change his first draft completely. Instead, Brian left his first draft more or less unchanged and simply added answers to the questions he wrote in his revision plan/goals. He also includes a substantial analysis of the story and values contained in the original draft. For some readers, this was an appropriate strategy since the story was so central an illustration of the argument in his paper. For other readers, this choice results in disunity and incoherence. Since this is a revision, not a final draft (the only draft in which Robert requires meshed texts to follow the rule-governed reality of all meshed textual elements), writing teachers who insist on code switching and surface correctness even on working drafts will wonder why the draft still contains so many of what they would see as sentence-level and editing errors not allowed in the academic prose of collegiate culture. Just like Adhita, Brian produced an outline for rewriting his second draft. Brian relied on the outline to guide him to genuine insights, not predictable truisms. What is perhaps most remarkable about this second draft is how willing Brian is to face what he regards as the ambiguity of the idea of "success" in our country. Here we can clearly see an example of a student's attempt to work their way out of the Shock Stage, an attempt was not as evident in Adhita's revision. We know from his essay that Brian really is trying to find his own place in a

US society that doesn't depend on crime and violence. In the end of his revision, Brian refers to "the big people on Wall Street" and comments, "But in some ways I am still a criminal. I still want self-advancement and I'll do whatever I can to get it now, like the big people on Wall Street. Are they really so different from me or the old me?" Brian says he is "still a criminal" in that he'll do "whatever [he] can" to gain success. Brian told his instructor that in his final draft, he would have to clarify exactly what certain phrases mean, especially "I'll do whatever I can to get [success] now" and "the big people on Wall Street. . . . Are they really so different from me or the old me?" Brian's essay ends with his continuing to question who he is becoming based on where he has been and where changes in life and even this essay will lead him. He's using the questions as a means for moving past writer's block, past the Shock Stage and toward Adaptation. Culture shock is always an emotional and epistemological challenge of dissonance with one's new culture in several, and perhaps many, ways. Whether we wish it or not, our writing always announces who we are and what we think and feel.

The answers to these two crucial questions can be constructed in the final draft, in which your students try to identify with their reconceptualization and become a center of communal responsibility. We are asking both you and your students to sky dive intellectually. We don't have to sky dive. We can drop the course. We can quit the job. We can turn away from the activist work of trying to save some element of life on this planet, or even the planet itself, and just quit. But we writers across cultures are brave folk who will probably jump out of the intellectual plane and hope our epistemological and ontological parachutes are sound and will get us to a safe and illuminating place. We writing teachers are constant intellectual skydivers on behalf of our students. We model the Shock Stage by judiciously sharing some of our own writing or orally sharing the dissonances we are trying to face in cross-group communication, which challenges us the most when we open to writer's block and culture shock, allowing us to change significantly, to be coconstructed by the rich, multivoiced environments we are working within in our writing-course community. Notice what the Shock Stage states on the left of the Eddy Model: "Must create a role acceptable to class." Each of us must be allowed to exist in our educational, employment, or activist settings. We must be at least functionally accepted by our groups. If we coconstruct writing communities in our courses, sites of employment and activist venues in which we can all be dynamically and complexly present, then that constitutes each of us having created a role acceptable to the group. For our group(s) in the middle of the Shock Stage, we must remember everything is up for grabs, no one is intellectually safe, and no one can hide. But—we can invent what we want. Students who turn the Shock Stage into a creative experience are those writers who accept the feeling of conceptual disharmony between their home and academic cultures and change their sense of self and society.

Brian is powerful and critically intelligent and will not accept second-class status whether in the street-drug trade or in supposedly legitimate professions within a white-supremacist system. What does college success or professional-group acceptance mean under conditions of white dominance for a determined black man like Brian? Robert and Brian had long mentoring sessions about writing but also about the street, boxing, and Malcolm X. Brian admitted to Robert that the reason he gave time to the mentoring sessions was not Robert's PhD, classroom-teaching experience, time in Africa, or any other professional qualification or experience Robert possesses. Brian said the only reason he was even talking to Robert on career and life choices was because of these things: Robert's being an undefeated former amateur boxer, a teacher of prison writing in several states, a long-term serious student of Malcolm X, and a practicing Muslim when Brian wanted to become Muslim but without giving up any behaviors Islam forbids or discourages. In their last mentoring session, Brian asked Robert, "Be straight with me. Am I a fool with my college success and engineering-company plans in a white-supremacist America that made sure Malcolm was stopped for good?" He and Robert looked at each other, separated by race, separated by generation, but connected by fighting, by intense experience of incarcerated spaces, and by love for Malcolm, and Brian said, "Straight. What are my chances? Am I a fool?" Robert didn't take his eyes off Brian and said, "You can't miss success in college if you keep at it. I would bet it all on that." Brian looked at him a long time. "What about the company deal? Can that happen? How likely?" Robert looked down for one second, and Brian noticed. Nowhere to hide here; only honesty would work. Robert said, "Not impossible but not likely. A black, small, new engineering company staffed by former convicts? Not impossible but not likely." When a student in the middle of college culture shock, especially a first-gen man-of-color former convict pushes for a teacher's real opinion about a life-changing question, issue, or life plan, we owe them our complete honesty, however difficult.

This is wicked-hard work we are asking you to do with students. It is work that affects teaching careers complexly. Your career may experience challenges, detours, and roadblocks because you will not be asking for routine engagement from students and self. It is human to scapegoat when we cannot meet a challenge. It is far easier to give A grades than to ask students to question their operative assumptions. You may see rosters shrink as some students choose lives of monocultural simplicity. This work requires serious engagement with human lives at vulnerable but potentially life-changing moments. Ask yourself what the operant ethos of your teaching is. Why are you teaching writing, which is married to epistemology? Just as the Shock Stage engages by having students question their home cultures, professors must question their pedagogy ontologically. Here is one example. What are our responsibilities to students who are literally migrants, whether documented or not? Some students, more than some writing teachers know, acknowledge, or want to know are economic or political migrants. How is their cross-cultural experience of crossing multiple dangerous borders with the danger of being undocumented at a US college vastly complicating their college work and identity decisions? As writing teachers supporting migrant students navigating risky cultural terrains, what are our responsibilities to them in the midst of their differential experiences of disorientation and alienation? To be writing teachers who do this work of shared fate and acknowledge the total humanity of the people we teach and learn with, in this case the extra vulnerable migrant student, whatever our precise answers to these questions are, the heart of the answer—so we can continue this work honestly—must be to give all we have got and realize their fate is our fate.

7

CONVINCING THE AUDIENCE BY USING EDITED AMERICAN ENGLISH

WHY TEACHING FUNDAMENTALS FOSTERS AUDIENCE AWARENESS

The previous two chapters looked at five types of audiences and how students could use feedback for revision and overcoming writer's block. The five types of audiences serve as wellsprings of response, in an Aristotelian sense, for understanding that language must be adapted for different purposes and different audiences. Now we shift the focus from who it is students are writing for and for what effect to a broader reading community. At some point we must engage students in a discussion of how and why detailed editing of their language choices is crucial not only for their growth as writers but also for their development into intercultural beings. The traditional skills this chapter discusses are reading, grammar, citation, and editing and how mastery of them has been the primary signifier of a writer's fluency with Standard American English. As a former writing center director, Amanda repeatedly had to field criticism from faculty and administrators about the lack of "quality writing" found on campus; this criticism mirrors comments Robert heard at the HBCU he taught at regarding some of his students' linguistic choices. Faculty who assign writing in discipline-specific courses often complain about having to teach or grade writing when their subject-matter expertise lies elsewhere, and they are angry someone else didn't already teach their students how to write. Providing your students with the task of further developing their fundamental composition skills might be crucial for their reception as writers, in the rest of college and in the world of work because humans have a tendency to mistake surface correctness for excellence in writing.

WHAT YOU MUST TEACH YOUR STUDENTS SO THEY ARE CONSIDERED SUCCESSFUL WRITERS

We have discussed composing, soliciting feedback, and handling that feedback when it causes your students to question old assumptions. We

DOI: 10.7330/9781607328742.c007

have talked about global issues. At some point, students must improve their ability to find grammar, citation, proofreading, and other sentence-level errors in their own writing if they want to independently switch back and forth between home and academic language varieties, if code switching is their choice. A continuing outcome of many FYW programs is students locating and editing local issues in their writing *on their own.*

This chapter discusses mastering EAE, the de facto language of white power. Just as your students are newly arrived members to the culture of college, you too may be newly arriving but to the culture of composition studies. Many new teachers, and quite a few who have been at it for years, come to the teaching of writing with preprogrammed assumptions, baggage if you will, about what they think it is they are supposed to teach their students in the weeks, even hours, that make up a semester or quarter. Just as we require our students to write about their own cultural assumptions, we invite you, our readers, to consider some of the assumptions about the culture of teaching FYW that continue to plague our discipline. We ask you to consider assumptions you and we have about the future of teaching EAE at all in FYW, and whether its time has passed.

A common assumption people have about writing professors is that we are not doing our jobs (or that we deserve to lose them) if we don't actively teach the following:

what a unified and coherent paragraph is
what a thesis (topic, transitional, lead-in) sentence is
what an introduction, body, or conclusion paragraph is
how to interpret a literary work
how to find and read professional, usually peer-reviewed, sources
how to fix mistakes like fragments, dangling modifiers, comma splices
how to use an LMS
how to write an email or text message
how to write a narrative or some other mode
how not to plagiarize
how to complete a timed essay
how to spell
how to interpret and respond to someone else's writing

Does your classroom deal with these "problems" day in and day out, or is your time spent asking students to engage in discussions about issues in written and spoken exchanges? In this era of standards and common-core curricula, FYW instructors are expected to assign this busywork. Students are also conditioned to expect to be assigned busywork. It seems that all the players in this game have been preprogrammed to accept this behavior as normal. The success of many FYW instructors' annual reviews have even been determined by their ability to evaluate their students' writing based mostly on the students' attention to surface features rather than on their reasoning. Accreditation and college-wide assessment, as well as *US News* rankings, ensure this behavior much more than can any scholarly research published to the contrary. Whether we accept it or not, students' imprecision with sentence-level errors, citing sources, and proofreading affects their credibility negatively. This is patrician and racist because it clearly values one variety of language use over another. Those who privilege EAE usage believe it must be learned by your students from you, and more important, must be valued by student writers just as it is by the professional world.

It is painful but necessary to remind all teachers of FYW that we must be consciously intentional about how conflicted our position is in a national structure of white dominance and violence. Laura Greenfield reminds us that

> language prejudice is not a figment of the imagination. People across the world form strong opinions in response to the negative assumptions they make about different languages, and those attitudes undoubtedly have material consequences for the opportunities made available to speakers. Nevertheless, a central argument of my chapter is that it is not the language which causes listeners to make assumptions about the speaker, but the attitudes held by the listeners towards the speaker that cause them to extend that attitude towards the speaker's language. Accordingly, changing the language would address merely the symptom of the racial prejudice—not the institutionalized cause. In other words, a stigmatized person will rarely lose her stigmatization completely by adopting—or speaking as a home language—a language of prestige because her body still carries with it the racialized markers people have used to relegate her to the margins to begin with. She may gain a minimal amount of access in certain ways by distancing herself from what white people historically associate with people of color, but doing so does not erase others' white privilege nor bring about institutional change to the larger system that held her up to judgment in the first place (2011, 50).

The question here is, Are we going to work with a racist system of Standard English and EAE or resist it? Amanda and Robert are both in total opposition to our national racist system. We agree that, as Greenfield puts it, "When it comes to 'Standard English' 'error' is racialized rather than seen as linguistic variable and an equal 'difference'" (47). Robert's informed response to the stark choice is to push code meshing and active resistance to EAE. Amanda's approach is connected to her informed commitment that as a professional woman of color, she feels she is leading her students, especially first-generation students, and certainly first-generation students of color, to rhetorical, assessment, and employment slaughter if she doesn't help them to construct as much fluency as they are able in EAE. She uses code switching to train students to intentionally choose which language to use with each audience in their future courses and professional work settings. Amanda believes this provides her students who cannot yet produce EAE the option of choosing meshing in the future. Robert says, in terms of his FYW courses, "If not now, when?" Amanda says, in terms of her FYW courses, "I help them understand EAE now so they can make viable choices for themselves later in courses and employment situations when it counts." Both Amanda and Robert are convinced that the other's position on error or difference and code switching or code meshing is based 100 percent on caring and commitment and a profound sense of responsibility to students, especially the most vulnerable students. Though they take opposite positions about response to EAE and how best to resist systemic racism, their commitment to pluralism and their commitment to their friendship have deepened as they struggle to construct their consciously intentional theory and practice of FYW in terms of language and power. So that's the deal. We ask our readers to be pluralist and respectful as you define or redefine your own positions on these large matters, and especially we ask that readers be understanding and open as early-career FYW teachers position themselves as conscience directs on the difficult matter of how to respond to language and power issues as systemic racism has more and more trouble hiding in a digital universe moving inexorably toward total surveillance. And, quoting J-Love Calderone, Robert says to himself and to other white readers of this book,

> **Don't think you are the exception to the rule; YOU ARE NOT THE COOLEST WHITE PERSON IN THE WORLD!** You are not so different and unique as to warrant a special "cool white-person" pass. Are you still trying to be the ONLY white person in the crew? Do you feel animosity when other "cool" white kids come around and deflate your ego? Do yourself a favor, instead of trying to diss that other white kid, explaining how they fake or whatever, maybe your should take the time to connect with someone who may be similar in some ways to you. Don't push them away or be ashamed, build with them and see them as part of a community within a community (2014, 300–1).

Amanda's goal is helping code-switching students get as close to fluency in EAE as they are able in their FYW course, which might be their last course opportunity to focus on this goal. Robert also wants his students to routinely reproduce the rules of EAE and the rules of AAE and the rules of any other languages they mesh. One category of Robert's vivid memories of the HBCU where he taught and learned for ten blessed years was both the humor and the enormous peer pressure of AAE users corrected the spoken or written errors of careless AAE users, which was frequently done in a not-gentle manner. Rules count in language communities, often in unforgiving ways.

There are better ways to achieve correctness in EAE or any other languages than through skill-and-drill busywork. White privileged views of language instruction hold that FYW instructors have a responsibility to make certain that students *want to produce texts with surface correctness* because of the positive effect it has on readers. The most obvious effect the mastery of correctness produces for students is good grades. We argue that what we really should spend our time teaching students to do can be summed up as

how to compose,
how to revise,
how to ask for help,
how to read,
how and why and when and what to cite, and
how to edit.

We have spent the last six chapters examining the first three items on this list because they are the bulk of what we do teach and are the subject matter in our courses. Attention to sentence-level conventions, and whether they should be addressed at all in FYW, is the focus of this chapter because we know that far too often those are the features the general public is referring to when they claim someone can't write, is illiterate, or is uneducated. These are also the features that carry economic and political power in our wider society. The fact is, people are judged by their language use and choices, especially their ability to use Standard English, so we have an obligation to give students, especially students of color, the skills necessary to master EAE for code switching and meshing.

As in sports, mastery of fundamentals is essential, but we also know the conventions of grammar and usage are arbitrary. No matter how nice the sentences look, how well the words are spelled, or how effectively sources are cited, surface-feature correctness will never carry rhetorical weight if it is used to express platitudes, oversimplifications, and incongruent thought. The arbitrary nature of language conventions is also why we believe that in the not-too-distant future, EAE is going to wind up like Latin. We all know Latin was once the language of power for a select few in the West. Today it is still studied, read, and even on a small scale spoken, but only by a privileged few. We suggest that by the middle of the twenty-first century, EAE is going to wind up like Latin, learned only by those who intentionally study it, leaving it to otherwise fade into oblivion. It won't be required because it will have been replaced with use of language varieties such as coding, visual rhetoric, multimedia authoring, and texting; the revolution has already started. EAE's power is constantly being eroded by a fluid vernacular that bends, breaks, and ignores conventions and rules all the time. Like Latin, EAE will lose its power as fewer and fewer people actually know, understand, or even use its conventions and rules. Each passing decade, as fewer new K–16 English teachers really study EAE grammar, much less understand how to teach it, the shelf life of those aspects of EAE is going to be shortened significantly.

This claim and prediction that EAE is going the way of Latin does not mean that those of us who reject racist structures can bide our time and simply wait until EAE falls or disappears while others do the work, take the risks of resistance, and pay the price of activism. Robert doesn't just "allow" code meshing; he urges all his students to seriously consider its use for their own linguistic, rhetorical, and human wholeness but also as active resistance and group responsibility in support of justice and fairness for all of us, especially disrespected sisters, brothers, and trans folks.

WHY READING MATTERS

All our students come to college already knowing how to read at least for basic comprehension. They could never have been admitted in the first place if they did not have this skill at some level. Even the teachers who claim their students can't understand a reading assignment must know comprehension is usually not the problem. Unfortunately, many professors don't realize our students' success with reading assignments depends on our helping them understand how to read. Too often students are assigned a reading and given no direction about approach. David Sumner notes, "Have we not pleaded with them to read 'critically' without thoroughly explaining the subtlety of the term? The costs of such bad reading habits are lack of understanding and absence of conversation" (2000, 61).

Critical reading is crucial for navigating college for two reasons. First, students will obviously read many and varied texts during their college years, mostly for information. They must read to take tests, engage the material in assignments, choose courses, follow directions, and gain the entry-level core knowledge of their majors. But they also must use reading as a means of being selective about what influences them. Students who are given an assignment without reading instructions allow their eyes to move across the pages and do not remember or internalize what they read. When discussion begins on Monday morning, and the instructor asks a question about the text, is it any wonder the response is a bunch of dead-eyed stares?

Clearly, providing students with reading directions is important for understanding and selecting what to notice about a text. Doing so especially helps students summarize texts. Students can't effectively analyze if they don't read critically. Amanda always tells students what they should look for as they read and asks students to write and share one- to three-sentence summaries of assigned readings before any discussion begins. This activity ensures that all have something to contribute and demonstrates that not all readers notice the same major points. When they find sources for their major essays, Amanda's students write annotated bibliographies, in class, to get more practice in summarizing and citation. Since her students know these activities will take place, they read sources and choose their research knowing they will use reading observations in their assignments. They select sources with a purpose.

Amanda also assigns group work tied to reading, such as a collaborative summary in groups. The first summary is done this way so students learn the skill together before having to do it alone. Amanda asks students to write a summary of a children's fable or story that is widely familiar, such as "The Three Little Pigs." Group members write a summary of the story. Each group shares what they wrote, and the class responds by asking questions about main points left out or places where the summary has too much detail. Then, each group contributes to the summary until the entire class has coauthored a new one using sentences from those written by the small groups. Although this activity may not seem like reading, it really is because they must read each other's summaries, evaluate them, and then coauthor and edit the one written by the entire class. This type of reading gets students to move from writer-based texts to reader-based prose. In this way, reading also plays a role in audience and revision. Students who are creating reader-based prose edit, revise, and are generally aware of how their linguistic and rhetorical choices affect their reader. If students are unable to read their own essays and locate the local as well as global issues to revise and edit, they will never become independent writers.

CONTEXT-BUILDING WRITING ACTIVITY 17
Critical Reading
What do you do when you read? Play music? Feed your cat? Watch TV? Cook dinner? Focus only on the following steps. I ask you to try this the first time you read an assigned text. If you find your old habits produce more successful reading comprehension, do your own thing, by all means. However, these steps ask you to really contemplate what you are thinking before, during, and after you read a text. Plan enough time to read the material more than once. These steps will help you become a critical reader.

Before you start reading the text, spend time looking it over and then do the following:

> Highlight who wrote it, where was it published, and when. Question the validity of the website where you find sources. Who produced the source website? Why? What does the title of the reading (and website) suggest? Do you see any headings, offset text (bold, caps, italics, etc.), key words? Do you need to look any of these up before reading sections of the text where they are used?

> Look for summaries, abstracts, précis, checklists, tables, charts, figures, images, conclusions. What do you notice about these? What major concepts do they introduce or discuss?

After previewing the text, begin reading the text to understand the content and do the following:

> Highlight unfamiliar words (see if you can figure out their meaning based on how they are used instead of stopping to look up every word you don't know). Look up their definition before you read the piece for a second time.

> Look for the author's main purpose and find sentences that demonstrate these.

> Examine the kinds of evidence the author uses. Is it biased? Convincing? Dated?

> Look for signaling of major points. These may serve as quotes in your future essays.

> Highlight any ideas you agree/disagree with, any ideas that surprised you, anything you had a question about or did not understand, any fallacious comments, and anything else that stood out.

After you finish reading the first time, do the following:

> Go over your notes and look at what you highlighted. Summarize, without using the text, the main points. What is your reaction? What do you remember as the main idea(s) you agreed with (or not)? How does the reading reflect your own experiences, home culture, values, and beliefs? What can you relate to in what you read? What did you learn from reading the piece?

Find the definition for each word you noted during your first reading of the text. Reread just those sentences with the definition in hand. Do you understand the word now? You may need to read a few sentences before and after the one that contains the word to get the context of how the word is used. Remember, words often have multiple meanings, so your first application of the definition you find may not be the appropriate one.

Reread the piece a second time. This time use your notes and let them help you get a better grasp of the meaning of the text. See if there is anything new that you learned or that you still need to look up to help you understand what you read.

WHY TEACHING CITATION MATTERS

Citation matters because it is part of the academic culture that promotes original scholarship and correct attribution of sources. It matters because it enables students to experience the pleasure of acknowledging indebtedness using the standards of the profession. If we want students to gain confidence with that most difficult genre of academic culture, the researched essay, it is imperative that they learn the customs of that culture, such as citing sources correctly. In doing so, your students will join the myriad conversations about the topics they explore in their essays. Most important, they won't be guilty of plagiarism. Many students flounder as they try to incorporate the ideas of brilliant others into their essays. Both Amanda and Robert have encountered students who claim that they copied and pasted directly from a source because it said a point better than they could. However, if students approach research as an opportunity to pursue *their own* interest in a required subject, the typical fear of research will dissipate. They will overcome fears of research by seeing it as a team sport in which they don't plagiarize what everyone else has said about the topic. Help your students see that their role is *adding to* an existing academic conversation instead of assuming they must try to create single handedly something called "new knowledge." Accordingly, your students must choose to research topics important to them.

USAGE: DISEMBODIED PARTS, OR THE SUM OF THE WHOLE

Erika Lindemann reminds us that "classtime is wasted when students spend too much time analyzing sentences someone else has written instead of generating their own. Classtime is also wasted if it's devoted exclusively to labeling sentence types or various phrases and clauses. Such lessons teach terminology—*what* to call the construction—not writing—*how* to create the constructions" (1987, 131). As a profession, we have concluded that students do not learn usage and grammar from worksheets and standardized tests, and yet they persist in teaching materials across the United States. Clauses, phrases, word choice, and the like are the limbs on the composition body. They work best when connected to other working parts. It is a waste of time, and for some students demoralizing, to be assigned workbook exercises that are decontextualized from their own writing.

The mistakes busywork is supposed to eradicate are actually usage errors. They are sentence fragments and misspelled or incorrectly used words. They are misplaced modifiers, vague referents, and tense shifts. They are often the sentence-level mistakes that are called *grammar errors* (we know they usually aren't) and that are used to justify lowering grades. Our students come to first-year writing assuming that if they can fix these errors, their essays will get As. We know better. Yet, as a profession, we continue to give this philosophy validity by devoting time and energy to sentence-level errors. We only have ourselves to blame for students mistaking editing for writing when the feedback we give leads students to believe that editing errors is the most important or valuable type of revision.

The best way to teach surface-error editing, such as removing comma splices, is by pointing them out once they are in the essay of a student who writes them. Since we are the subject-matter experts, we must find the patterns of error our students commit individually and make them aware of those errors. When she grades the first essay in her classes, Amanda always adds an end comment that includes a list of the three errors that are repeatedly present. Then she explains why and where those errors appear in the essay. During conferences, she even demonstrates multiple ways of rewriting the sentence to remove the error(s). This activity is important so authors see there is rarely just one way to rewrite something. After helping with the first sentence, Amanda asks the student to find the next error and rewrite the sentence, demonstrating applied learning. While this method is time consuming, it works. Robert uses a similar method. Before he returns final drafts, he circles surface errors so students can see them. Then he requires the students to find, using their textbook, the rule the error violates. Then students must explain the error and are told they can't use excuses like "I was lazy or drunk." He expects answers like "I confused the EAE rules of contraction with possession" or "Though it is my native language, I messed up the AAE subject-auxiliary inversion in the embedded wh-clause." They then are expected to edit those errors in this correction list before the final draft is accepted and the paper assignment is completed. Since Robert is committed to code meshing for students who freely choose it, this correction list includes not just EAE but any and all Englishes and languages the writer meshes. If there is a form of English or a language Robert does not know, he gets help from colleagues. Robert suggests to readers of this text who support code meshing that when colleagues accept employment in a new location, their planning and adjustment must include arranging a formal agreement with other colleagues committed to meshing that they will share their language literacies in responding to student drafts and help each other cover areas of nonliteracy. But how does a novice teacher differentiate between EAE and correct usage in another variety of English? In keeping with the above advice of literacy sharing with colleagues, novice teachers of FYW who for the first time are inviting students to code mesh must formalize a shared collegial exchange in which several novice teachers share the challenge of perceiving and appreciating differences in correct usage in several varieties of English. Some of the best "consultants" such two- or three-person teams of novice teachers can add to their resources are the students who do the meshing. Seek their help, even in front of the class, in determining differences in correct usage in their varieties of English meshed in the student text. Robert still uses such teamwork to remind everyone we are all teachers and students together. Some of the best moments of simple discovery and understanding of difference happen at such simple moments of human sharing of words, identity, and meaning beyond rigid "teacher" and "student" designations. Robert highly recommends this activity.

Although usage errors should not be the primary focus of our evaluation of students' writing, Amanda believes they should affect the grade only in a revision because the expectation is they will be edited out. Robert, who does not grade until the final course portfolio, accepts the correction list, when done correctly, as relieving him of the task of lowering the final course grade, especially when the final research writings of the course have few or no usage issues in any of the meshed languages.

WHEN WRITING ISN'T WRITING:
GRAMMAR, USAGE, AND HISTORY

Much of the feedback most students have received on their writing before taking our classes is commentary about usage errors. Too often instructors unpack their old baggage, giving undirected feedback just like they themselves received from their primary- and secondary-school English teachers. Although we have over fifty years of published scholarship about this issue, there are thousands of English teachers at every academic level who still refer to sentence-level errors as grammar errors when we know full well that 90 percent of those errors are actually usage errors. No wonder our students are worried about their grammar and think that if they just fix their grammar errors, they will earn As. In her seminal work, *A Rhetoric for Writing Teachers*, Lindemann provides both an historical overview and a literature review of the major composition studies that explain the difference between usage and grammar; most conclude that formal grammar instruction not only does not improve writing ability but takes time away from writing. She notes, "People who don't understand linguistic principles generally confuse the terms *grammar* and *usage*" (1987, 99). Few instructors actually teach their students the difference. Lindemann explains that humans acquire their "intuitive" grammar skills "by about age five" (99), and these skills should be understood as distinct from "traditional grammar, for example, [which] represents an accumulation of terms, rules, and methods for analyzing what we do when we use language" (99). The studies all reveal that the teaching of grammar is only useful for learning grammar, not for learning to compose. Richard Braddock, Richard Lloyd-Jones, and Lowell Schoer (1963) conclude that unless grammar instruction occurs within the context of discussing actual student drafts, it has no effect on the teaching of writing. This lack of contextualization also accounts for why so many students can "pass" standardized tests, such as Compass and Accuplacer, but have trouble writing coherent paragraphs. Anyone who has taught for more than one academic year has encountered a student in first-year writing who clearly isn't prepared but was placed into the class based on a standardized test score. Often teachers use the term *grammar* when they are actually referring to usage. Lindemann describes usage as "linguistic etiquette" (99) or "so-called standard English, implying that there's an absolute right and wrong way to use the language" (100). Lindemann was one of the first scholars to note that judging a student's usage as right/wrong or standard/nonstandard is a form of linguistic imperialism and intolerance. She writes, "Generally, the value judgments we make about another's [language use] are ethnocentric; that is, they assume the superiority of our own dialect . . . [and question] the intelligence or heritage of others. It is this tendency we must resist, in ourselves and in our students, for the judgments we make about another person on the basis of language reflect personal values, not linguistic facts" (1987, 102). While these studies are obviously quite old, we revisit them for two reasons. First, they go to our claim that the rules of EAE have always been arbitrary and used to undervalue other language varieties. Second, EAE's time may have passed when its rules are not being directly taught because even the teachers don't understand them.

THE LAST STEP: HOW EDITING CAN
DEHUMANIZE OR EMPOWER STUDENTS

At the end of the previous chapter, we ask why you are teaching. We ask because your teaching philosophy determines how you approach this chapter and whether you are ready to embrace an intercultural pedagogy by rejecting the presumption that EAE is the only valuable variety we should teach. Robert and Amanda are experienced writing teachers and are no longer uncertain about their philosophies of teaching. Otherwise, they would never have coauthored this book. They are certain students learn to write by reading and writing a lot and from receiving genuine feedback on their writing from multiple audiences. Students also learn by understanding that their agency as writers reveals itself when they choose to use whichever variety of English they wish while also understanding that doing so may result in a less-than-desired effect. Students learn to write by being allowed multiple opportunities to rewrite and even to fail. Students learn to revise by learning to critically read their own writing for its successes and failures. Both Amanda and Robert provide a type of correction list of usage errors in formal papers because if a student linguistically explains an error, they enrich their control of the rule-governed human languages they use and are judged by. Just as genuine revision and feedback must be taught, so too must genuine editing.

The academy and the world in general judge us by how we write. For students of color, this is particularly true. Recent composition scholars, such as Vershawn Young and Cristina Kirklighter, have noted how, in crucial ways, mastering editing in several Englishes, including EAE, means affirming that "multidialectical literacy is where our culture is headed" (Young et al. 2014, 7). The inherent value of any text is culturally constructed by those with the most power. Mastery of the text is a sign of privilege. Students from underrepresented backgrounds most need to learn to edit and proofread for surface errors because those are the first things readers notice about a text and may be the only thing they remember. Readers don't want to struggle with texts; they can't and won't bother getting past surface features to your point if they don't have to. Surface errors often lead to negative first and last impressions. This aspect of editing is also important to us as teachers in regard to peer response. We must ask ourselves how and when the gender or race of the author affects the feedback they receive from peers. How does the race, gender, or other identity marker of a respondent affect the feedback they are able to give? Mastery of usage, then, presents a final marker of students choosing when to accept the new academic culture.

THE SHOCK STAGE FOR TEACHERS

Early in this book, we used the metaphor of culture as a backpack of essentials. We noted how some suggest, especially assimilationists, that people must "lose their baggage" in order to grow. We also said we disagree with that notion since it suggests people must lose or give up part of who they in order to change. Instead, we believe that if we extend this metaphor, we don't replace bags but instead continually add to our collection of them. In other words, we may start out life with just a backpack, but over time, we add specialized luggage such as hat boxes, trunks, carry-on roller bags, duffles, briefcases, and the like. Just as different writing styles and types and modes won't work for all situations, we know some bags suit a purpose better than others. As with travel luggage, we believe life and learning are additive processes of accumulation, adding to our base, not merely tossing out all we had before. However, even this metaphor only works so well. If we go through life constantly adding on new types of luggage, we won't learn to evaluate which are the most valuable for our needs. We suggest an alternate metaphor: the operating system.

Students aren't the only ones who need to question their role and world. Novice teachers might be entering a Shock Stage of their own about their own pedagogy instead of the Shock Stage of the writing process your students experience. Unlike luggage we purchase, we get our operating system from family, friends, and the home culture we were raised in. In the case of teaching, your operating system came with programs from your training, your own days as a student, and education. You have been programmed to teach using certain methods and materials, often based on your own experiences as a student. These experiences may explain your compulsion to hang on to EAE for dear life. Historically, computers ran off code that was placed on either punch cards or magnetic tapes. More recently, operating systems have been hardwired onto motherboards and serve as the command centers for computers. They determine which programs run or don't run. A computer has its own operating system that can't be discarded because the computer depends on it. As teachers, too often we fall back on the old operating system and would benefit from an upgrade in our programming. We hope this book helps make that happen.

We believe the purpose of learning is creating independent, critical thinkers who can question their own and others' assumptions of how the world operates. It is an operant ethos for human interaction. James Baldwin writes, "The paradox of education is precisely this—that as one begins to become conscious one begins to examine the society in which he is being educated. The purpose of education, finally, is to create in a person the ability to look at the world for himself, to make his own decisions, to say to himself this is black or this is white, to decide for himself whether there is a God in heaven or not. To ask questions of the universe, and then learn to live with those questions, is the way he achieves his own identity" (1985, 326). Practicing intercultural teaching has led Robert and Amanda to realize we are all wayfarers. We know we have a vocation, and it is our job to help our students discover, develop, realize their potential, embrace failure, and share their tentative grappling with academic culture. We know critical thinkers use writing as a way of understanding the world and our place in it. If teaching first-year writing becomes more than a job or career for you too, you will also have to continually learn again how to teach writing. "If you accept this profession—this calling, this vocation," as Donald Murray writes, "you [will] have apprenticed yourself to a lifetime of learning" (1985, 5). Just as culture is not ideologically safe, neither is teaching. Enjoy the highs as well as the challenges; they will both continue to shape who you have been, who you are, and who you are becoming.

8

THE ADAPTATION STAGE
Final Drafts and Congruence

The Adaptation Stage of the Eddy Model of Intercultural Experience is the point in the Eddy method at which students produce a final draft. Here they become a center of communal responsibility to the course and culture. They become a spokesperson for their subject and point of view. This new culture, for which they are now, in part, responsible, includes their composition classmates and instructor but is not limited to one exclusive classroom. The American college learning space in general is their new culture, and its academic language includes the key characteristics of being skeptical, analytical, and critical.

By finishing paper one at all well, students will have learned more than they realize about their topic and about the methodologies of academic thinking and writing. To a far greater degree than will be apparent to them yet, academic language is becoming their language; it is becoming the way they look at the world of ideas and at everyday life.

Being skeptical, analytical, and critical means taking nothing at face value, especially our own points of view. We subject them to constant scrutiny and revision as new knowledge is acquired and as new theoretical or hypothetical positions become known to us. We look for ways to clarify, deepen, and expand our thinking, even at the cost of having to challenge old and even beloved attitudes that simply can't stand up in the face of careful and systematic academic analysis.

In the Adaptation Stage of finishing paper one, students in very real ways become a center of communal responsibility to their classmates and instructor. They probably ended up knowing more about the subject of paper one than anyone in the course. In writing the paper, they needed to be fair to all sides and open to new knowledge, but, in addition, they needed to be aware of what is at stake when writers even indirectly challenge conventional and comfortable thinking about any widely held beliefs. Their responsibility of taking readers beyond comfort zones into the uncertainty of real questioning, where they really don't know what answers, tentative positions, or disconcerting issues might emerge, is the

DOI: 10.7330/9781607328742.c008

essence of academic analysis and of their responsibility to their readers. Moreover, your students need to make it clear what their own position is on the subject they are writing about rather than claiming an objectivity only a computer can assert. Rather than claiming objectivity and then conveniently hiding their own point of view and how it influences the way they gather evidence, students decide what to look at and what to ignore. How the "knowledge" they affirm in their paper upholds their own preferred beliefs is crucial in demonstrating their claim to be fair, open, and honest.

To many faculty, academic discourse should be the scientific method of society at large and of democracy in general. But this faculty ideal is often oppressive. Academic discourse rejects more than what it considers poorly argued. It also rejects what it considers unimportant or undesirable. Unusual voices that try to enter the academic conversation, especially those that try to change it, do not have an easy time. On the one hand, this difficulty is as it should be. Ideally, academic discourse—which is the scientific method "objectively" pursued, scientists would say, or "fairly" pursued, humanists would say—wants to weigh the evidence carefully and fairly before it accepts opinions as facts or considers new theories and interpretations as worthy of further attention and development. Academic discourse, if it is to be truly scientific and if it is to stay healthy and open to new points of view, requires perpetual review. Academic discourse, thus, is characterized by both the need for criticism and the fear of it. It needs criticism and constant review because if we are to make sense of the world, we cannot have faith in those in power and in the status quo; we must question them constantly. But academic discourse fears criticism because of loss of power if other voices become influential or even simply heard in the academic conversations in books, journals, conventions and, most especially, college courses.

Unusual voices that try to enter the conversation of academic discourse, especially those that try to change it, are excluded, ignored, attacked, or misrepresented in our systemically racist structure. Here the dissonant voice of the Eddy chart is crucial, and the next chapter focuses on the dissonant voice. But having experienced the Shock Phase and taking paper one through revisions, with responses from family, friends, classmates, tutors, and instructors, your students will have joined conversations that can become coalitions of activism in students' possible futures. By talking to people from different groups, your students will have begun situating themselves formally, theoretically, and practically in the conversations in, through, and by which our society evolves a continuing or changing sense of who we are, what kind of society we want to be or become, and what kind of society we are right now. They might think these issues of definition are settled or beyond their control. They are not. Any national culture trying to become a multiracial democracy is constantly defining itself. As your students continue to evolve a sense of what their college major will be, and to focus the possibilities of their future career or careers, they must consider where the dissonant voice comes from and what roles they play, or should play, in academic discourse and in conversations outside the academy. In the next chapter, we come back to dissonant voices when we discuss the Reentry Stage.

ADAPTATION AND RECONCEPTUALIZATION

In the previous two chapters, we dealt with students' increasing participation in the college writing processes as they obtained responses to drafts and learned the value of editing. As they received feedback, students needed to judge it. To comprehend such responses, students began to understand that they had to make a deeper effort to interpret interactions in class. After analyzing all responses to their draft, they needed to decide which they should reject as irrelevant or not helpful and which to accept. They also needed to consider which they would partially accept, in altered form. To answer these questions required more than analyzing the paper. They asked themselves, What did I accomplish and fail to accomplish in each draft? What do I want to aim for in further drafts? To arrive at the strongest possible final draft, which is the subject of this chapter, they need to do more than ask questions about their paper and subject. They must also ask questions about audience: minimally, their audience is their classmates and instructor. In the broader sense, it is the academic community itself, which is why editing is so important. Sloppy or inattentive editing usually causes readers to dismiss any author's claims outright.

In chapter 6 we dealt with the Shock Stage of the writing process: culture shock and writer's block. Your students came face to face with the inescapable reality that they had to create a role acceptable to the class. What does that mean? They had to take a stand in their revised draft. They had to declare themselves, to say, "Here I am; this is what I am arguing." They had to be allowed to exist in the community. They realized they would not be allowed to argue a position that was counter to the ideals of the academic community: dispassionate search for truth, assemblage of evidence others can scrutinize, arrival at reasonable conclusions others might agree or disagree with. What would be an example of a role and argument that would put a writer outside the academic community? Here's one: any attempt to argue that the Holocaust did not happen. Such a stance screams ignorance and prejudice over inescapable historical truth.

Why are culture shock and writer's block connected? In trying to create a role acceptable to the class, to the ideal of college work at its best, your students naturally fear self-exposure and real questions. They ask themselves, Will I be accepted as a member of the group? Will someone respond to my draft by pointing out that I am stupid, racist, sexist, classist, or homophobic? They especially fear the reconceptualization they must construct in order to revise their writing because it leads them to wonder, Where will reconceptualization lead me? Who or what will I become?

In this chapter, we deal with the Adaptation Stage, the time when, and place where, students create a role as a center of communal responsibility. They demonstrate responsibility for classmates on their topic. The subject matters; the people in the course matter. They are interacting with classmates in such a way as to affirm the search for more truth in their subject and their classmates' subjects. Hopefully they are learning respect for other voices and other viewpoints, so long as everyone remains committed to search for truth, the bedrock value of academic discourse.

In this Adaptation Stage, your students will produce a final draft through identification with reconceptualization, which evolves in response to the varied feedback they receive. The final draft represents the optimum degree of congruence they can develop at this time and place with their chosen subject.

What is congruence? How much can you aim at? How much should you be satisfied with? What might complete congruence look like? Congruence, according to Edward T. Hall,

> is a pattern of patterns. Congruence is what all writers are trying to achieve in terms of their own style, and what everyone wants to find as he moves through life. . . . Complete congruence is rare. One might say that it exists when an individual makes full use of all the potentials of a pattern. Lincoln's Gettysburg Address is an example. . . . Usually it is a matter of going over and over a statement and making it clearer and clearer so that finally everything fits and nothing comes between what is being communicated and the audience. (1973, 134)

If complete congruence is "full use of all the potentials of a pattern," what response in writer or reader might complete congruence create? Hall answers that on the "highest level the human reaction to congruence is awe or ecstasy" (135). Every writer would surely love readers to respond with "awe or ecstasy," but Hall uses such extravagant language because he believes "the drive toward congruity would seem to be as strong a human need as the will to physical survival" (139).

It is a large claim to say the "drive toward congruity" is as strong as the will to survive. But let us at least acknowledge that the desire to achieve congruence brings out the best in us. Moreover, the group behavior of a student-writer, moving toward congruence, seeing the self as a center of communal responsibility, encourages classmates to develop teamwork that will be vital to their individual college and career successes. We need to work together for a future of multiracial equality. Striving for congruence, which finally is a social experience, is the key to the team spirit we need to develop in this country. Each student can make a difference in their own life by reorienting or reinventing the self as a team player.

For now it is important to realize that in some powerful ways, the Adaptation Stage is a useful fiction or an unreachable but encouraging ideal. In intercultural experience or in writing, do we ever attain complete congruence? Even when we complete a piece of writing with a group, and we are done and it went well, do we experience total identification with the reconceptualization? Probably not. We are historically contingent, dialogical beings who are multiple amphibians forever bending and flowing in multiple environments of competing ideologies, so, yes, congruence isn't complete and total. However, one thing is for sure: there are deadlines and there are "final drafts." A final draft means "I, we, cannot make the text any stronger" and/or "We ran out of time because of the deadline." Final drafts are real. As the section on the left side of the Eddy Model about self as center of communal responsibility shows, our final draft, our best effort at congruence, is profoundly communal. We complete the work for our activist group, for our employment team's collective success, for our writing course to see and approve our best effort. In these ways we each in our turn become, yes, temporarily but meaningfully and in a real world, self as center of communal responsibility.

BLOCKS TO CONGRUENCE IN THE FINAL DRAFT

Someone who has produced a revised draft after having gone through the Shock Stage of Intercultural Experience and writer's block is close to being finished with their paper. This writer has faced the questions, Where will reconceptualization lead? and Who will I become? The writer seeks to become a center of communal responsibility on their subject.

What blocks congruence for this writer is an undefined abstraction, a logical fallacy, or an unexamined alternative explanation. Let's look at these concepts.

Undefined Abstractions

It is best to use concrete and clear language. Undefined abstractions are vague. They indicate the writer assumes their connotation of the abstraction is the only one or the correct one. This is a form of talking to yourself and assuming there is agreement about the meaning of the word when there might be little or none. In the revised draft of Adhita's paper, some undefined abstractions remain, and they weaken her argument. Let's look at them.

We'll begin with the title. What does "Being" mean? Does it refer to the religious status quo? Does "Being" indicate hatred of any change? Wouldn't we appreciate a clear definition early in the paper? In paragraph six we get a pretty good definition, but would most readers be willing to wait that long? Similarly, in the third paragraph, Adhita introduces the phrase "the realms of God's absolute reality." We have no clear sense at all of what the phrase means. Paragraph three also presents the following undefined abstractions: "cultural suicide" and "neo-colonial." They must be defined if Adhita is to complete her analysis. Writers should not make their reader wait to receive concrete definitions of their key abstractions unless there is a good rhetorical reason. Abstractions should be defined when first introduced.

Before the writing the final draft, Adhita visited her composition professor and a professor of Islamic studies during their office hours. Both pointed out the need to clarify abstractions. To clarify "Being" in her title, Adhita added one sentence to the end of the first paragraph of the paper. After you read these paragraphs, ask yourself whether this change is enough or whether you want/need a more developed discussion than either version provides the reader?

Old Form of Paragraph One

> The Islamic attitude toward modernization is greatly affected by their belief in the purity of the soul and the beauty of creation. It is affected by the concept of being in God's world now, and perceiving its reality. If all and everything are pure creations of God, then where is the need to change?

New Form of Paragraph One

> The Islamic attitude toward modernization is greatly affected by their belief in the purity of the soul and the beauty of creation. It is affected

by the concept of being in God's world now, and perceiving its reality. If all and everything are pure creations of God, then where is the need to change? The word "Being" in my title and in this paper does not imply an unthinking Islamic rejection of change, but instead points to the Islamic emphasis on the unfolding of one's consciousness of God's perfect being in this world.

How does this revision work for you as a reader? As an instructor of writing? If you prefer one version over the other, why? Adhita dealt with the three abstractions in paragraph three by simply eliminating the first abstraction—"the realms of God's absolute reality"—altogether and by defining "cultural suicide" and "neo-colonial." Let's again observe the changes she made and ask ourselves if the changes ring "true" or seem forced onto the rest of the paragraph.

Old Form of Paragraph Three

> If the Islamic nations are to modernize with the consent of their populations at large, then they must modernize Islamically. The process must work within the realms of God's absolute reality, or else modernization will lead to religious and cultural suicide. It is neo-colonial to expect western modernizations to work in Islamic cultures.

New Form of Paragraph Three

> If the Islamic nations are to modernize with the consent of their populations at large, then they must modernize Islamically. This process must embody Islamic emphasis on God's primacy in human consciousness, or else modernization will lead to religious and cultural suicide. Cultural suicide is the act of ignoring the key values of your culture when it is influenced by Western technologies. It is neo-colonial to expect western modernizations to work in Islamic cultures, if imported wholesale and with little or no regard for Islamic values. Neo-colonial here means assuming the absolute superiority of Western Technological culture compared to other cultures that are less technologically advanced. Technological advances, whether Western or otherwise, do not necessarily demonstrate moral, social or cultural superiority.

Instead of accepting the feedback as a way to reconceptualize who she will become, congruence is blocked in Adhita's final draft because she is unable or unwilling to interrupt Shock Stage thinking to realize a student-writer's full analysis of her subject. She will repeat this pattern when attempting revision due to the other blocks as well.

Logical Fallacies

Logical fallacies are reasoning errors that prevent or weaken clear thinking. There are books that name, categorize, and define dozens and dozens of errors in logical thinking. Often in logic or critical-thinking textbooks, the logical fallacies retain their Latin names. For those of us who see logic as an integral part of teaching the rhetorical situation, notations in the margins of your student's papers that their analysis is based on the post hoc ergo propter hoc fallacy aren't unheard of. The Latin here—"after this, therefore because of this"—is the fallacy of assuming a cause-and-effect relationship exists simply because of a chronological relationship. Your students, however, might be tempted to respond to your comment with tu quoque, or "you too!" However, they then would then be guilty of committing the fallacy of charging an opponent with a similar crime.

Some logical fallacies are well known, and their names are self-explanatory: *distortion, false analogy, hasty conclusion, name calling, over-simplification,* and *sweeping generalization.* Other logical fallacies are associated with debate and politics, although they too appear in college papers. Examples are *red herring* and *slippery slope.* A red herring is a concern put forward to divert attention from the real issue. Slippery slope is a scare tactic that tries to appeal to "common sense." It is the fallacy that a certain vote, choice, or action will inevitably lead to future more negative actions. An example might be lowering the drinking age. A slippery slope argument is the argument that such a change in the law would create more alcoholics in society. This claim is easily disputed using the evidence provided by societies like France, where significant numbers of young children drink wine at meals with their families yet do not become alcoholics. Each act or potential act must be judged on its own merits. Unsupported assertions must be rejected.

Each logical fallacy is a different form of the act of refusing to acknowledge complexity. Each fallacy is also a failure to admit one's opponents might have some truth that should be presented to see a subject fully and fairly. As we continue examining drafts by Adhita and Brian, we will see which fallacies they commit and how they remove or choose not to remove these errors in logic from their essays. It is crucial to affirm that revising for errors in logic is an important part of teaching our students ethos.

Perhaps the three most common logical fallacies in first-year college papers are ad hominem, appeal to authority, and either-or. The ad hominem fallacy, sometimes called *poisoning the well* or *genetic fallacy*, involves attacking your opponent's character rather than ideas or argument. The literal Latin is "against the man."

The appeal-to-authority fallacy is the other side of the ad hominem fallacy. Here one implies that an eminent person's views are true simply because of the person's great reputation. Ideas and arguments must be judged on their merits, not by the public's often-shifting judgments of a famous person's character or celebrity.

The either-or logical fallacy is common in first-year college papers and is the most serious in preventing balance and insight because it precludes middle ground. Either-or thinking avoids different voices. It divides the world into only two voices, and actions are limited to this or that. The world and most subjects are wildly too complex to be stereotyped in this way. Either-or thinking is an intellectual closet shutting out the fresh air of the many voices and human texture of complexity and nuance.

The either-or logical fallacy is labeled as the *false dilemma* because there are more than two possibilities to most debates. Such oversimplifications lead to obscuring rather than opening up the full landscape of a subject.

Adhita was asked by her composition professor whether she was engaged in either-or thinking in her title itself—"Being Vs. Becoming." She decided to "think about it" and resisted the urge to give an instant answer of self-justification. She reread her paper to answer the question fully.

In deciding whether her paper and title were either-or thinking, Adhita began to have a powerful sense of her communal responsibility to her subject and audience, especially to her classmates, who might indeed be influenced in fundamental ways by her treatment and presentation of Islam. She had a renewed desire to be fair and thorough. Adhita remembered her interactions with classmate Karen in their travelog journals in which Adhita began to feel she needed to open up her thinking more and admit how complicated her subject is. Adhita knew she needed to avoid stereotypical thinking, to resist blinking away complexity and hiding from life in the mole-like attempt to produce certainty where an open give and take is what's needed. Real academic discourse is concerned with relationships of fact and theory. It does not accept an idea without vigorously looking at the evidence from as many sides as possible.

After many additional readings, Adhita decided her paper was not based on either-or thinking and that it acknowledged the complexity of her subject with as much thoroughness as she could muster at this point in her college career. Although Adhita did compose additional material to add to her ending, she felt her fundamental distinction of the religion of technological progress in the West that causes a worship of change and becoming for their own sakes was accurate, and that Islam's sense of Being is an ideal that—to varying degrees of course—structures the identity of Islamic communities in the Middle East and perhaps elsewhere. When we examine Adhita's final draft in this chapter, you can consider whether her conclusion and additions adequately resolve her errors in logic.

CONTEXT-BUILDING WRITING ACTIVITY 18

Identifying Fallacies

This activity allows students to work together to apply their understanding of the definitions of various common fallacies. Assign yourself into groups of three. Work together and identify all the possible fallacies committed in the following essay. Make sure one member is the note taker. Another person should fact check the definitions of the fallacies. Another person should act as the spokesperson who will share your answers with the entire class when we discuss our findings. Your group must state/identify each fallacy in each sentence by name. Then, explain how the sentence commits each of the fallacies. Label the sentences with numbers. Don't list the fallacy unless you are sure it is being committed. Some sentences have no fallacies in them; most are guilty of committing multiple fallacies. Be sure and identify all of them.

Example of answer format:

Paragraph four
Sentence one: appeal to authority; Ruth being woman of the year
Sentence two: fallacy name; reason
etc.

WHY I THINK ABORTION IS SWELL

Sally L.

First of all, let me get right to the point without beating around the bush and mincing words: I like abortion. All abortions should be free for all women. The government should pay for it. After all, the government pays for everything else we use to make life easier, such as highways and Amtrak. Abortions certainly do more good than trains.

If women could get free abortions on demand, the birthrate would drop. This would cause the population to decrease and therefore the crime rate would drop. With fewer people in the world, there would be less pollution and the lines at the bank would be shorter too.

I know some people are opposed to abortion because they think it is murder, but no woman has ever been convicted of murder for having an abortion. Besides, God must allow unborn babies to die because he invented miscarriages. You can't argue with God.

My cousin Ruth had an abortion once and she was later named "Woman of the Year" by her bridge club, so abortions don't make you a bad person. Anyone who thinks abortions are a sin is obviously an uneducated cretin who is living in the past. Just because they didn't have abortions in biblical times doesn't mean it's evil. Jerry Falwell said, "What if Mary had had an abortion? We would have no Jesus!" All I can say is that if Mrs. Falwell had had an abortion, we would have no Jerry. I rest my case.

Unexamined Alternative Explanations

The third and final category of blocks to congruence in a final draft, after undefined abstractions and logical fallacies, is unexamined alternative explanations, which block the student's full analysis of the subject. We look at three alternative explanations Brian needed to consider in order to achieve congruence in his final draft:

1. apparent absence of a sense of guilt
2. his self-definition as a "veteran of the war of the streets"
3. the issue of personal and group suicide

Brian said very little about feeling any guilt for the harm he caused people directly through overt violence and indirectly through selling drugs. At the following point in his paper, he does admit to feeling guilt:

I'm still not comfortable sitting with my back to doors, even in college classrooms. There are a lot of people from my past that have a reason to get even with me, especially the children of the people who bought drugs from me. I have children of my own now. When I look at them I think too often about the children I hurt indirectly. That's when I do feel like an animal.

Brian drops the subject just at the point at which he might have helped himself and readers understand that guilt could represent conscious commitment to going straight and living a constructive life to make amends for the trauma and destruction he caused.

Brian's comparison of the illegal drug trade to Wall Street represents a rejection of guilt and therefore a refusal to accept full responsibility for what he did. Such serious blurring of key distinctions opens a door to future possible relapses into crime.

When Brian's writing teacher made the above comments to him in a private meeting during office hours, Brian was annoyed and angry at first. Even though the professor, whom Brian felt closeness to and trust in, tried to be earnest, professional, and sensitive, but not censorious, Brian still reacted to the profoundly personal and quietly challenging nature of the criticism of his paper and of his past with anger and frustration. Several days after the meeting with his professor, Brian composed an additional paragraph to end his essay because he felt it was necessary to address and not ignore his professor's comments. As we saw with Adhita, the additional material becomes the essay's conclusion. When you read the final draft later in this chapter, ask yourself whether it seems fully integrated into the essay or more tacked on.

In response to the issue of the second unexamined alternative explanation—his self-definition as a "veteran of the war of the streets"—Brian responded to comments from a peer tutor about the explanation of the shooting-scene portion of Brian's revised draft. The peer tutor, whom Brian had grown to admire, made the following comments about that section of Brian's paper:

> In the material you showed me from your composition instructor, he refers to the need for you to consider "unexamined alternative explanations" of key points in your revised draft before you could feel that you had truly finished your paper. Brian, you asked me to respond in writing to what I consider the most important place in your paper where you need an alternative explanation. You asked me to be straight. Here goes. . . .
>
> I find it outrageous when you compare a shootout in the street to pledging a fraternity. I can guess why you did it. Every once in a while you hear in the news about a fraternity going too far with hazing or some related foolishness. But when you say that protecting your drug money by risking the lives of all the people present at that scene, money gotten from pathetic drug addicts whose children are pushed to the limit, or beyond, of hunger, abuse or rage, in part because of the action of wolves like you were, to me it just is too much to accept. You need to produce an alternative explanation, or at least an additional one. I really think you need to face the music and tell the truth, not try to beautify or rationalize a fire fight as somehow comparable to innocent or juvenile college socializing. They are as different from each other as death is from play.

Brian thought through this response, as much because he respected the peer tutor as because of feeling the sting of the tutor's reply. As you will see when you read Brian's final draft below, he decided to add a paragraph to his paper, right at the point at which the shooting scene from his paper ends. Again, ask yourself whether it seems integrated with the essay or not.

In response to the issue of the third unexamined alternative explanation—"the issue of personal and group suicide"—Brian listened to and read responses from a professor, a peer tutor, and two classmates. He decided that to respond to their readings would put him into the writing of a new and different paper. He felt he had said enough about suicide when he added this in his revised draft:

How can my experience help other criminals to go straight? It can show them that if they stay the way that they are, anything can happen. They will be put in situations where they will have to make quick crucial decissions like life or death just to protect their name or reputation. At some point they have to get knocked off the hill. It's inevitable. It's actually a form of suicide. An ugly death must come. Its only a question of when.

Brian's journey through the Adaptation Stage is more intense than Adhita's. Unlike her, Brian is more willing to explore unexamined alternative explanations. We see Brian making deliberate choices in his revision that lead to congruence. As you read Brian's final draft, observe how much additional material he chose to include and ask yourself whether it works.

FINAL REVISIONS FOR STYLE AND PROOFREADING

We have reached the point at which Adhita and Brian finished revising the substance of their papers. The only responsibilities they had before declaring their papers done, other than handing them in, was revising for style and proofreading. Revising for style essentially means having variety in sentence structure and length, avoiding unnecessary wordiness, and communicating the actual complexity of one's subject in the simplest and clearest language. Your students should strive for complexity of thought but simplicity of language. Inexperienced writers often try to impress readers by using the most complicated words their thesaurus can suggest, but experienced writers choose the simpler of two words if it will do the job of concrete communication. Experienced writers use erudite or showy words only when they know their audience is familiar with and uses a specialized jargon or when no other word will work.

Proofreading, on the other hand, focuses on correcting grammar, punctuation, spelling, and usage. Publishers always give writers at least one copyeditor who assists with proofreading. If published writers receive such support, don't first-year college writers need it too? Our brains quit noticing errors when we have spent a lot of time with a text. Our brain thinks it sees a punctuation mark that isn't there, so your students must be sure to find at least two friends, classmates, or roommates to help proofread. At this point, a second or third visit to the writing center could move from discussing global issues to focusing on sentence-level issues. Encourage students to use software that helps with spelling and grammar, but remind them not to let such support replace the traditional, live, and present aid of real people by their side. There is no substitute for the human eye when it comes to locating errors like awkward sentence structure, wrong word usage, or contraction errors.

Notice how, first, Adhita, and then Brian—who both received focused editing and proofreading help from peer tutors, classmates, and friends—revised their final drafts for style by varying sentence structure, eliminating wordiness, and trying to choose clear and concrete language. Notice proofreading and inclusion of their revisions for congruence. Adhita ended up deciding that the elimination of wordiness, in only a few places, was all she had to do. Notice how few strikeouts she made. She also had distinctly fewer proofreading errors to correct. These proofreading corrections are indicated on both essays by the striking out of the original and placing the corrections in square brackets in bold characters. Are there any parts of the essay that need additional editing for style?

Islam, Memory and Modernization: Being Vs. Becoming
Adhita
[final draft]

The Islamic attitude toward modernization is greatly affected by their belief in the purity of the soul and the beauty of creation. It is affected by the concept of being in God's world now, and perceiving its reality. If all and everything are pure creations of God, then where is the need to change? The word "Being" in my title and in this paper does not imply an unthinking Islamic rejection of change, but instead points to the Islamic emphasis on the unfolding of one's consciousness of God's perfect being in this world.

Western generated scientific and technological advances are impregnated with western cultural values, which interfere with the balance of nature and the relationship of people with the balance of the world as it was first created. For example, large, obtrusive western buildings defeat the purpose of the marriage of beauty and functionalism of traditional Islamic architecture and public planning. The humanly created landscape in Islam is suppose to mean something more than efficiency and cost-effectiveness. It has to show the culture's priorities. It has to be a form of worship.

If the Islamic nations are to modernize with the consent of their populations at large, then they must modernize Islamically. This process must embody Islamic emphasis on God's primacy in human consciousness, or else modernization will lead to religious and cultural suicide. Cultural suicide is the act of ignoring the key values of your culture when it is influenced by Western technologies. It is neo-colonial to expect western modernizations to work in Islamic cultures, if imported wholesale and with little or no regard for Islamic values. Neo-colonial here means assuming the absolute superiority of Western Technological culture compared to other cultures that are less technologically advanced. Technological advances, whether Western or otherwise, do not necessarily demonstrate moral, social or cultural superiority.

As the west leads in science and technology now, (just as Islam lead previously, during the Middle Ages), the west thinks that its way is the "right" way, and that it will work for every other culture. This cultural or technological arrogance leads to increased international instability, as it oftentimes seems that the western powers cannot respect a culture so different. The differences are not respected, and one being stronger than the other physically, leads to the attempt of domination. In the American media, the "arab" is reduced to one of two stereotypes, the imbecile or the terrorist, which the author of the medieval text *The Song of Roland* would recognize and approve. The Crusades still go on, but in ways that pretend not to be about religion.

So what are the key differences between Islam and the west when it comes to memory, being and becoming? Imagine for a minute if we could remember everything that we have experienced since our birth. It would be ~~hyperintense,~~ [**hyper intense**] hyperactive, drowning in a sea of sensations and rushing thoughts which are unconnected. Insanity surely. Certainly there could be no "meaning" or relationships because we would see everything, but one at a time, chaotically. So, therefore memory must (1) be *selective* and it must involve (2) the *making of meaning*. The selectivity creates the meaning. I think our culture tells us what and how to select; what and how to "see." The west and Islam "see" different worlds. What's the Islamic world look like?

In Islam there is no concept of Original Sin. No Fall. No corruption. This is a profound difference between Islam and the west. ~~A giant difference. Thus, the core of human nature is pure and heavenly.~~ According to Islam, we carry paradise at the Center of our Being. The key Arabic words are:

> *Fitrah* [our true, pure original nature]
> *Dhikr* [remembrance of God as context of all meaning (memory)]
> *Jihad* [struggle, "war," striving to open up completely to the memory of *fitrah*]

The outline above suggests that Being, our original nature, *fitrah*, is more important than Becoming. In the west, Becoming, Progress, is more important than Being; Progress is more important than our original nature.

In my opinion western science and technology deny or submerge Being, the idea of a pure soul, and replace it with John Locke's tabula rasa, blank slate, a person *becoming* more and more progressive. But I ask one question, toward what ideal or utopia is scientific-technological "Progress" heading? What are we going to become? I think it is best for the reader to fill in the answer or answers. There are terribly negative possible answers: a nuclear holocaust, planetary death through environmental catastrophe, etc. But let's leave the negatives aside. What is the most positive "final" result we can imagine? By asking a half-dozen of my dormmates, I discovered that I'm not the only person who has trouble answering this question of *positive* final outcomes of the scientific-technological religion of Progress.

Here I bow to the reader and ask for an answer.

Islam's sense of time is very different. Time has meaning as the unfolding of Being, not as becoming. Being, the eternal divine nowness, is all that matters. *Fitrah*, our original nature, is spontaneous joy and creativity. Paradise here and now.

Fitrah is the pure natural state of Islam. The word "Islam" is derived from the Arabic root "slm," which means *peace, purity, submission* to God's will. The whole Islamic enterprise is to remember the pure spontaneity of our original nature. How does one try to accomplish this goal of total memory, or return to *fitrah?* The answer is the five pillars of Islam in their outward and inward forms.

The five pillars of Islam are (1) the declaration of faith: "There is no god but God" and "Muhammad is the Prophet of God." (2) prayer five times per day; (3) fasting, especially during the month of Ramadan; (4) alms giving; (5) pilgrimage to Mecca. As in all religions I know of, there is a tension in Islam between its outer and inner dimensions. This tension between external rules and inner commitment is the arena for the struggle of *jihad*. The outer *jihad* is the defense of Islam, such as the Russian invasion of Afghanistan, which was an attempt to destroy an Islamic society. Fighting the Russians was a true *jihad*. But the outer *jihad* is also the seeking of social justice. Economic actions have to be sought in which remembrance of God is kept in mind and material welfare does not become an end in itself. Greed is not good in Islam, compared to certain American movies about the stock exchange!

The *jihad* for the inner self is the recognition that whatever one wants most, whatever one gives most of one's time to, is what one truly worships. Many people worship wealth as their only true god. They might give some time or a little time to Allah, but such people are not fighting an inner *jihad*. To the one who fights the inner *jihad*, God is everything. Such a Muslim tries to see Allah in every dimension of existence.

In Islam total memory is in theory possible. *Jihad* can lead, at least temporarily, to total recall, total *fitrah*. In the Islamic tradition, certain great poets like Rumi or Ibn 'Arabi, who are also spiritual teachers, report in their poetry, moments of total memory. I will give some examples of what the world looks like when one has "remembered" divine vision: when the "ordinary" is seen to be extraordinary: concrete, simple, beautiful, divine. Here are the quotes:

> The intense, terrible beauty of perceiving everything as divinely
>   beautiful—
> a woman's spit
> the pain of sexual desire
> the unbearable nostalgia of memory
> the fragrance of an oasis after a sudden rainstorm
> the texture of bare flesh
> the croak of a raven
> the startling joy of lightning flashing over the desert
> the ecstacies [**ecstasies**] of the visionary, the poet, the scientist, at the
>   moment of insight
> the cool serenity of a shrine deserted by all pilgrims in the hour
>   before dawn.

Such unbearable beauties are what matter in a perfect world—this world when perceived correctly, openly and with the giving away of your life to the experience of total recall of God, who is the beauty of ancient days, forever new.

Total memory in Islam is possible because the core of our Being is divine, if we overcome the dream of forgetfulness, of thinking money, success, practicalities, being "special" are what really matter in life. The dream of forgetfulness is a nightmare of materialism, selfishness, loneliness, violence and imprisonment of the human spirit.

Total memory in Islam is possible because the soul is pure, not corrupt, as is taught in the Christian doctrine of the Fall, and thus provides the context that *organizes* all of our memories since birth into an unbearably beautiful perceptual tapestry of ordered experiences that turn out to be a face of God, our deepest conceivable joy and connectedness with the natural world, all other people and with Allah. The only response to such beauty, to such total meaning, to such ordering and arranging of all of our experiences and memories is the shout of joy, in Arabic: "El Hamdu l'Allah: thanks be to God."

Conclusion

It is possible to find groups of people in the West who care more for being than becoming. In these groups we might include environmentalists and Native Americans who care more about nature's Being than about technological becoming. These groups might also include people with a deep religious devotion to God's Being, whether Christian, Jewish or the mystics of other religions.

It is also certainly true that there are many individuals in the Middle East, especially the more Westernized, who share the West's worship of technological change and its utopian dream of perpetual progress.

Cultures, thank God, are not monolithic, but interactive and thus experience at least some change, sometimes dramatic amounts. But such varieties in a culture's characteristics and values, and exceptions to mainstream cultural rules, don't change the fact that there is a mainstream, whether we like it or not. I believe the essences of the West and of Islam are as I have presented them, and that Being vs Becoming is a fundamentally accurate way to understand the deep and powerful tensions in their relationship. I think Islam wants to say "modernization but not westernization!" The West wants to say "modernization is westernization. You have to do it our way because it's the only way!"

In this paper I have written about what I think is the essence of Islam and why this essence is so centrally different from what I take to be the nucleus of the west's worldview. So, do we need a synthesis from these opposites or the continuation of such dramatically different visions of how best to live? Since technology continues to shrink the planet, and no nation can really be isolated anymore, does that mean modernization is inevitable and thus we must seek syntheses and not respect or even accept elemental cultural differences? Is one world culture desirable or perhaps even inevitable? The answer to that question is another paper—paper two perhaps?—but as we, the college students of the present, and the future leaders of tomorrow think about such crucial questions, we better remember that, as the Islamic thinker Ziauddin Sardar says,

Technology is a human activity: there is nothing neutral or value-free about it.
It develops in a society according to its needs and requirements, social pressures
and political priorities. It solves the problems that it was designed to solve. For
example, the contemporary building technology with steel, glass and concrete as
its raw materials has developed out of social and material concerns of Europe
and America. They have evolved to build a typical, standardized Western city.
It is unrealistic to expect modern building technologies to produce something
else. One would need a totally different kind of building technology, based on
different social assumptions and using different materials, to produce a differ-
ent kind of city. Technologies developed to build airports cannot be used in a
conservation area for it will end up resembling an airport. The evidence, and
the supporting literature, for the social and cultural bias of technology is now
so strong that we can ignore it only at our peril. (298)

Brian's final revision for style and proofreading was complicated by the essential place in his paper of what he continued to name "street language,"
which illuminates the world-view within which he lived during his criminal
period. As he revised for style, and especially in proofreading, he had to
decide where that language should be retained for the paper to be true
to his past experience. Should such language be eliminated when Brian is
talking about the present and the future? This was tricky for him because
it had profound identity implications, not only about race but also about
social class. He wants to give up the criminal life but not reject his roots
and past entirely. Moreover, he told his composition professor, a peer tutor he grew close to, several classmates, and friends that he did "not want
to begin only using the language of successful people and begin slowly to
look down on people like I was before." Notice the compromises he made
in style revision and in proofreading as he produced his final draft.

Another Night in the Hood
Brian Jones
[final draft]

It looked like just another Friday night in the hood. I quickly walked
around the corner to the game room. As I walk I pass the same old routine
people. I was in a hurry to meet my partner at the spot. When Mike and I
were in juvenile detention together we decided when we got out we were
going to get paid. We are both sixteen now so the law considers us as adults.
So as far as we see it we are not taking no shorts and no shit! When we are
on the corner one of us holds the other one sells the drugs. This night it
was my turn to hold the gun and watch Mike's back. We were already told
by some kids out there to watch out for a blue 4 door Chevette. They said
it was some stick up kids from Brooklyn. About two hours later things were
going as normal. We had been doing good this night. There had been no
police and definitely no sign of any stick up kids. But I guess our good luck
was due to end. Before I knew it there was the blue Chevette. Two kids had
jumped out and grabbed my partner Mike. They had not noticed me off

to the side of the game room. In my mind I knew I had to make a ~~decission~~ [**decision**] and do it fast. I could just stay quiet and let them get the money. I could run half way down the block and get some more of our homies. Or just come from around the corner shooting at them.

If I decide to go get help I have a better chance of having the odds in our favor. Plus if I get the homies we can run these kids off our corner for good. But this could take to [too] long and they could be gone by the time I get the homies and back. Even worse by the time we get back Mike could be dead. And if Mike gets shot he would be wondering ~~were~~ [**where**] I was at. And if he was shot I would have to put up with all the homies in the hood.

I thought about just not saying a thing and let them get what they came for. This way both of us would be alive to see ~~tommorrow.~~ [**tomorrow.**] And as they were leaving I could come out from the side and surprise them. But if so this means they would already have our money and have a good chance of getting away. I might hit one of them, but what if he is not the one with the money.

The thought of just coming out shooting was a choice too. This way I would catch them off guard before they got the money. If I hit first then most likely Mike and I would not get shot. I would also let them know that we are not two little punks on the corner just waiting to be robbed. We already decided that we were going to be serious about getting money when we are out there on the corner. But this will mean I would have to take a chance at killing someone. Since I am sixteen the law would deal with me as an adult. As of now the going rate on murder is about 20 years!

Its funny how fast your mind moves when you are under pressure or just ~~press~~ [**pressed**] for time. I don't know if I really made a ~~decission~~ [**decision**] or if my actions were just forced out of me due to my tight situation. If I could compare my actions to someone I guess it would be a person by the name O-Dog from the movie Menace 2 Society. The ~~charcter~~ [**character**] in this movie was just buck wild. He never really thought ~~to~~ [**too**] much about anything he did. He really used to just do things by the speare of the moment. ~~Nothig~~ [**Nothing**] mattered to him. He was the kind of person you could be cool with, but at the same time he was capable of causing trouble. He was nothing but a real product of his environment. Since his living conditions were bad he too was bad. Plus the fact that this person really ~~nevers~~ [**never**] thinks about the things he is about to do. He pretty much does it by the moment. And since his personality is always wild, [**added comma**] whenever something is about to ~~happend~~ [**happen**] he will always be the aggressive one.

All I remember is stepping out and hearing rounds of gun shots. The next thing I knew I was dragged in the game room and my partner kept asking for the gun. All I could remember is the pain that ran all up and down my leg. I knew I had been shot but it did not seem as important to me at the time. My mind was really on the money. I wanted to know if the money was still ours. I kept wondering if I had hit one of them. I had already been known in the hood to have a gun. And I was also known to have the heart to pull it out and shoot. But this was my first time getting shot and my first time being in a shootout so close. Most of the time when I had to use my gun I would have them foolsrunning once I began shooting. But this time I was right there in the middle of the whole thing. My eyes were open the whole time the shooting was going on, but it all seemed to be a ~~blurr~~. [**blur**]

I never feared for my life as I think about it. See when you play the game in the concrete jungle death is one of your chances. I knew that I was subjecting my self to either getting caught by the police or I could be shot and killed. I never would think about it when I was at work. But after hanging out some late nights and someone either got shot it would make me think. I just would rather get shot for a reason than for nothing. I was looked upon by the kids in the hood as ~~I~~ [**a**] tough guy or some kind of hero. See I stood up for our hood or our corner. ~~Thats~~ [**That's**] what one needs out here in the streets. In the streets your name and your reputation takes you a long way. My man Mike until this day says he owes me his life. I feel I did the thing I had to do. I really don't think my choice was thought out it just ~~happend~~ [**happened**] that way. The way I see it is if I'm going to go out from this world I'm going out fighting. I'll never let it be said that I was afraid of anything not even death itself!

But how did this event of me [**omit word**] getting shot change me? It made me realize at the time that this was no game. I was really that drug dealer that would kill if I had to protect my investment. This event put me to the test. ~~to see if I really was going to "take no shorts and no shit."~~ I had already said that we were going to be serious about getting money, but this event made words into actions. I was now that criminal in the statistics of America. You can say that this event made me into an O.G. ("original gangsta" or veteran to the war of the streets). It was like when you pledge a fraternity. The ~~delima~~ [**dilemma**] of whether or not to come out shooting was the pledging part, and my decision was what determined whether I went over into the fraternity of the hood. You can say that I got my letters (O.G.). The event was like a trial of my manhood, like what the Indians, I hear, went through. Now I was looked upon as a man of the hood or a warrior. This event actually put me deeper into the game, because it earned me respect.

In response to an earlier draft of this paper, a great peer tutor, who wishes to remain unnamed, complained strongly that comparing the shooting scene to pledging a fraternity was a big mistake. The tutor said that "they are as different from each other as death is from play." The peer tutor is right of course that they are as different as death and play, but what he forgets or fails to understand is that some forms of play are deadly and that there was a real level of play—of distance from reality and understanding but still a form of play—in the life I was living or playing then. Also, at that time in my life I would have paid any price to get into the "fraternity of the hood," just as I've noticed that a lot of first-year students seem to be ready to pay any price to get into fraternities. They are interested in fraternities not only to get into the "in-group" in college for social reasons in the present, but also because of future career and economic networking reasons. In terms of improving status in the present and enhancing future economic prospects the comparison is exactly accurate.

In this country, people who have never been without the safety zone of a legal job and a home in a safe neighborhood need to work hard to understand what this country looks like from the perspective of grinding poverty and the violent street culture it produces, or at least encourages. I'm not claiming that my total situation of poverty and a dangerous environment gave me the right to become a criminal and prey on the weak and helpless, or on other criminals. No. It didn't give me any such right. Yes. No such right exists. Yes. I became a criminal and an animal. But believe me. If we want to lessen the possibility of aggressive young men (and women), from seeing the fraternity of the hood as their only realistic alternative to poverty and hopelessness, mainstream America better see that my comparison can teach us something important about what the world looks like to the havenots compared to the haves.

How this event changed me is not the same question as **why** it changed me. I was only 16 at this time and everybody looked up to me like I was some kind of tough guy or hero or something. I fell in love with my new found fame, and I wanted more fame, and to keep my reputation. To keep my reputation of not being afraid of anything, not even death, I had to not care about consequences at all.

When did this event change me? It was all at once and yet slowly too. They are both true, even though logic says its impossible. I was only 16 when this event happened, and it changed me in a negative way. Though I had the body of a man, I was only a child, and a child's mind is very easily manipulated. See, my mind was manipulated by money but also by fame and respect. The way people looked at me—fear, respect, envy—was an incredibly powerful drug for me. Man, [**comma added**] I didn't want to lose it at any cost. To keep this fame and respect, I had to not care about anything or at least act like I did not care, because you know that no one wants to die or go to jail. As I got older this event along with many others lead me to believe that my life would not last long the way that I was going. I had to change my mentality of not caring about consequences and only caring about self-advancement, to caring about my life along with the lives of others. Else I'd be a dead man.

What does memory include and ~~what does it leave out~~? [**overlook?**] What did I leave out in the writing of this story? I didn't say much about my fears. I was afraid that if I didn't come out shooting it would really hurt my reputation and make me look like a ~~punk~~ [**coward**] to Mike and my homies. I didn't talk about how even if I ran to get my homies I would still look like a punk [coward]. I really felt at the time that I had no choice but to come out shooting. In the first draft I didn't emphasize that I was backed into a corner and had no real choice about what I could do and still live in the only world I knew at that time. I said that O-Dog, the movie character, was a product of his environment, but I didn't talk about how I too was a product of my environment. Notice that I didn't talk much about whether I hit one of them, and about how this whole kind of life is a form of group suicide.

Why did I omit the things I left out of the first draft? Now I think there were two main reasons why I omitted what I didn't want myself or my reader to see. First, I didn't want to look like a punk or coward. And more importantly, I left out some things ~~so that it did not come back on me politically~~. [**to protect myself in a legal sense**].

How do I feel now about the person I was before, and is part of me still a criminal? ~~The person that I was before, some people would call an animal.~~ When I was in prison I read Malcolm X's autobiography. Looking back from prison on his life of crime, Malcolm referred to his pre-Muslim self as "an animal." I don't know if I was an animal, but I do know that the life I lived before was a constant ~~hustle and~~ struggle. I did not care about anything, not even death. I was not looking out for our (~~me and Mike~~) well being when I came out shooting, because we both could have been shot. If I ~~would've punked out and~~ let them get what they wanted, I would have been looking out for our best interest. I hated living in fear of it all ending at anytime. I always had to watch my back and live with caution, like a wolf being hunted by men. This is how I made it so long, and I still live with caution even now. ~~You can say that in some ways I am still a criminal.~~ I'm still not comfortable sitting with my back to doors, even in college classrooms. There are a lot of people from my past that have a reason to get even with me, especially the children of the people who bought drugs from me. I have children of my own now. When I look at them I think too often about the children I hurt indirectly. That's when I do feel like an animal.

~~But in some ways I am still a criminal.~~ [**But I am still aggressive**.] I still want self-advancement and I'll do whatever I can to get it now, like the big people on Wall Street. Are they really so different from me or the old me? Before, I did whatever it took to get self-advancement. It took, at first, being the best hustler I could be, but now I do whatever I can, like going to college. Patience is needed in college to help me get through hard times, because college almost guarantees me in the future what ~~criminology~~ [**the criminal life**] promised quickly (but at too high a cost). The only difference is the speed of my advancement, because I am going to advance. I also still have the desire for fame and respect. Doesn't everybody?

How can my experience help other criminals to go straight? It can show them that if they stay the way that they are, anything can happen. They will be put in situations where they will have to make quick crucial ~~decissions~~ [**decisions**] like life or death just to protect their name or reputation. At some point they have to get knocked off the hill. It's inevitable. It's actually a form of suicide. An ugly death must come. Its only a question of when.

My life can also show them that there are other ways to get the things that they want. It only takes patience. If the dedication they put into ~~their name and reputation was put into getting advancement in whatever,~~ [**crime was put into legal activities**,] they would not have to put their lives at risk. For a criminal, the price of success on the streets is too high. You can never really enjoy what you get. You know in your heart that ~~its~~ [**it's**] not really yours. It's a price no one will want to pay if they really start to think about it. The problem is, how do we get them to think? Mike is very intelligent, but his thinking will only go in certain channels. How do we get Mike and other criminals to see the big picture? Our society has to find an answer or continue to build more prisons than any other "free" country in the world!

To those who would say, and have said, that I have shown too little guilt or grief over what I have done, and that because of this refusal to fully admit my wrongdoings that I might backslide into a life of crime again, I just want to say that I have thought seriously about this point. Sure, I am responsible for my illegal activities. Yes, I really am sorry for the lives I have damaged or destroyed, and for the pain I have caused. But though I wish I could, in real life there is no way to rewind the video of my life and change the violence that I committed and the violence that I responded to. But although I can't change the past, I most definately [**definitely**] have the chance to change the future for the better. Isn't that all anyone can do?

The completion of your students' first college paper is a big deal! As with Adhita and Brian, your students' final drafts will probably end up stronger than the students thought they would be at the beginning of the process. If your students work at all hard and engage the intercultural writing process presented in this book, they will have not only a true introduction to the culture of college but will become active members. Adhita and Brian both ended up with substantial papers that fully engaged them as people and as scholars in training. In one sense, when your student's first paper is done, your journey is done. You and your students have worked, struggled, and begun to master the various stages of intercultural experience in college and especially in the college writing processes. Your students have adapted somewhat to college by finishing discovery, working, and final drafts. All the papers your students write henceforward, in your classes and beyond, will be further developments of the processes, experiences, behaviors, and methodologies they engaged as they drafted, rewrote, revised, edited, and finally completed their first college paper. Thanks for helping guide your students as junior colleagues to arrive at and take their place in college culture.

9

THE REENTRY STAGE
Future Compositions and Dissonant Voices

What is a dissonant voice? Ideally, it is the perfect embodiment of skepticism, the analytical impulse, and critical consciousness. On the face of it, the dissonant voice seems the opposite of congruence, the goal of the Adaptation Stage of Intercultural Experience, which we discuss in the previous chapter. But notice that although congruence is the ideal of the Adaptation Stage, we are still talking about a stage. Congruence, even to the most sublime degree, can never be a permanent condition. Congruence of a permanent kind is a necessarily unreachable goal, a useful fiction. Permanent congruence would be oppressive because it would be an attempt to silence the other voices that constitute the life, strength, and source of innovation of democratic societies. These other voices are led, inspired, encouraged, or responded to by dissonant voices.

Why should we have congruence as a goal if it is both unreachable and, even if it can be reached, constitutes an eventually oppressive structure? Congruence represents the optimum harmony potentially present in any academic or other group setting, but since all groups are historically contingent with cross-currents of multiple sites of the politics of representation under conditions of unequal power, even locations of considerable congruence must interrupt the unearned privileges of the main constituent group or groups of that location of congruence. Since every democratic setting, to remain democratic, must support the conversations and voices that lead to change and renewal—sometimes drastic amounts of change—then structures that seek congruence must change in a fluid and open manner. Such continuing changes do not make a permanent goal any less worthy of pursuit by academic and democratic societies.

Even though the dissonant voice seems to be the opposite of the congruence of voices since it seeks to open up the existing harmony of the status quo, it is not the enemy of congruence so much as it desires greater degrees of congruence, a congruence inclusive of as many voices

DOI: 10.7330/9781607328742.c009

as possible. If, as chaos theory demonstrates, order and disorder are not opposites but are dimensions of each other, then change, disruption, and disputes are inevitable characteristics of all complex systems. We must encourage and prepare for the chaos and creativity of dissonant voices while understanding that such voices are unavoidably disruptive and produce disorderly events.

Is this dissonant voice speaking in the tones of an original genius, the extreme individualism of the "star" performer, athlete, or artist? Or to use a religious context, is this a voice crying out in the wilderness? All such voices could be considered monologues that claim special power all to themselves. They imply uniqueness, a special star status. In this sense, since they are monological, such voices are antidemocratic. They try to hold all power to themselves. Simply put, such voices are literally talking to themselves and want to be idolized as stars. They are not interested in what others say; they want to be agreed with, if not venerated. They believe in a complete and separate individuality, and they are convinced they are the preeminent example.

Is this what is meant by dissonant voices, especially in cross-cultural settings? No. Exactly the opposite. The dissonant voice is dialogical and is interested in the dynamic multiple and continuing exchanges by which groups define themselves, define what they do, and understand who should and does benefit from group work. The dissonant voice that functions through dialogism—the emphasis on the conversations of groups, not on stars' voices within those conversations—argues for the letting go of the intention of complete control of the definition and sense of self. Such an intention of complete control of the definition of self is regarded by the dissonant voice as pure selfishness, as pretending we each live on a deserted island. Instead, the dissonant voice argues for acknowledgment of the permeable boundaries between self and other and, therefore, that the future is beyond our individual or primary group's control. Those of us involved in the reality-defining conversations of group life will become cocreators of our own sense of self and that of others. This process is not the end of self, self being a social construction always involved in the process of the politics of representation of our multiple group identities, but instead it is the end of the illusion of complete individuality.

The dissonant voice also sees and defines knowledge in a different way, as a contesting multiple-team sport. Knowledge is always contested ground. Yes, there are some basic facts that everyone agrees on, such as that the Japanese bombed Pearl Harbor on December 7, 1941. But as soon as we ask *why* questions, we are on contested ground again. The dissonant voice wants to add new points of view and new voices to the conversations that produce human knowledge so the process of knowledge construction becomes more open and democratic.

The dissonant voice, in dialogue with the power structure, has this fundamental conviction: that everything is up for grabs; no one is safe, and no one can hide in the twenty-first century. But—we can invent what we want. The basic question always is, Who do we want to be or become? What coalitions of a shifting shared fate, ultimately on a planetary scale, and its complement in classrooms and learning spaces do we want to work for and build, and how do we stop excluding undesired others? We welcome the migrant as the dissonant voice, as our colleague, and as the fully human person displaced by political-economic conditions in a previous home culture.

What does the dissonant voice have to do with you personally as a writing teacher? How is it connected with your need to plan and produce the best curriculum and writing work you are able, and does it help your students move in college? The contribution of the dissonant voice is to provide any conversation and any structure with confrontation and innovation.

You should aim at providing for and enabling such voices in your writing pedagogy so your students can do so in their final drafts and subsequent writing assignments. Since dissonant voices belong to team players who are not looking for personal glory but for the human interests of all involved in the issues at hand, the confrontation and innovation such voices help produce are ultimately constructive, although along the way they might occasion a lot of disruption. The confrontations are not a form of showing off, an attempt to grab some glory, but instead a voice of the unmanifested, potential congruence inherent in the situation. Any student who can fully articulate, or even suggest as best they are able, the innovation and confrontation that seeking congruence for all involved in the paper subject or issue under review could produce, can be an important voice for the group and increase the student's chances for success in college and in future work or activism. You as teacher must make clear to the entire learning group, and individually to students manifesting the dissonant voice that, of course, some group members who resent a dissonant voice's pedagogical team spirit and seeking of congruence will be offended by attempts at truth telling and by the dissonant voice claiming to see, or be part of, the big picture. Thus, the shifting dissonant voices and the group overall needs to be reminded fairly often that dissonance will set up a lot of turbulence, some of which will rock the boat of group and individual consciences and of the commitment to the academic search for truth and fairness.

Ultimately, one side effect of students being constructive voices for creative confrontation and innovation is that such dissonant voices will be admired and valued by those people of vision in the group who want the subject and group to move forward, and who therefore see teachers who foster dissonant voices and students who manifest democratic dissonance as people who embody the commitment crucial to progress. What honest and forward-looking peers and supervisors would not profoundly value such voices?

REENTRY STAGE AND RETURN SHOCK

In the interim between separate papers or projects, something quite subtle but important happens to the evolving intercultural and critical consciousness of your students. On the one hand, your students will have just experienced the positive rush of finishing paper one, and on the other, the first draft of paper two is not yet due. They are in an especially dynamic intercultural space and consciousness. Their potent foray into the culture of academic discourse through writing and finishing paper one has resulted in their internalizing more of the language and values of academic skepticism, analysis, and critical thinking than they are yet aware. Their conscious awareness cannot keep up with the subtle, yet far-reaching, changes they are experiencing. As they begin to look at the world of ideas, of everyday life, of family, of friends, and of their sense of self through the language and perspectives of academic discourse, they intensify the creatively ambiguous relationships they are developing with their original or home culture as a result of their increasing adaptation to the ways of their new college culture. What are the practical results of these changes and this sense of ambiguous relations with their home culture? The main answer is return shock. For most first-year college students who do not drop out and return home, college probably represents the end of the exclusive dominance of their home culture in their lives. Most of your students will never live at home again after college. This certainly does not mean they are going to lose or give up all of their home culture. Such is not even possible. We cannot cancel history. But polyculturalists are intellectually alive and are therefore changing and reinterpreting the past and present, and your students are subtly becoming polycultural thinkers and producers. They must be open to change, but they also must try to understand and direct their own changes as much as they are able so they are not being redefined by others against their will under conditions of unequal power in a racist national culture.

So what exactly are the Reentry Stage and return shock? The Reentry Stage of Intercultural Experience involves returning to one's homeland. Imagine a return home after a considerable time spent internationally. There are excitement and anticipation as one leaves the new culture for the return home. But two giant facts condition what one experiences on the return:

1. One's home has been changing while one was away.

2. One has become a subtly yet significantly different person because of adaptation to the new culture(s).

There is almost always a period in which one is out of harmony with one's old home culture, including family and friends, and both sides are to varying degrees surprised and uncomfortable and don't really know why. Moreover, both sides are often reluctant to talk things over, at least at first, because each assumed the reunion would be smooth, joyous, and automatic.

Since your students' home cultures were not in suspended animation while they were away, and since they obviously want to share their many powerful experiences in the new culture with old friends and family now that they've returned, the two sides seem to be speaking at cross purposes or in disoriented ways. Each side tends to feel, rather than consciously think, that a significant dimension of their personhood is being ignored. Actually, there is often considerable justification for this perception, although neither side intends to create this response. If your students stop to think about it, how could even significant members of their home culture continue to show an interest in what was for the student powerful experiences in a new culture after a couple of conversations on the subject? The students have been permanently transformed by their foreign experience, but members of the home culture tend to see it more as a merely exotic interlude from "real life" at home. Likewise, our students probably show too little interest in what their families want to tell them about their life while the students were away because to the students, such happenings seem unremarkable or even routine compared to the intense ups and downs of foreign living. The excitement and even the danger of foreign experience are more vital and real to students than the "routine" of home. Each side here is insufficiently fair and insufficiently attentive.

This culture shock in reverse is return shock. Return shock, lack of harmony with one's original culture, is especially troublesome, even hurtful, because it is totally unanticipated. It is an accurate general-ization to say that the greater the degree of adaptation to one's new culture, the more considerable the degree of return shock one will experience. Each side should show sensitivity, but especially our first-gen student travelers, because they know both cultures and their family and friends might not. The students need to respect the deep complexity of each of these cultures and know when to keep silent. They also must learn when to compare the two cultures and when not to. Too much comparing, especially since the comparisons usually disrespect the students' home culture because they are missing their foreign culture, can be boring, arrogant, and insulting, or can demonstrate a feeling of polycultural superiority. This is not a time to use the dissonant voice of confrontation and innovation. Save that for public and professional settings. Your students now know much about their immersion in a new culture and have a sense that the self is capable of profound transfor-mations. Yet this inherent capacity of the sense of self to change creates in many people fear (and sometimes terror) of losing their "real" self. Because many people tend to fear change since they know on some level that the self is finally fragile and so is easily insulted if our values are called into question too frequently by friends or family returning from a foreign sojourn, we must be diplomatic and respectful ambassadors, especially at home.

Remember, too, that because your students have a second culture with which they can now compare their home culture, they probably perceive the positive and negative dimensions of their home culture much more clearly than those who lack foreign experience. Consider these lines from T. S. Eliot's poem "Little Gidding":

> And the end of all our exploring
> Will be to arrive where we started
> And know the place for the first time. (V)

What do the Reentry Stage of Intercultural Experience and return shock have to do with your students' college situation of having finished paper one but possessing a bit of time before they jump into the writing of paper two? Just as in intercultural experience, the return home causes inharmonies for the reasons developed above; likewise, when your stu-dents finish paper one and relax a bit before jumping into paper two, they have a sense of being between two worlds. They don't fit perfectly in any one place anymore. When they can begin to see clearly the negative side of their home culture, added to the fact that they are now adapt-ing to another culture, they have a beginning sense of transcendental homelessness, however slight. There is no one place where both or all sides of their evolving self can manifest easily anymore. They begin to understand Thomas Wolfe's often quoted line: "You can't go home again." Likewise, their growing academic critical consciousness, when added to their increasing ability to see beyond binaries to the many sides of arguments they used to perceive as black and white, means now they don't really know where they stand when they are asked by others, or by their transforming or conflicted self, questions like these:

Are you still my friend? Or brother, son, daughter?

You've changed a lot. Who are you now?

You've changed a lot. Do you think you're better than me, than us?

What do you believe in now?

Do you believe in anything? Everything?

If you can see both or all sides of this subject, does that mean you have no commitments?

Do you change into whatever the people around you want you to be?

Are you losing yourself or forgetting who you are?

Who are you?

Who are you becoming?

These questions, or questions like these, are existential and real. They must be faced directly or indirectly, now and later. Encourage your students to dialog with a couple of classmates they feel comfortable with, especially in written form. Using the discussion feature of their LMS (so they have a written record of the exchanges) is an excellent way for students to continue to explore the changes students they are undergoing. Such digital discussions are often productive.

But there is one more thing your students might like to do, in addition to an LMS exchange and beyond telling their friends and family members they value their relationship with them and that they need to understand that the student's expanding horizons are a challenge for your student as well as for family and home friends. Take another look at the Kluckhohn Model. Where, in each of the categories, does the dissonant voice fit into that model? Where does your student fit in? Is it the same place? What are their key cultural assumptions now? Finally, how is their developing critical consciousness inviting them to interrogate the structure of the Kluckhohn Model itself, and what does such an activity of interrogating models teach your students about the dissonant voice? Invite them to create their own model to replace the ones in this book.

We also want to present you with an activity that brings us literally to reentry.

Early in this book, we looked at Robert's key-cultural-assumptions assignment and followed Adhita's and Brian's processes in taking their work on it from brainstorming to a finished draft. Since we have come full circle, we now present Amanda's version of this assignment that her first-year writing students complete.

CONTEXT-BUILDING WRITING ACTIVITY 19

Key Cultural Assumptions: Essay Two

RESEARCH

Print a complete copy of each of the professional sources you will use for this project. You are required to use two professional sources for this assignment. One source must defend your assumptions; the other should challenge your assumptions. Highlight or underline directly on the copies the passages or relevant data that will be used to prove your claim. Your annotated sources **must** be turned in with the essay on the due date.

DRAFTING THE ESSAY

This essay requires you to analyze the origins and validity of multiple assumptions you currently hold about a specific culture. Your introduction should state the specific culture being discussed and identify at least five assumptions you hold about that culture. Next, the body paragraphs of your essay will focus on discussing each of these assumptions in depth. Each body paragraph will discuss each assumption in turn and discuss the reasons you continue to hold on to these assumptions. These paragraphs should explain the origins for each assumption. You may want to use your history, background, or education to discuss the origins of each assumption. Next, your essay will discuss the sources you found about the assumptions. These paragraphs will demonstrate how/whether each source supports or challenges your assumptions. You must use two sources. Each source may defend or challenge one or more of your five required assumptions. Your goal is to find sources that discuss more than one assumption so one source can be used to discuss multiple assumptions. If you can only find sources that each discuss only one assumption, that is fine, but not ideal. Finally, the essay will draw conclusions about the assumptions. What have your sources taught you about your assumptions? Do you still hold them? Why? Has your research led you to rethink your belief in these assumptions? How? If you plan to continue believing these assumptions (or if you choose to abandon them), explain why in your conclusion. The essay will include all these steps, using professional, published sources as backing to support the reasons you hold or have these cultural assumptions. If your essay includes all these elements, it will have met the major assignment requirements.

Last, how would your students respond to the message contained in the end of Aesop's fable "The Bat, the Birds, and the Beasts"? The fable argues for an insular, tribal monoculturalism. The birds and beasts are going to have a war. Each tries to get the bat to join their side. He refuses. War is avoided at the last minute, and each side celebrates peace. The bat tries to join the birds' celebration, then the beasts' celebration, but is turned away by each. The fable ends with this sentence:

> "Ah," said the bat, "I see now, he that is neither one thing nor the other has no friends."

Ask your students to respond to the view in the world of this fable that we must of necessity stay within our original group identity? Does remaining in our original group identities honor group ideals? Is it cultural imprisonment? Is such monocultural provincialism appropriate to a society that calls itself *democratic* and *open*? Are we, or should we be, free to become who we want to be or who we want to try to become? Which of our group identities or "homes"—racial, cultural, class, gender, sexual, religious, or political—should we leave and which should we remain within? Who should make such decisions of culture maintenance or culture change? How should the groups to which we belong participate in such decisions and how should individuals? If a student's answer to this momentous question is "individuals," your student is Aesop's bat: neither bird nor beast but a border crosser, a stranger, an Other, a foreigner, different, and perceived by every form of tribal consciousness as dangerous. Georg Simmel's 1908 essay "The Stranger" opens with the traveler, willing to become the stranger, the dissonant voice, the person who writes an original script of their life and is described this way:

> If wandering, considered as a state of detachment from every given point in space, is the conceptual opposite of attachment to any point, then the sociological form of "the stranger" presents the synthesis, as it were, of both of these properties. . . . The stranger will thus not be considered here in the usual sense of the term, as the wanderer who comes today and goes tomorrow, but rather as the man who comes today and stays tomorrow—the potential wanderer, so to speak, who, although he has gone no further, has not quite got over the freedom of coming and going. He is fixed within a certain spatial circle—or within a group whose boundaries are analogous to spatial boundaries—but his position within it is fundamentally affected by the fact that he does not belong in it initially and that he brings qualities into it that are not, and cannot be, indigenous to it.

The stranger, or the dissonant voice, represents the drama and power of writing: not knowing what will be revealed next on the page, on the screen, or in our lives. Writing and living have no essential or absolute boundaries. Yes, there are genres and countries and mixed media, but they are ultimately permeable. What we write has a way of influencing who we become or reveals the complexity of our present selves.

Which writing or voices have a right to speak? To be heard? To be published? Or simply, What are the politics of writing and identity and representation? Do we want as many kinds of voices as possible in the public arena and in learning spaces? If we want no limits put on voices, and since we are living in an increasingly transnational world where borders are crossed and all sorts of structures transformed by the multi-perspectivism of our multiple settings, it is crucial to ask how academic discourse is challenged and changed by the plurality of voices. How are African Americans, Asian Americans, Latinx Americans, and Native Americans changing the existing rhetoric of academic discourse? What kinds of changes are multiracial and multicultural rhetorics bringing to academic discourse? Do these various groups—African American, Asian American, and so forth, themselves fluid and open—merely add something to the tone of academic discourse, or are we challenging and changing the actual methodology of academic discourse? What are these challenges and changes? What might they mean for your theory and pedagogy as a writing teacher?

What are these challenges and changes for your students? How about this one in terms of how you imagine your students articulating it to themselves? Is storytelling, as a form of writing, necessarily less persuasive than supposedly "objective," "impersonal" scientific prose? Is telling stories fundamentally different from constructing arguments? Is it right to combine autobiography and scholarship in critically conscious ways? Is academic discourse itself a "story" of how white rhetoric defines itself and polices it boundaries against what it regards as illegal immigration?

Here are three questions to invite your students to ask of any rhetoric, especially the most powerful one, the one that controls, or attempts to control, all the other rhetorics:

1. What constitutes knowledge according to the rhetoric? (Or, What is excluded as unfounded suppositions, as propaganda, as superstition, or as countercultural?)

2. Who has the right to speak as an expert or as a knowledgeable person? (Or, Who is excluded as a lay person, as a nonspecialist, as an outsider?)

3. Who benefits from knowledge in a field? In a profession? In a rhetoric? (Or, Who is regarded as rhetorically impoverished, as unworthy?)

What's at stake in the politics of academic discourse as your students pose these questions? In the final chapter, we look at the heart of the adjustment and opportunity we all face in a color-majority United States.

10

CULTURAL MESHING OR SWITCHING IN POLY- OR INTERCULTURAL WRITING CLASSES

As our text and journey end, we revisit the major points we each want our readers to reconsider. Amanda is hopeful that in the future, the teaching of FYW will be approached using poly- and intercultural methods such as the one Robert developed that we present in this book. She is also skeptical about the long-term future of Edited American English given that living languages are in constant flux, so contemporary vernacular will continue to erode the power we presently assign to increasingly arbitrary usage rules. Using our activities and the Eddy Model invites students to enter academic culture with far less conflict than currently exists in most FYW classrooms. The Eddy Model makes possible for all students, but most especially students of color, a way into linguistic agency and independence. Students who use this method will come to understand that their decisions as writers influence not just their grades but their future classes, careers, and interpersonal communications as well. Teachers who adopt the method will learn with their students, and not just because of the tasks they design or ask of their students. The method works when teachers participate in the interrogation of white privilege themselves, and even their own complicity in it, no matter their ethnic, racial, religious, or other background/identity markers. This text provides tools everyone engaged in academic culture can use, regardless of role, to make deliberate decisions about the use and value of language varieties, including but not limited to EAE. Amanda also wants readers to realize more fully that the challenge of choosing one language variety over another never ends. Linguistic choice is always political and always comes with consequences. Some are wonderful and some are disheartening. Amanda has witnessed numerous colleagues and former students who embraced this ideology only to have to repeatedly defend their promotion of their students' right to use their own language instead of or in tandem with EAE. They have had their jobs

DOI: 10.7330/9781607328742.c010

threatened, their bodies beaten, their citizenship challenged, and their patriotism questioned, even by fellow composition faculty who should know, as we outlined in chapter 7, that there is not an inherent standard variety of English. She has also seen the pride and sense of accomplishment in the eyes of students who, after embracing the challenges of code switching and meshing, felt liberated by using the activities outlined here. Polyculturalism flourishes when teachers and students alike interrogate the power dynamic of the white privileged classroom.

What Robert wants readers to consider at the end of this book is that writers decide whether to code mesh or to code switch and that people who are able to do both sometimes choose one and sometimes the other. If it is true as this book argues that we should see self and other and all of us as almost infinitely complex, and that the people who know us best barely know us, then it follows that what we should want as teachers, students, researchers, and scholars is to increase our ability to be more consciously intentional. A writer's decision to code mesh or code switch in response to a particular writing task is rhetorical—persuasion in multiracial settings of unequal power relations; ideological—an expression of our set of strongly held beliefs, values, and world-view; and involved with the politics of representation—how we are, whether we like it or not, in terms of our audience: a representative of our race, religion, sexuality, nationality, or immigration status.

Since it remains true that the overwhelming majority of college writing and multimedia authoring teachers are white but that students are increasingly of color, and that these same white writing teachers are often early-career writing professionals who might "graduate" out of teaching first-year writing after a few years, these white writing teachers, and certainly white students as well, need to embrace the challenge and exciting opportunities of instructing in multiracial writing spaces. Our white teaching and student colleagues need to learn to evaluate code meshing, not just code switching, and do that dynamically and with some fairness. White teachers especially must extend, or in some cases initiate, code meshing in their own oral and writing work in the course. Writing teachers should share, or, if they have never done so before, compose a code-meshed text of the work of the course: perhaps a writing prompt for a formal paper or in-class group activity, a draft of their own current scholarship, or, best of all, a composition produced with students in class as a literal writing community. Kim Brian Lovejoy reminds us that any code-meshed text, but especially a teacher's code-meshed text, must aim at being "intelligible, purposeful, and effective"

(Young et al. 2014, 144). We can all become more effective at producing dynamic meshed texts by asking these audience questions: "In what ways and how much will my audience participate? How far will I push the stakes?" (Canagarajah 2011, 409).

CODE-MESHING ACTIVITY 5

Teacher and Students Code Mesh Together in Class

Whether all, most, some, few, or none of you in the class have code meshed or continue to code mesh any of the required writing in this course, whether formal papers or informal writing tasks responding to readings, responding to multimedia texts, or producing creative or speculative writing, as in-class-right-now writing, share a memory, however small or anecdotal, about your home language. Write about this home-language memory using your home language by itself or meshed with EAE. This memory can be very brief, a paragraph, but it must be a complete anecdote/brief story with an opening, middle, and ending. Your teacher will also be code meshing their own brief memory connected to home language. For a teacher or student who doesn't know how to proceed, consider these steps:

1. If you think rightly or wrongly that your home language is EAE in written form and "Standard English" in spoken form so you have nothing to mesh because you live entirely in one language, which might or might not be the case, a simple home-language memory, perhaps from childhood or teen years when you "noticed" more than previously the power of language, is what you need to focus on here. What about the way you talked with friends when puberty was heating up and you wanted to sound cool or special?
2. Consider nicknames.
3. Consider sport or club language.
4. Consider peer or street terms and cussing.
5. Consider a memory in which someone tried to put you in one group through language when you thought you belonged elsewhere or in "both" or "several" language groups.
6. Just try to mesh a paragraph memory; it will be cool, even if it ends up entirely one language.

MULTIPLE AMPHIBIANS IN COLOR-MAJORITY CLASSROOMS IN COLOR-MAJORITY UNITED STATES

The coauthors of this book insist that we are all multiple amphibians already and that we must become more consciously intentional, critically conscious, and more fully open to multiple amphibian environments and learning spaces. The preface of this book asks, "What are we, then?

We are—all of us—multiple amphibians living in many worlds and communities at once who badly need to be recognized as vast and complex. All of us."

All teachers and students, especially white teachers and students, and especially in first-year writing courses and their assessment, must actively be preparing or more dynamically interacting with color-majority classrooms and learning spaces in our soon-to-be color-majority United States. This rapidly approaching demographic reality should best be seen as an opportunity for emerging possibilities of coalition building and shared fate in classrooms and beyond. How do teachers and students, especially white teachers and students, prepare to flourish in this emerging environment of multiracial complexity? Our answer in this book is that we do so by becoming more consciously aware multiple-amphibian beings, dynamic and present in all our many environments.

Sheryll Cashin argues that the United States is bifurcating into two groups: generally older monoracially provincial whites who want to separate from everyone of color and white allies of folks of color and live alone in fear of everyone else, and a second group she calls the "culturally dexterous." This second group, Cashin predicts, will increasingly gain political power. She says the culturally dexterous reject fear, enjoy bending and flowing in complexity, and are focused on "economic justice and combating racism" (2017, 169). This is the group Robert considers multiple amphibians.

The heart of this adjustment from white privilege, white-majority status, and white isolation to polycultural openness to a multiracial focus is something all of us will be challenged by but also opened up by. The heart of the adjustment and opportunity we all face is focused in this question and its evolving answers:

> How do your racial identity and comfort level influence the people you work or study with, especially the people of races other than your own whom you teach or otherwise supervise and work with?

The subset issues from the above overall question invite some difficult but necessary questions white teachers and all of us must ask in FYW contexts when we consider code meshing, code switching, and writing assessment as we approach Cashin's "culturally dexterous" United States:

> How do I romanticize whiteness?
>
> What are my feelings and comfort level for discussing unearned white privilege?
>
> Has my teaching perpetuated the exploitation of people of color by reifying myths, such as saying things are getting better over time?

Do I try to render students of color obedient to white rhetorics by rejecting code meshing literacies they already possess?

Do I notice how I racialize students and how that racialization influences my expectations of their academic success or failure and my manner of interaction/noninteraction with them?

If I were wired to the best lie detector and asked whether I have the same academic expectations for my white students and students of color, what would be demonstrated?

In attempting to become more intercultural in complex multiracial settings, how should I alter my critical gaze?

When I am composing teacher commentary on the work of students of color who challenge me indirectly or directly, do I use white authorial embellishments rather than respond openly? What else would the comments reveal about my reification of existing power dynamics or my own use of power as an instructor?

Have I considered the implications for my academic responsibilities in James Baldwin's famous judgment that the only thing whites have that people of color need is power?

Do I ruminate about how systemic white privilege conditions white people to be blind to students of color? Or how it conditions students of color to perform racist inter- and intracultural acts?

Do I engage in an evolving analysis of how systemic racism has a sophisticated self-adjusting organization and that educational outcomes are a main structural location where white innocence is constructed?

Have I considered the possibility that for many people of color, systemic racism involves a constant near-death experience?

How do I design course materials that invite students of color to actively resist the sociopolitical and economic forces that challenge them to just code switch instead of engage code meshing?

What is at stake in the political economy of white privilege for FYW teachers in the midst of code-meshing considerations as part of fair and representative multiracial assessment in the fast-approaching white-minority United States? Here is one small but significant example from one of Robert's classes. Imagine a first-generation Latinx student with language resources from both Spanish and English. Imagine this student of color who is experienced and adept at meshing, as Victor Villanueva puts it, "codes, languages, dialects in both English and Spanish, registers of formality and informality" (2014, ix) proposing the following item as one yardstick by which all students in an English department course in first-year academic writing are evaluated and graded: Does the course portfolio of a student's writing challenge conventional forms of English by engaging in code meshing rarely? Sometimes? Often? How might white, middle-class,

English-only students or teachers react to such a course portfolio rubric requirement? Is the requirement fair to such mainstream, white students who will soon be part of color-majority United States? Should first-generation students of color whose code meshing is sophisticated, complex, critical, and creative be judged by that real-world criterion? If writing assessment must be an "antiracist project" (Inoue 2015, 293), as surely it must in a racially just society, how could the student's request be denied? The rubric item was proposed in a multiracial class where there were eight students of color and nine students who self-presented as white, and Robert requested a class vote on inclusion of the code-meshing item. The students of color all voted in favor, and white students voted against it, except for the two first-generation white students who voted with the students of color.

Here is another example of what is at stake in fair and representative multiracial assessment in our FYW courses. Brian said he felt like a "new and completely free man" after he finished his final draft of paper one. He felt that he now "saw the big picture" of taking control of his language and life. Brian felt that with the completion of this paper, he had adapted to the new world of college and its culture of skepticism, analysis, and critical thinking. He had constructed a "new home" where he was "as good as all the other college students." He said his next task was to help change academic discourse to let in more formerly excluded voices, especially of previously incarcerated people.

Brian sent his teacher a note after he completed his final draft. We quote a portion of Brian's note, with its use of the poem "I, Too" by Langston Hughes. After thanking all the people who had helped him, Brian said, "Here is the new me in the words of brother Langston":

I, too, sing America
. . .
Tomorrow,
I'll be at the table

. . .
They'll see how beautiful I am
And be ashamed—
I, too, am America.

The Eddy Model ends with the dissonant voice, the voice of the outsider looking toward the next writing task and intending to divide up resources and power with more justice. The dissonant voice affirms the "teeming diversity of the natural world" and the "tremendous potentiality of human nature to evolve freely its own capacities and powers" (Harvey 2014, 261). We end this book with several final context-building writing activities. These tasks affirm the seriousness of the work that lies ahead of us as writing teachers and writing students, and as residents of this nation as we live the challenge and opportunities of writing across cultures in our soon-to-be color-majority country. We end the book looking to the migrant, and to new naming, and with a meshed rhetorical analysis of one electronic site that constructs future possibilities.

CONTEXT-BUILDING WRITING ACTIVITY 20

The Migrant as Our "Rescuer" in Our Course and in Our Country

THE TASK

In the post-9/11 nationalistic and xenophobic United States, popular consciousness imagines the economic migrant as originating in Central America and the Caribbean and political migrants—Muslims—as originating in the Middle East. But in Saleem Peeradina's poem "Reflections on the Other," we meet the migrant with a different sense of origin: "an uninvited/guest from a future age who could have been/your rescuer" (2014, 146–47). The migrant is a human being in extreme need of support in our classrooms and in our country and might be any one of us in an uncertain future. Peeradina helps us see that any of us could become migrants, and if we react in fully human ways, the migrant could become our "rescuer." The migrant could be the "rescuer" in classrooms by being the dissonant voice of democracy that "rescues" us from the tribal, the monocultural, and the racialized stereotype. Consider the scene from *The Day After Tomorrow* (2004) a climate-fiction disaster film in which US survivors of a sudden new Ice Age rush south over the Rio Grande to illegally enter Mexico to escape extreme cold.

THE METHOD

Recorder_____

Member_____

Member_____

(each class member signs own name)

Form groups of three people; choose a recorder, who will not answer individually but will instead note the collective opinion of the group. If class racial demographics allow it, each group of three should be composed of three different races based on how class members self-present their identity.

Take the task outlined above and reflect in your group on the task of seeing migrants as "rescuers" in classrooms and in our country. Outline a situation in a classroom or in our country generally in which a migrant or migrants become "rescuers." **You have only twenty minutes to complete this assignment**, and each group's recorder will present the classroom or national scenario in as detailed a way as time permits and will invite questions from the front of the room, where all group members will be present addressing the entire class.

Exact wording of your "rescuing" scenario. **(Be CLEAR and CONCRETE; no vagueness.)** _____

_____

_____

_____

Rhetorical justification of your scenario. _____

_____

_____

CONTEXT-BUILDING WRITING ACTIVITY 21

Renaming the United States of America

THE TASK

If we do not collectively rename the United States, we will remain locked into the slowly spreading poison of genocide and slavery effects, and locked into the endless reproduction of the systemic racism of the school-to-prison pipeline for black and brown Americans, the new racism, most recently including Islamophobia. We will also be locked into the separation of the races and antipathy of the races for each other, especially the antipathy of white Americans for people of color. Most important, if we do not collectively rename the United States, we will remain locked into a nonadaptive rigidity at a time when all human populations must unbind from death-affirming hate and war-based social structures and transform to social structures of shared fate, sustainability, and polyculturalism.

Will the renaming of this large North American human population be enough to transform us into a true team? Of course not, but it is a necessary step. Naming matters and is a form of evolving collective justice. We must acknowledge vastly more complexity in the peoples of this nation, the extraordinary incompleteness of the white story of "America" that leaves out so much human activity by Americans of color. This white national story erases, glosses over, or justifies behaviors by the group in power that any nation espousing equal access and opportunity will find impossible to justify: unearned white privilege in exact proportion to the systemic discrimination against people of color in housing, hiring, tracking in schools, and all the other routine ways. It is time to invite everyone and every group equally to the table of US democracy and US collective identity and shared fate. *What should the new name be?* It is for all of us together to name who we truly are together as cherished equals on one uncertain life boat collectively on a sea of troubles politically, economically, and environmentally. Systemic racism must go, and our new name must arrive.

THE METHOD
Recorder _____

Member_____

Member_____

(each class member signs own name)

Form groups of three people; choose a recorder, who will not answer individually but will instead write down the collective opinion of the group. If class racial demographics allow it, each group of three should be composed of three different races based on how class members self-present their racial identity.

Reflecting on the task of renaming the United States for racial justice and shared fate, your group should **ask** and **answer** an important question—agreed upon as important by the group of three—inspired by your collective analysis of <u>what question must be asked and answered first</u> before the country can collectively be renamed by all our constituent racial groups. **You have only twenty minutes to complete this assignment**, and each group's recorder will present the question and the heart of the response and will invite questions from the front of the room, where all group members will be present addressing the entire class.

Exact wording of your question: **(Be CLEAR and CONCRETE; no vagueness.)** _____

_____

Group answer to your question: _____

_____

Rhetorical justification of your answer: _____

_____

CODE-MESHING ACTIVITY 6

Rhetorical Analysis of a Code-Meshed Academic Website: Education, Liberation, and Black Radical Traditions for the Twenty-First Century

Sara Michael-Luna and Suresh Canagarajah remind us that "code meshing is a communicative device used for specific rhetorical and ideological purposes in which a multilingual speaker intentionally integrates local and academic discourse as a form of resistance, reappropriation and/or transformation of the academic discourse" (quoted in Williams-Farrier 2017, 255). Academic discourse, since it reflects and supports the systemic racism of this country and other countries, certainly must be resisted, reappropriated, and transformed. Do a code-meshed rhetorical analysis as follows:

1. Tune to http://carmenkynard.org/.
2. Do a meshed rhetorical analysis of how this site resists current US academic discourse.
3. Do a meshed rhetorical analysis of how this site reappropriates current US academic discourse.
4. Do a meshed rhetorical analysis of how this site transforms current US academic discourse and gives glimpses of what we might be and do in color-majority countries of social justice that were formerly white.

REFERENCES

Alizadeh, Ali. 2006. "Your Terrorist." Poetry International Web. http://www.poetryinter nationalweb.net/pi/site/poem/item/14577.

Baldwin, James. 1985. "A Talk to Teachers." *The Price of the Ticket: Collected Nonfiction 1948–1985*. New York: St. Martin's.

Barron, Nancy, and Nancy Grimm. 2002. "Addressing Racial Diversity in a Writing Center: Stories and Lessons from Two Beginners." *Writing Center Journal* 22 (2): 55–83.

Bizzell, Patricia. 1992. *Academic Discourse and Critical Consciousness*. Pittsburgh, PA: University of Pittsburgh Press.

Bonilla-Silva, Eduardo, and Tyron Forman. 2000. "I Am Not a Racist but . . . : Mapping White College Students' Racial Ideology in the USA." *Discourse and Society* 11 (1): 50–85.

Braddock, Richard, Richard Lloyd-Jones, and Lowell Schoer. 1963. *Research in Written Composition*. Urbana, IL: NCTE.

Calderone, J-Love. 2014. "White Like Me: 10 Codes of Ethics for White People in Hip Hop." In *A Language and Power Reader: Representations of Race in a "Post-Racist" Era*, edited by Robert Eddy and Victor Villanueva, 297–302. Logan: Utah State University Press.

Canagarajah, A. Suresh. 2009. "Multilingual Strategies of Negotiating English: From Conversation to Writing." *JAC* 29 (1/2): 17–48.

Canagarajah, Suresh. 2011. "Codemeshing in Academic Writing: Identifying Teachable Strategies of Translanguaging." *Modern Language Journal* 95 (3): 401–17.

Cashin, Sheryll. 2017. *Loving: Interracial Intimacy in America and the Threat to White Supremacy*. Boston, MA: Beacon.

Comfort, Juanita. 2001. "African-American Women's Rhetorics and the Culture of Eurocentric Scholarly Discourse." In *Contrastive Rhetoric Revisited and Redefined*, edited by Clayann Panetta, 91–104. Mahwah, NJ: Lawrence Erlbaum.

Condon, Frankie. 2012. *I Hope I Join the Band: Narrative, Affiliation, and Antiracist Rhetoric*. Logan: Utah State University Press.

Davidson, Cathy, and David Theo Goldberg. 2010. *The Future of Thinking: Learning Institutions in a Digital Age*. Cambridge, MA: MIT Press.

Eck, Diana L. 2006. "What Is Pluralism?" Pluralism Project Harvard University. http://pluralism.org/what-is-pluralism/.

Eddy, Robert, ed. 1996. *Reflections on Multiculturalism*. Yarmouth, ME: Intercultural.

Eddy, Robert, and Victor Villanueva, eds. 2014. *A Language and Power Reader: Representations of Race in a "Post-Racist" Era*. Logan: Utah State University Press.

Esters, Jason B. 2011. "On the Edges: Black Maleness, Degrees of Racism, and Community on the Boundaries of the Writing Center." In *Writing Centers and the New Racism: A Call for Sustainable Dialogue and Change*, edited by Laura Greenfield and Karen Rowan, 290–99. Logan: Utah State University Press.

Fowler, Shelli, and Victor Villanueva, eds. 2002. *Included in English Studies: Learning Climates That Cultivate Racial and Ethnic Diversity*. Urbana, IL: NCTE.

Goldberg, David Theo. 2009. *The Threat of Race: Reflections on Racial Neoliberalism*. Malden, MA: Wiley-Blackwell.

Greenfield, Laura. 2011. "The Standard English Fairy Tale." *Writing Centers and the New Racism*, edited by Laura Greenfield and Karen Rowan, 33–60. Logan: Utah State University Press.

DOI: 10.7330/9781607328742.c011

Guerrero, Lisa, ed. 2008. *Teaching Race in the 21st Century: College Teachers Talk about Their Fears, Risks, and Rewards.* New York: Palgrave Macmillan.

Hall, Edward T. 1973. *The Silent Language.* New York: Anchor Books.

Harvey, David. 2005. *A Brief History of Neoliberalism.* Oxford: Oxford University Press.

Harvey, David. 2014. *Seventeen Contradictions and the End of Capitalism.* Oxford: Oxford University Press.

Hernández, D., and Bushra Rehman. 2002. *Colonize This! Young Women of Color on Today's Feminism.* New York: Seal.

Inoue, Asao, and Mya Poe, eds. 2012. *Race and Writing Assessment.* New York: Peter Lang.

Inoue, Asao. 2015. *Antiracist Writing Assessment Ecologies: Teaching and Assessing Writing for a Socially Just Future.* Fort Collins, CO: WAC Clearinghouse and Parlor.

Jamila, Shani. 2002. "Can I Get a Witness? Testimony for a Hip-Hop Feminist." In *Colonize This! Young Women of Color on Today's Feminism,* edited by Daisy Hernández and Bushra Rehman, 382–94. New York: Seal.

Johnson, Gaye Theresa, and Alex Lubin, eds. 2017. *Futures of Black Radicalism.* Brooklyn, NY: Verso.

Johnson, Michelle. 2011. "Racial Literacy and the Writing Center." In *Writing Centers and the New Racism: A Call for Sustainable Dialogue and Change,* edited by Laura Greenfield and Karen Rowan, 211–27. Logan: Utah State University Press.

Jordan, Zandra. 2012. "Students' Right, African American English and Writing Assessment: Considering the HBCU." In *Race and Writing Assessment,* edited by Asao Inoue and Maya Poe, 97–109. New York: Peter Lang.

Justin, Tyrone Aire. 2014. "Raps: Suite Brown and Black." In *A Language and Power Reader: Representations of Race in a "Post-Racist" Era,* edited by Robert Eddy and Victor Villanueva, 34–40. Logan: Utah State University Press.

Kells, Michelle Hall, Valerie Balester, and Victor Villanueva. 2004. *Latino/a Discourses: On Language, Identity, and Literacy Education.* Portsmouth, NH: Boynton/Cook.

Kirklighter, Cristina, Diana Cárdenas, and Susan Wolf Murphy. 2007. *Teaching Writing with Latino/a Students: Lessons Learned at Hispanic-Serving Institutions.* Albany: SUNY Press.

Kirsch, Gesa, and Liz Rohans, eds. 2008. *Beyond the Archives: Research as a Lived Process.* Carbondale: Southern Illinois University Press.

Kohls, L. Robert. 1984. *Survival Kit for Overseas Living: For Americans Planning to Live and Work Abroad.* Yarmouth, ME: Intercultural.

Kumar, Deepa. 2012. *Islamophobia and the Politics of Empire.* Chicago, IL: Haymarket Books.

Kynard, Carmen. 2013. *Vernacular Insurrections: Race, Black Protest, and the New Century in Composition-Literacies Studies.* Albany: SUNY Press.

Kynard, Carmen. n.d. "Education, Liberation & Black Radical Traditions for the 21st Century: Carmen Kynard's Teaching & Research Site on Race, Writing, and the Classroom." http://carmenkynard.org/.

Kynard, Carmen, and Robert Eddy. 2009. "Toward a New Critical Framework: Color-Conscious Political Morality and Pedagogy at Historically Black and Historically White Colleges and Universities." *College Composition and Communication* 61 (1): W24–W44.

Lewis, Tom, and Robert Jungman. 1986. *On Being Foreign: Culture Shock in Short Fiction.* Yarmouth, ME: Intercultural.

Lindemann, Erika. 1987. *A Rhetoric for Writing Teachers.* 2nd ed. New York: Oxford University Press.

Malcolm X. 1965. *Autobiography of Malcolm X.* New York: Grove.

"Malcolm X on Progress." 2008. YouTube video, 0:20. Posted April 21. http://www.youtube.com/watch?v=cReCQE8B5nY.

Michael-Luna, Sara, and Suresh Canagarajah. 2008. "Multilingual Academic Literacies: Pedagogical Foundations for Code Meshing in Primary and Higher Education." *Journal of Applied Linguistics* 4 (1): 55–77.

Murray, Donald. 1985. *A Writer Teaches Writing.* 2nd ed. Boston, MA: Houghton/Mifflin.

Nasr, Seyyed Hossein, Caner Dagli, Maria Massi Dakake, Joseph E. B. Lumbard, Mohammed Rustom, eds. 2015. *The Study Quran: A New Translation and Commentary.* New York: HarperCollins.

National Council of Teachers of English. 1974. "Resolution on Students' Right to Their Own Language." Position Statements. http://www2.ncte.org/statement/right toownlanguage/.

Panetta, Clayann Gilliam, ed. 2001. *Contrastive Rhetoric Revisited and Redefined.* Mahwah, NJ: Lawrence Erlbaum.

Peeradina, Saleem. 2014. "Reflections on the Other." In *A Language and Power Reader: Representations of Race in a "Post-Racist" Era,* edited by Robert Eddy and Victor Villanueva, 143–49. Logan: Utah State University Press.

Powell, Malea. 2004. "Down by the River, or How Susan La Lesche Picotte Can Teach Us about Alliance as a Practice of Survival." *College Composition and Communication* 56 (1): 38–60.

Prendergast, Catherine. 2003. *Literacy and Racial Justice: The Politics of Learning after Brown v. Board of Education.* Carbondale, IL: Southern Illinois University Press.

Royster, Jacqueline Jones, and Gesa Kirsch, eds. 2012. *Feminist Rhetorical Practices: New Horizons for Rhetoric, Composition, and Literacy Studies.* Carbondale: Southern Illinois University Press.

Said, Edward. 1994. *Orientalism.* 25th anniversary ed. New York: Vintage Books.

Schroeder, Christopher. 2001. *ReInventing the University: Literacies and Legitimacy in the Postmodern Academy.* Logan: Utah State University Press.

Schroeder, Christopher. 2011. *Diverse by Design: Literacy Education within Multicultural Institutions.* Logan: Utah State University Press.

Shen, Fan. 1989. "The Classroom and the Wider Culture: Identity as Key to Learning English Composition." *College Composition and Communication* 40 (4): 459–66.

Smith, David Livingstone. 2011. *Less Than Human: Why We Demean, Enslave, and Exterminate Others.* New York: St. Martin's.

Smitherman, Geneva, and Victor Villanueva, eds. 2003. *Language Diversity in the Classroom: From Intention to Practice.* Carbondale: Southern Illinois University Press.

"Spotlight Journalists Illuminate Boston's Unique Racial Disparities." 2017. *PBS News Hour.* https://www.pbs.org/newshour/show/spotlight-journalists-illuminate-bostons-unique-racial-disparities.

Sumner, David Thomas. 2000. "Starting the Conversation: The Importance of a Rhetoric of Assent When Teaching Argument." In *In Our Own Voice: Graduate Students Teach Writing,* edited by Tina Lavonne Good and Leanne B. Warshauer. Boston, MA: Allyn and Bacon.

Trimbur, John. 2011. *Solidarity or Service: Composition and the Problem of Expertise.* Portsmouth, NH: Boynton/Cook.

Villanueva, Victor. 2008. "Colonial Memory, Colonial Research." In *Beyond the Archives: Research as a Lived Process,* edited by Gesa Kirsch and Liz Rohans, 83–92. Carbondale: Southern Illinois University Press.

Villanueva, Victor. 2014. Foreword to *Other People's English: Code-Meshing, Code-Switching, and African-American Literacy,* edited by Vershawn Young, Rusty Barrett, Y'Shanda Young-Rivera, and Kim Brian Lovejoy. New York: Teachers College Press.

Williams-Farrier, Bonnie J. 2017. "'Talkin' Bout Good & Bad' Pedagogies: Code-Switching vs. Comparative Rhetorical Approaches." *College Composition and Communication* 69 (2): 230–59.

Yamamoto, Eric. 1999. *Interracial Justice: Conflict and Reconciliation in Post–Civil Rights America.* New York: New York University Press.

Yen, Hope. 2012. "Census: Minorities Now Surpass Whites in US Births." NBCNews.com. http://www.nbcnews.com/id/47458196/ns/us_news-life/t/census-minorities-now-surpass-whites-us-births/.

Young, Jennifer Rene. 2002. "Using Assessment Techniques in a Racially and Ethnically Diverse Classroom." In *Included in English Studies: Learning Climates That Cultivate Racial and Ethnic Diversity*, edited by Shelli Fowler and Victor Villanueva. Urbana, IL: NCTE.

Young, Vershawn, Rusty Barrett, Y'Shanda Young-Rivera, and Kim Brian Lovejoy. 2014. *Other People's English: Code-Meshing, Code-Switching, and African-American Literacy.* New York: Teachers College Press.

Yu, Han. 2014. "How to Define a Teacher." Translated by An Lan Zhang. In *A Language and Power Reader: Representations of Race in a "Post-Racist" Era*, edited by Robert Eddy and Victor Villanueva, 165–72. Logan: Utah State University Press.

Zhang, An Lan. 2015. *Flowers in Chinese Culture: Folklore, Poetry, Religion.* St. Petersburg, FL: Three Pines.

INDEX